D0073507

Frontispiece: Elgar at Severn House, Hampstead, c. 1915

Elgar Studies

Edited by
RAYMOND MONK

40157

Scolar Press

© Each essay copyright © its contributor 1990

All rights reserved. No part of this publication may be reproduced, stored in a retrieval system, or transmitted in any form or by any means, electronic, mechanical, photocopying, recording, or otherwise without the prior permission of the publisher.

Published by
SCOLAR PRESS
Gower Publishing Company Limited
Gower House
Croft Road
Aldershot
Hants GU11 3HR
England

Gower Publishing Company
Old Post Road
Brookfield
Vermont 05036
USA

British Library Cataloguing in Publication Data
Elgar studies.
1. English music. Elgar, Edward, 1857–1934
I. Monk, Raymond
780'.92'4

ISBN 0–85967–810–5

Printed in Great Britain by
Billing & Sons Ltd, Worcester

The Elgar Society exists to honour the memory of Edward Elgar and to promote a wider interest in his life and music. It was founded in 1951 at the suggestion of Sir Adrian Boult who became its first President. The Society has expanded from modest beginnings to become the largest composer society in the United Kingdom with more than 1200 members. Full membership details may be obtained from: John R. Greig, Orchard Barn, Derringstone Street, Barham, CANTERBURY CT4 6QB. The Society has an International Sub-Committee which looks after the interests of a wide overseas membership.

Contents

List of plates

Frontispiece: Elgar at Severn House, Hampstead, c. 1915

(between pages 108 and 109)

1 The fall of Simon Magus: Pollainolo relief, c.1480 (see page 124)

2 Elgar in 1880 (aged 23)

3 Elgar in 1896

4 Elgar in 1904

5 Elgar at Severn House, Hampstead, 1913

6 Elgar at Severn House, Hampstead, c.1915 (with Anthony Goetz, son of Muriel Foster)

7 Elgar with Algernon Blackwood, London, c.1916

8 Friends pictured within

9 Elgar with John Coates, Gloucester, September 1925

10 Elgar with Bernard Shaw, Malvern, 1932

11 Elgar at Marl Bank, Worcester, 1932

12 The last photograph: Elgar with Carice Elgar Blake and Fred Gaisberg, Worcester, 12 December 1933

Notes on Contributors

Robert Anderson, M.A., F.S.A., D.Mus. (Hon.), was born in India, and educated at Harrow School and Gonville and Caius College, Cambridge. Director of Music at Gordonstoun School, he was also an assistant conductor for Gian-Carlo Menotti at the Spoleto Festival. For eighteen years he was an associate editor of *The Musical Times* and has broadcast frequently. He has conducted the St Bartholomew's Hospital Choral Society in a number of Elgar performances at the Royal Albert Hall, London. He is now co-ordinating editor of the Elgar Complete Edition published by Novello, and a visiting fellow at the City University.

Peter Dennison was educated at the Universities of Sydney and Oxford. He lectured in music at Glasgow University and then at Cambridge. He has been Professor of Music at the University of Melbourne since 1975, and Chairman of the Board of the Melbourne Symphony Orchestra since 1986. Peter Dennison has published several articles, a monograph on Pelham Humfrey, and is currently writing a study of the music of Elgar.

Michael Kennedy O.B.E. was born in Manchester and educated at Berkhamsted. He has been staff music critic on *The Daily Telegraph* since 1950, northern editor from 1960 to 1986 and joint chief critic from 1987. He has written biographical studies of many composers and conductors and is the author of the *Oxford Dictionary of Music*. A frequent broadcaster and record reviewer, he is also a vice-president of the Elgar Society.

John Knowles was born in Loughborough and educated in Manchester, Oxford and London. Since 1984, he has been Vice-Master of Queen Elizabeth's Grammar School, Blackburn. He was treasurer of The Elgar Society from 1976 to 1984, during which time he masterminded the production of the first two records to appear under the aegis of the Society, who also published in his *Elgar's Interpreters on Record*, the first complete

Diana McVeagh studied at the Royal College of Music. She works as a freelance, reviewing for various periodicals including *The Times*. She was assistant editor of *The Musical Times*, and has written articles on Elgar. Her book *Edward Elgar: his Life and Music* (Dent) was published in 1955. She was chairman of the London Branch of the Elgar Society (1980–86). She is a vice-president of the Elgar Society and of the Royal Musical Association.

Jerrold Northrop Moore was educated in the United States and has lived in England since 1970, by which time he had begun work on *Edward Elgar: A Creative Life* (OUP, 1984). He is also author of *Elgar: A Life in Photographs, Spirit of England*, editor of the Oxford Edition of Elgar's Correspondence, co-editor of *The Elgar Edition* (Novello) and author of books and articles about the history of gramophone recording. Jerrold Northrop Moore is an occasional broadcaster and lecturer and a vice-president of the Elgar Society.

Ian Parrott was born in London, studied at New College Oxford and was Gregynog Professor of Music at U.C.W., Aberystwyth from 1950 to 1983. He has won various awards and has been a vice-president of the Elgar Society since 1973. One of his first contributions to Elgar scholarship was 'Variation for a Dog?' in *The Music Teacher* and his Master Musicians volume on the composer appeared in 1971. Professor Parrott's book on musical patronage in Wales, *The Spiritual Pilgrims*, was published in 1987. He has recently been on a lecture tour of the USA and Canada, lecturing on 'Elgar's Enigma Solved'. Elgar's peculiar brand of harmony and attitude to text-books has always fascinated him.

Michael Pope, born in London, was educated at Wellington College, and studied at the Guildhall School of Music. He joined the staff of the BBC in 1954, and subsequently became responsible for producing many revivals on the Third Network, including *Caractacus* (1974/5) and *King Olaf* (1976/7). He has written, lectured, and broadcast on Elgar and his contemporaries, and was chairman of the Elgar Society (1978–88). He is active as a choral conductor, and is a vice-president of the Elgar Society.

K E L Simmons, M.Sc., Ph.D., is a research zoologist, with a long list of scientific publications and an international reputation in the field of behavioural ecology. He was co-editor of the first three volumes of *The*

Birds of the Western Paleartic (OUP, 1977–83). As a boy, he wanted to be a musician but the war intervened and he became a teacher instead. He took early retirement in 1980 and is now writing a biography of the naturalist Edmund Selous. He has done much research into the background of the Elgar family of Worcester, where in 1945 he heard Heddle Nash and Astra Desmond sing in *The Dream of Gerontius*.

Ronald Taylor was born in Southgate, Middlesex, in 1928. For over twenty years he was a director of the booksellers Bertram Rota Ltd. He is now the proprietor of a specialist record shop in Central London and has been the Editor of the *Elgar Society Journal* since January 1977. He has researched BBC broadcasts of Elgar's music 1922–34, and a discography of Columbia Records in Britain (with Frank Andrews), both for future publication.

Percy M Young M.A. (Cantab), Mus.D, D.Mus. has spent a lifetime in music. His interests are represented in various musical works, many books, of which the best known concern Handel, Elgar and Kodaly. He is currently occupied with critical edition of *The Spanish Lady*, Elgar's opera of which Young's performing edition was heard for the first time in 1986. He is a vice-president of the Elgar Society.

The editor

Raymond Monk is a Trustee of the Elgar Birthplace, a Governor of the Elgar Foundation and a member of the National Committee of the Elgar Society. He is a Fellow of the Royal Philharmonic Society. Elgar has been an important part of his life since the age of twelve when he heard a performance of the Second Symphony and he is currently engaged in compiling a major iconography of the composer.

Foreword

Sir Yehudi Menuhin, O.M.

These illuminating 'Variations' on Edward Elgar are in a way a mirror-image of *Enigma* – a commentary by friends rather than of friends.

Together they make a most revealing and integrated picture, Elgar's image losing neither dignity nor humour – rather, it is enhanced by both, inseparable from genius, an unfailing and trustworthy intuitive lead, backed up with equally unfailing dedication, zeal, passion and hard work – from his earliest years a man, in his heart of hearts absolutely sure of what he was and of what he always would be to us. He was considered by his friends to be affectionate and possessed of that very British quality of unassuming command, radiating this to humans and animals alike both through his music and simply by being himself.

To be so English (and yet to have studied so deeply and faithfully his contemporaries and predecessors, both German and French) always struck me as remarkable. Perhaps, as Goethe said, one can only begin to understand one's own language when one can speak a foreign one.

My own indissoluble bonds with the English people were forged when I played his glorious violin concerto, with the composer conducting, in July 1932 for a recording and a few months later at the Royal Albert Hall and thus became through his music a voice of his people.

A lifetime is insufficient to express my gratitude (and throughout the more than five decades which separate me from that day) I come ever closer to a musical score which is as mystical as it is full-blooded, as cultivated as it is 'folk', as elegant as it is rumbustious, festive and humorous.

It is wonderful when a people can recognize themselves in the music of a great composer, not only the individuals of *Enigma* but the collective soul of a race, set in its own climate and landscape.

And privileged though I am by the passage of years, I still hear his voice, I see him among my family as he knew them in my parents and my two sisters. The living memories crowd in – London, Worcester, Paris, Ville d'Avray; with Enesco, with Beecham, with English and French orchestras and with Fred Gaisberg and the old-timers at HMV (now EMI).

I am happy to say that Sir Edward's music is gaining rapturous audiences from Paris to Tokyo and in the Germany of his beloved Schumann and Wagner.

As I told the wonderful musicians of the New Japan Philharmonic in Tokyo a short while ago after we had rehearsed Sir Edward's First Symphony: Now you have come to know the English soul as our audiences will shortly and better and more truly deeply than all your fellow-Japanese. For only great composers can 'speak' without barriers to another people. Only a great composer can speak with that true voice which survives wars, fear, hatred and all demeaning human passions.

I am happy and thankful that this so valuable book has been compiled by Raymond Monk and his friends and brought out for the Elgar Society, of which I have the great honour of being President.

Editor's preface

From the very beginning Elgar has been able to reach the hearts and minds of those people with whom he shared a common heritage. Today it is much wider than that, and perhaps it always was. In the past, Englishmen have tended to regard Elgar as being their own exclusive property – the Shakespeare of their music. But Shakespeare has a world-wide audience, and so I firmly believe does Elgar. Recent performances of *The Dream of Gerontius* in the Soviet Union and Japan may be seen as being part of a continuing process of international acceptance which can be traced back to the famous 1902 Düsseldorf performance of that work which did so much for Elgar's reputation at home and abroad. The cataclysmic events of this 20th century may have slowed the process down, but proof that it continues may be found in the ever increasing number of European, American and Far Eastern visitors who make the pilgrimage to Elgar's Birthplace at Broadheath, near Worcester, each year. Without doubt these visitors reflect the wider and more frequent representation of Elgar in concert programmes, radio schedules, and record catalogues throughout the world.

On the 28th May 1931, in a letter to his biographer Basil Maine, a diffident and disillusioned Elgar had written: 'I fear the interest in my music is too slight and evanescent to be worth such concentration as you propose to devote to it'. Well, countless Elgarians since then have disproved that statement and I am confident that future generations will continue to do so. Elgar bibliography has come a very long way since Maine's *Elgar: His Life and Works* first appeared in 1933 and it is now very extensive. I make no apology for adding to it and this present volume of essays seeks to embrace analytical, biographical, textual, and critical aspects of our great composer. To have been able to call upon so many fine Elgarian writers is a matter of great satisfaction to me. I believe that their work will have permanent value, and that it will contribute handsomely to an even wider interest in Elgar. Each of these distinguished contributors has

given their services and all royalties from the sale of this volume will
go to the Elgar Society. This is their book and I salute and thank
them all.

One essay began life as an A T Shaw Memorial Lecture and I am grateful to
Michael Pope, former Chairman of the Elgar Society and fellow Birthplace
Trustee, for allowing it to form part of this book. I must especially thank
Sir Yehudi Menuhin for his finely written Foreword. Recently I sat with
him in the concert hall of the Royal College of Music to listen to his
famous 1932 recording of the Elgar Violin Concerto. This was a deeply
moving experience, never to be forgotten by those fortunate enough to
be present.

Let me also thank John Knowles for his splendid discography and
John Fletcher for invaluable help in the preparation of the type-
script. Antony Wood provided advice and encouragement at precisely
the right time and I shall long remain grateful to him. I am also
indebted to James Bennett and Christopher Bennett of the Elgar Birthplace
Museum and to Lewis Foreman, Dr Christopher Kent, Dr Donald Hunt,
Harry Windsor-Sharpe, Lindsay Wallace, Marion Simmons, Carol Holt,
Mary Moore, Derek Tomkins, Peter Hinchcliffe and Robert Knight, who
were helpful in so many ways. Grateful acknowledgements are made
to E Wulstan Atkins and the Elgar Foundation, the Elgar Will Trust,
the British Library, the National Portrait Gallery, the Royal College
of Music, the Mansell Collection, and to EMI Ltd. for permission to
use the various photographs and plates which are reproduced within
these pages.

For other help and advice I have to thank Dr K E L Simmons
who has been a source of constant support during the time which
I have devoted to this undertaking. And a particular word of gratitude is due to Professor Brian Trowell whose kind understanding of
a difficult editorial decision deserves special mention here. Professor Trowell's 'Elgar and Literature' was commissioned for this collection of *Elgar Studies* but it soon became clear that his monu-
mental work would need to be published as a separate book in its
own right. He has done full justice to a fascinating subject and the
Elgar bibliography will be greatly enriched by this further publication.

It remains for me to express my very special thanks to three great
Elgarians: to Dr Percy Young for his friendly encouragement and continuing
advice; to Michael Kennedy for his kindness and generosity in providing a
second invaluable essay; and to Jerrold Northrop Moore who has chosen to
end this volume with a most eloquent and moving tribute to the power of
friendship. Elgarians owe Dr Moore a great debt and they will understand
and cherish his closing words.

This book is dedicated to the memory of Sir Adrian Boult who was a good friend to many of its contributors and to myself. Sir Adrian made a very special contribution to the musical well-being of our country and this volume of *Elgar Studies*, completed in 1989, the centenary year of his birth, is an expression of gratitude for his life and work.

RM

1 Elgar's musical apprenticeship

Peter Dennison

When in 1900 the University of Cambridge conferred an honorary doctorate of music on Edward Elgar, the Public Orator referred to him as 'autodidactos', and from that time, when he was on the threshold of a widely-acclaimed mastery, Elgar was often described as self-taught. This was an epithet that he himself endorsed, and a few years later he elaborated on its significance in his career.

> When I resolved to become a composer and found that the exigencies of life would prevent me from getting any tuition, the only thing to do was to teach myself. I read everything, played everything, and heard everything I possibly could ... I am self-taught in the matter of harmony, counterpoint, form, and, in short, the whole of the 'mystery' of music.[1]

Elgar had resolved to become a composer by 1873, the year in which he turned sixteen. From that time, and propelled largely by his own instincts, he began a thorough study of music, its techniques and language through playing, principally as an orchestral violinist, and through voracious listening and reading.

Elgar's musical apprenticeship can be said to have virtually concluded by 1899, the year of the *Enigma Variations*, his first unqualified masterpiece. Nevertheless his style remained susceptible to major external influences until about the end of 1902. In that year he made his last visit to Bayreuth and also came to know Richard Strauss and a number of his major works most closely. It was also the year of the first performance in London of an orchestral work by Debussy, *Prelude à l'après-midi d'un faune*, music with which Elgar shared some common lineage from Wagner but with which he felt little empathy. Throughout the years of his apprenticeship Elgar had avidly sought out music from Europe and Russia, but now for the first time the work of a major new European composer did not attract him. By this stage his particular canons of taste had been formed and his

1

musical apprenticeship had finally come to an end. Elgar's mastery, which was achieved finally at the age of 42, was a product of his emerging genius and those diverse musical experiences that he had been pursuing with such singularity of purpose since the early 1870s. It is an investigation into those musical experiences, and their role in the making of his mastery, that is the subject of this study.

Through the preservation of a wealth of material, largely at the Elgar Birthplace Museum at Broadheath, one can build a substantial picture of his formative musical experiences.[2] Elgar kept the programmes of most of the concerts that he attended as listener and performer, and in his earlier years he annotated some of these. Appendices 1 and 2 list the most significant and substantial works by other composers, British and European, as far as it has been possible to trace, that Elgar heard or performed in public up to about 1902, and particularly significant works heard or performed between 1902 and 1913.[3] The tables omit only works of the type that Elgar himself dismissed as without interest. They list in bold type all the works that he is known to have performed; before 1897 he usually performed as a violinist but from that year he conducted the work in question. There remain at the Birthplace only a selection from Elgar's library of scores and books on music, but these too give some insights into his musical concerns, and some are sporadically annotated. Appendix 3 lists the significant books on music, Appendix 4 scores and parts, and Appendix 5 opera librettos that have survived there. From the time of their marriage in 1889, Elgar's wife Alice kept diaries,[4] although for the first ten years or so these do little more than record that Elgar attended a concert or an opera. But sometimes they do express a musical opinion and these are probably those of Elgar himself. Valuable, if biased memoirs of Elgar were written by Rosa Burley, who first met Elgar in 1891, and by Mrs Richard Powell, Dorabella of the *Enigma Variations*, who first met him in 1895. Both give some insight into Elgar's musical tastes. Finally there are the letters that Elgar wrote to friends expressing something of the excitement of musical discovery, and the aspirations and apprehensions of the composer in his formative years.[5]

In the second half of the nineteenth-century, until the death of Queen Victoria in 1901, the predominant foreign influence in England ranging from royal connections to spheres of the arts came from Germany. In many respects, the English musical establishment was an outpost of the Leipzig school where the influences of Mendelssohn, Brahms, Joachim and Clara Schumann were dominant. Prompted initially, no doubt, by this prevalent German bias the young Elgar turned his attentions towards the most advanced music that was emanating from Germany. This is confirmed by Adolphe Pollitzer with whom Elgar studied the violin in London in August 1877. Pollitzer encouraged his pupil to pursue composition and later observed that 'although leaning towards the modern German school,

[he] does not lose either his love or respect for the composers of the past.'[6] Besides the Germanic school, however, there were the riches of the British choral tradition in which Elgar had had his earliest musical experiences, and also French, Italian and later Russian music, all of which he explored with characteristic zeal.

The focal point of the musical year in the west country in Elgar's youth was the Three Choirs Festival. By the nineteenth century this was taking place annually early in September and rotating between the cathedral cities of Worcester, Hereford and Gloucester. On each of the four days of the Festival there was a morning concert of sacred works for chorus and orchestra held in the Cathedral, and in the evening a concert of orchestral works, selections from opera and miscellaneous vocal and instrumental items held in a prominent hall sometimes within the Cathedral precincts. The backbone of the Festivals was the sacred choral and orchestral concert. In 1878 Elgar, then aged 21, joined his father and uncle in the Worcester Three Choirs Festival orchestra, and was listed as 'Mr Elgar jun.' among the second violins. At the next Worcester Festival in 1881, he was promoted to the firsts where he remained at the Festivals of 1884, 1887, 1890 and 1893.

The repertory of the Three Choirs Festivals in these years was dominated by the oratorio, those inherited from Händel and Haydn, those elicited from Mendelssohn and those expected from any aspiring English composer. Händel was the cornerstone of the repertory and it was a performance of *Messiah* in 1869 that precipitated Elgar towards a musical career. In his memoir of Elgar, W H Reed, a close friend and professional colleague for almost thirty years, recalled how, even in his latter years, Elgar's love of *Messiah* remained undiminished, and how he revelled in Mozart's 'exquisite but audacious variations'[7] of scoring. Händel's music left an indelible impression on Elgar, and Herbert Howells remembered how as a young man he had heard 'the man of unsurpassed sonority in string writing himself declare that Georg Friederich Händel was the true source of all such opulence.'[8] Elgar maintained a comparable enthusiasm for the other perennial of this repertory, *Elijah*, and W H Reed again remembered in particular his love of Mendelssohn's deft scoring in its fugal overture and the quartet in Part I.[9]

A number of more modest musical enterprises in his local area gave Elgar opportunities to arrange and compose music for limited resources. For the ensembles with which he was associated, he arranged light music by composers like Balfe, Bellini, Bishop, Hérold and Rossini, and he composed quadrilles, polkas and minuets. Between 1878 and 1881, Elgar composed a more substantial body of music for the wind quintet in which he played bassoon. In 1877 Elgar was appointed Leader and Instructor of the Worcester Amateur Instrumental Society which in the early 1880s gave some of his first orchestral pieces a performance. Elgar was much in demand as an orchestral violinist in the 1880s and he led a number of these orchestras. Their programmes were sometimes orchestral, sometimes choral and orchestral, and to a large extent they duplicated the repertory of the Three Choirs Festivals. As early as 1872 the young Elgar first played the organ for Mass at St George's Roman Catholic Church in Worcester, and in November 1885, he succeeded his father as organist of the church, a position he held until he moved to London in 1889. Well before 1885 he was composing and arranging music for the choir of St George's.

For some years from 1891, Elgar taught music rather unwillingly at 'The Mount', a fashionable school for girls in Malvern. There he supervised an orchestral class. Rosa Burley, the headmistress and a violinist herself, remembered how Elgar would fill in the missing parts on the piano playing from full score.[10] She felt that the music hired for the class was often selected by Elgar more because of his desire to study a particular work than because of its suitability for the limited resources of the class; this included such obscurities as the overture to Gounod's *Mireille.*

During his early Worcester years, Elgar acquired a number of books concerned with musical composition, and those that have survived from his library are listed in Appendix 3. Later in life he could be sceptical of what value these had been, and many years afterwards he told George Bernard Shaw that *Succinct Thorough-Bass School*, which he believed to be by Mozart, 'was the only document in existence of the smallest use to a student composer.'[11] On 27 May 1882, Elgar acquired a copy of the newly-published translation of Berlioz's *A Treatise on Modern Instrumentation and Orchestration to which is appended The Chef d'Orchestre.* He went through it meticulously making corrections and a table of its musical examples. Despite his remarks to Shaw, he described this treatise as 'inspiring' in a lecture at Birmingham University on 1 November 1906.[12] In the same lecture, he said that Prout's *Instrumentation*, which he had acquired on 7 October 1878, could 'be recommended for beginners.' The scores which have survived from Elgar's collection are listed in Appendix 4, but he owned or had access to more than these, and a study of scores would have played a vital part of his self-education.

One of the most enterprising concert series in the Midlands outside the Festival circuit were the regular orchestral concerts in the Town Hall Birmingham conducted by W C Stockley. In November 1882 Elgar joined the first violins of the orchestra and played regularly until November 1889. The repertory was more progressive than that of the Worcester Three Choirs Festivals, and here he played works by Beethoven, Mendelssohn, Schumann (a composer conspicuously absent from the Three Choirs programmes), and Wagner. There were also works by Dvorak, Berlioz and other French composers but almost none by Brahms.

These performing experiences in Worcester and Birmingham confronted Elgar in his most formative years with the art and craft of the composer from within. From the late 1870s, however, he broadened his experience yet further by attending concerts in London. Many years later, when considering the advantages of the gramophone, Elgar recalled and perhaps exaggerated the comparative difficulties of gaining musical knowledge in those earlier years, but none the less confirmed the importance of those experiences in his own creative development.

> If London in 1877–8–9 was scantily supplied with orchestral concerts, the provinces were in a worse plight.
>
> The Crystal Palace concerts, under the direction of August Manns, were undoubtedly the best, and many new works were produced and compositions of established repute were played which I wanted to know. I say 'know' and not 'hear'; it is possible to do either or both, but the scores were not easily obtainable; if they had been procurable a reading would have satisfied my immediate wants.
>
> But the actual procedure was on many occasions as follows – I lived one hundred and twenty miles from London, I rose at six, – walked a mile to the railway station; – the train left at seven; – arrived at Paddington about eleven; – underground to Victoria; – on to the Palace, arriving in time for the last three quarters of an hour of the rehearsal; if fortune smiled, this piece of rehearsal included the work desired to be heard: but fortune rarely smiled and more often than not the principal item was over. Lunch, – Concert at three; – at five a rush for the train to Victoria; – then to Paddington; – on to Worcester arriving at ten-thirty. A strenuous day indeed; but the new work had been heard and another treasure added to a life's experience.[13]

The earliest programmes of London orchestral concerts that survive in Elgar's collection date from 1881, and in addition to the Crystal Palace Saturday Concerts, Elgar regularly attended the St James's Hall Richter Concerts conducted by Hans Richter. Both series were particularly enterprising in programming the most recent German and French music, and it was here that Elgar's extensive knowledge of Schumann, Liszt, Brahms, Wagner, Dvorak, Berlioz and Saint-Saëns had a major source. Both series of concerts offered detailed programme notes with a generous number of music examples to aid the enquiring concert-goer. Between November 1878 and March 1899 Elgar sporadically attended the St James's Hall Popular Concerts, which offered chamber music by the greatest classical and romantic-Germanic composers. From 1889, after their move to London, Elgar and his wife periodically attended the opera, principally at Covent Garden.

Elgar travelled abroad first in August 1880 when he went on holiday to Paris. While there he heard Saint-Saëns play the organ at La Madeleine and bought a piano score of Delibes's *Sylvia*. By about 1872 it was Elgar's ambition to study in Leipzig, an uncharacteristic reflection of what English musical opinion would have considered proper for a gifted aspiring composer. By the early 1880s, however, this strategy had been reshaped, but at the beginning of January 1883 Elgar spent two and a half weeks in Leipzig and enthusiastically heard as much music as he could. He heard concerts at the Gewandhaus and the Musikverein and saw operas at the new theatre in Leipzig. Writing to his friend Dr C W Buck about Leipzig on 13 May 1883, Elgar reported: 'I heard no end of stuff. Schumann and Wagner no end. They have a good opera in Leipzig and we went many times.' Buck must have asked for more details as on 1 July following Elgar elaborated:

> We used to attend the rehearsals at the Gewandhaus; 9 a.m. . . . The first thing I heard was Haydn Sym. in G. – the Surprise: fancy!! . . . After that I got pretty well dosed with Schumann (my ideal!) Brahms, Rubinstein & Wagner, so had no cause to complain.

Elgar's most regular trips abroad were made between 1892 and 1902, years in which his own musical techniques and style were making their greatest consolidating advances. In that decade he made six trips to Germany, and on each he saw productions of operas by Wagner and occasionally by other composers.

Further evidence of works by other composers that may have had some particular influence on Elgar is provided by the contents of concerts that he conducted well into his mature years. He conducted the Worcester Festival Choral Society briefly in 1897, and in 1898 the Worcestershire Philharmonic Society was founded specifically to give him a platform as a conductor. He remained with the Society until 1904 conducting twelve concerts in all. Under him, the Society performed music by Beethoven, Brahms, Wagner, Verdi, Berlioz, Grieg, Tchaikovsky, Wolf, Humperdinck, Bruch, Wolfrum and Berger.

In the early years of the new century Elgar periodically conducted professional English orchestras. These engagements became more regular between June 1911 and October 1913 when he conducted (usually in London) and principally with the London Symphony Orchestra by whom he was engaged for two seasons. It can be assumed that as conductor Elgar played some part in selecting the programmes. The works included were drawn from the European repertory of which he had made himself so rich an heir.

Elgar was introduced to much European choral music and to some European instrumental music in the west country, but his knowledge of both expanded considerably through his experiences in London and abroad. The earliest composition model that he set himself in matters of structure and fine detail was Mozart, and as late as 1904, he could still affirm that 'Mozart is the musician from whom everyone should learn form.'[14] He first encountered Mozart's Symphony in G minor K 550 as a performer on 11 September 1878 during his first season playing in the Three Choirs Festival orchestra. He marked it in his programme for particular attention, and during the rehearsals he set himself the task of composing a symphony closely modelled on K 550. Although he completed only sections of a first, second and third movements, and none of the finale, he remembered the value of this exercise well into his maturity. In 1904 he recalled:

> I once ruled a score for the same instruments and with the same number of bars as Mozart's G Minor Symphony, and in that framework I wrote a symphony, following as far as possible the same outline in the themes and the same modulation. I did this on my own initiative, as I was groping in the dark after light, but looking back after thirty years I don't know any discipline from which I learned so much.[15]

Elgar lectured on this symphony at Birmingham on 8 November 1906 when he endorsed its reputation as 'amongst the *noblest* achievements of Art.'[16] He went on to conduct it with the LSO three times between 1911 and 1913. The Elgars saw a production of *Don Giovanni* at Covent Garden on 21 June 1889, and reacting probably more to the plot than to the music, the newly-weds' diary notes 'first time (*and last*)'. But it was not the last time, nor did Elgar's attitude remain negative. On 1 September 1897 they saw it in Munich conducted by Strauss when the verdict was 'lovely', and at a performance in London on 19 July 1902, they 'Enjoyed it much'. In a programme note for the Worcestershire Philharmonic Society on 7 January 1899, Elgar described *Don Giovanni* as 'Mozart's finest Opera', although there is no evidence to suggest that he had seen any other opera by Mozart.

By the latter decades of the nineteenth century, the music of Beethoven had assumed a central place in the English instrumental repertory, and Elgar heard and played much of it during his apprentice years. He remembered that 'the first [scores] which came into my hands were the Beethoven symphonies',[17] and that would have been before July 1873 when he quarried a Credo for his father's church choir largely from themes in Beethoven's fifth, seventh and ninth symphonies. By the 1880s, he was studying Beethoven's motivic intricacies. At a Crystal Palace Saturday Concert on 26 March 1887, when he heard the complete incidental music for *Egmont*, Elgar wrote on his programme that part of the second subject of the Allegro of the overture at bar 117 was derived from the first subject in the cellos from the 28th bar. Between October and December 1892 Elgar as violinist played all ten of Beethoven's violin sonatas and lectured on them in Worcester. During this series he also lectured (30 November) on Beethoven's Piano Sonata in C minor, the *Pathetique*.

There were four Germanic composers who exerted a particular and lasting influence on Elgar: Schumann, Brahms, Dvorak and most pervasively Wagner. Elgar's first real exposure to the music of Schumann came during his visit to Leipzig in January 1883. He was enthusiastic enough about the *Overture, Scherzo and Finale* to transcribe the first 17 bars of the

Scherzo in short score.[18] Writing to Dr Buck on 1 July 1883 about his musical experiences in Leipzig, Elgar described Schumann quite simply as 'my ideal!' Rosa Burley remembered Elgar playing the piano part in Schumann's Piano Quintet in the ensemble class at 'The Mount' in the early 1890s, and Elgar owned a volume of the most important of Schumann's piano works. Many years later W H Reed recalled that Elgar

> loved Schumann, and would discuss his symphonies at great length. The music entranced him; but he felt the weakness of the orchestration. He often surmised how certain other composers would have scored this or that passage – what Wagner would have done with it, or Berlioz, or Richard Strauss.[19]

Elgar mentioned the weakness of Schumann's orchestration in his lecture at the University of Birmingham on 1 November 1906 suggesting that Schumann, like Rubinstein, approached the orchestra through the piano and forgot that in playing the piano he used the sustaining pedal.[20]

On 12 May 1884, a week after he had travelled up to London to hear Richter conduct Schumann's 'Rhenish' Symphony, Elgar returned to hear Richter conduct the English premiere of Brahms's Symphony no 3. From this time Brahms quickly came to occupy a central and lasting place in Elgar's musical affections, and no work by Brahms more prominently than this symphony. Against the third movement, which was encored on that occasion, Elgar wrote 'lovely' in his programme. He chose it as the subject of his third lecture as Professor of Music at Birmingham University in November 1905, and at the same time he conducted it at a number of concerts in provincial cities. He conducted it again several times during his seasons with the LSO in 1911–13, but its strongest reverberations (and behind it those of Schumann's 'Rhenish') are found in his own Symphony no 2.[21] Elgar heard and played much of Brahms's music both during his years of apprenticeship and later, and he absorbed much of its spirit and technique into his own music. In a letter to the Malvern *Advertiser* dated 21 December 1886 he expressed his belief in the greatness of Brahms whom he described as

> the classical composer *par excellence* of the present day; one who, free from any provincialism or expression of national dialect ... writes for the whole world and for all time – a giant, lofty and unapproachable ...[22]

At the time when he was most occupied with integrating vocal and orchestral resources into a tightly organised unity in *The Dream of Gerontius*, Elgar could write of Brahms's *Schicksalslied* in the programme for his performance with the Worcestershire Philharmonic Society on 5 May 1900: 'The importance given to the orchestra in this work would almost justify its being called a "Symphonic Cantata".'

The highlight of the Worcester Three Choirs Festival in 1884 was the visit by Dvorak on 11 September to conduct his Symphony no 6 in D and *Stabat Mater,* and Elgar played in both. He was entranced, and wrote enthusiastically to Dr Buck on 28 September:

> I wish you could hear Dvorak's music. It is simply ravishing, so tuneful and clever and the orchestration is wonderful; no matter how few instruments he uses it never sounds thin. I cannot describe it; it must be heard.

Dvorak returned to conduct his Symphony no 6 in Birmingham on 21 October 1886, and Elgar was once more in the orchestra.

The single most influential composer on Elgar's formative years and maturity was Wagner. Elgar inherited from him some of the most significant innovations made in the language of music in the second half of the nineteenth century.[23] The earliest evidence of Elgar's association with the music of Wagner is at a concert of the Worcester Glee Club on 23 October 1876 for which he made an arrangement from the overture to *The Flying Dutchman.* Hubert Leicester remembered about the same time Elgar playing some of the overture to *Tannhäuser* on the organ. His first involvement with Wagner's music on a grander scale was at the Three Choirs Festival on 6 September 1881 when he played in the march and chorus 'Hail bright abode' from Act II of *Tannhäuser.* During his visit to Leipzig in January 1883, Elgar saw productions of *Lohengrin* and *Tannhaüser,* and at a concert he heard the Prelude to Act I of *Parsifal.* About this time he made a transcription in short score of the thirty-bar 'Entry of the Minstrels' from Act II of *Tannhäuser.*[24]

Elgar played some of the more popular orchestral excerpts from Wagner in Stockley's Birmingham orchestra, but during the 1880s his knowledge of Wagner grew most fully through the London concerts conducted by Manns and Richter. On 3 March 1883 Manns conducted a memorial concert for Wagner who had died in Venice on 13 February. Elgar was present and annotated his programme with comments intended perhaps for a companion, but affording his earliest specific reactions to the music of Wagner. He pencilled expression marks on the Siegfried motive in the Funeral March from *Götterdämmerung,* and 'beautiful' against *Siegfried Idyll.* Beside the Prelude and Liebestod Elgar wrote 'This is the thing!', and against the text of the Liebestod he continued 'This is the finest thing of W's that I have heard up to the present. I shall never forget this'. The spell that *Tristan und Isolde* continued to exert over him is confirmed by a note that he wrote on the blank page facing the Prelude in his vocal score of the opera acquired on 1 June 1893.[25]

> This Book contains the Height – the Depth, –
> the Breadth, – the Sweetness, – the Sorrow, –
> the Best and the whole of the Best of
> This world and the Next.
> Edward Elgar:

The music of Wagner was played frequently at the St James's Hall Richter concerts, and Richter included not only Wagner's concert pieces and orchestral extracts from the operas but also whole operatic scenes. On 23 May 1887 he conducted the Ride of the Valkyries, and the love scene from Act I of *Walküre*. Elgar put three ticks beside the former in his programme and wrote:

> brass telling through all the strings – most weird & witchlike hurry scurrying through the air and the battle in the rushing wind embodied.

Against the text of the love duet he noted striking characteristics of scoring, and pencilled a vertical line beside the fourteen lines where Siegmund draws the sword from the tree. From about 1889, the year in which he moved to London, productions of Wagner's operas became more frequent in the capital and Elgar saw a number of these. In July 1889, soon after the move, he saw *Die Meistersinger* at Covent Garden no fewer than three times.

Elgar's knowledge and understanding of Wagner deepened most markedly during the crucial decade 1892-1902 when he travelled to Germany six times and on each occasion saw productions of operas by Wagner. In July 1892 the Elgars visited Bayreuth where they saw *Parsifal* twice, *Die Meistersinger* and *Tristan und Isolde*; the last Alice Elgar noted in her diary as TRISTAN. Before making this pilgrimage Elgar acquired analyses of the three operas. He made a detailed collation of the motives included in these with vocal scores of the operas. On each of their subsequent visits to Germany in August and September 1893, 1894, 1895 and 1897 they saw productions of Wagner's operas in Munich. In 1893 the Elgars were joined by Rosa Burley, who later wrote an account of the pilgrimage. On 17 August the party saw *Die Meistersinger*, and Rosa Burley recalled how Elgar loved the part writing in the quintet. She remembered also that Elgar made extensive notes on what he had heard, and that they had detailed discussions about the performances and Wagner's technical means of achieving his dramatic effect. On the following evenings they saw *The Ring*; poor Miss Burley, apparently overcome by its length, confessed that she was quite unable to understand Elgar's enthusiasm for it. She described the effect of *Tristan und Isolde* on all three of them, however, as 'shattering'.[26] On 29 August 1893 Alice Elgar wrote in her diary 'and then the great opera Tristan und Isolde at 6'. Elgar returned to Bayreuth in July 1902 at the invitation of Hans Richter who that year was sharing the conducting of *The Ring* with Siegfried Wagner whom Elgar met.

At the time when he was planning the trip to Munich in 1893, Elgar explained the basic principles of Wagner's operas to Rosa Burley who later remembered how he:

> plunged ... into an exciting lecture on the theories behind the new music-drama, its divergence from the older Italian opera, its use of

leading-themes – which he illustrated on the piano with the 'gaze' motive from *Tristan* – and the welding which was attempted of musical, plastic and dramatic elements into one art-form.[27]

Elgar's recognition of the importance of Wagner's innovations, and in particular of the creative interaction between music drama and symphonic music are incapsulated in a programme note that he wrote for the Worcestershire Philharmonic Society on 5 May 1900.

> It is unquestioned that the modern methods of writing music destined for the stage are the outcome of the symphony. For instance, the second act of 'Tristan' may be viewed in this light as a symphonic movement very much extended, and the tendency nowadays is to seek for continuity in the expression of ideas in place of a patchwork of such accepted 'forms' as the duet, aria, and so forth.

In his friend August Jaeger, Elgar found an ardent Wagnerian whose enthusiasm he was keen to share. In the postscript of a letter to Jaeger dated 18 October 1897, Elgar wrote: 'I forgot if I told you I am appreciating your Wagner letters very much: go on. It is nice to be told I am a sheep.'[28] But he was not happy to be so categorized by a wider public. In *The Musical Times* of October 1900 he is reported as protesting:

> I became acquainted with the representative-theme long before I had ever heard a note of Wagner, or seen one of his scores. My first acquaintance with the *Leitmotiv* was derived (in my boyhood) from Mendelssohn's *Elijah*, and the system elaborated from that, as my early unpublished things show.[29]

Despite this disclaimer with its defensive tone, Elgar's experience of the leitmotiv (as distinct from the Mendelssohnian reminiscence motif), and its wealth of dramatic and structural potential were inherited directly from Wagner. Elgar's genuine appraisal of the leitmotiv, its techniques and artistic value, can be gathered from the note that he wrote for a performance of Humperdinck's cantata *Die Wallfahrt nach Kevelaar* by the Worcestershire Philharmonic Society on 7 May 1898.

> In Hänsel and Gretel ... HUMPERDINCK employed the 'representative theme' in quite as elaborate a way as WAGNER, illustrating character and idea in as marked a manner. In the present work, the same intricacy is displayed; not, be it noted, the intricacy of the mere contrapuntist, but elaboration abounding in poetic and suggestive touches.

Elgar was grateful to receive from Schott & Co on 26 April 1902 an orchestral score of *Götterdämmerung* to complete his set of *The Ring*, and on 30 December 1902 an orchestral score of *Parsifal*. That December he also received, as a Christmas present from Mr and Mrs Edward Speyer, the eight volumes of Wagner's complete prose works in the translation by W A Ellis. Eight years later there is a glimpse of the respect that he maintained for Wagner in a letter to his revered friend Hans Richter dated 9 November 1910. 'I have been reading a book by Judith Gautier about the "Meister" and you. The book is … bald and poor, but it talks about you and the "Meister", and that would redeem anything.'[30] As late as 1926, Elgar was defending the inclusion of an excerpt from *Parsifal* at the Worcester Three Choirs Festival.[31]

Although the music of Liszt seems not to have been programmed at all in concerts in the Midlands, Elgar got to know a good deal of it in London in the 1880s. He was present, for example, at the all-Liszt concert at the Crystal Palace on 10 April 1886 at which the composer himself, with not four months to live, was present. Elgar owned full scores of the twelve symphonic poems although when he acquired them is not known. Elgar did not become familiar with the music of Tchaikovsky until towards the end of the 1890s, but its impact on him then was immediate. In a programme note for the first concert of the Worcestershire Philharmonic Society on 7 May 1898 Elgar described Tchaikovsky as 'the great emotionalist'. By then he had heard the fifth and sixth symphonies, and about this time as a 'jape' he contrapuntally combined the opening of the 5/4 second movement of Symphony no 6 with the British national anthem.[32] Elgar appears to have heard music by Bruckner only once, but at that Richter concert on 23 May 1887 the Symphony no 7 was played and Elgar noted against the opening of the first movement given as a music example in his programme 'fine intro'. There is no evidence of Elgar having heard or known any music by Mahler.

Of the major European composers active after 1900, Elgar became most familiar with the music of Richard Strauss. He first encountered Strauss conducting *Don Giovanni* in Munich in September 1897, and on 19 May 1902 became irritated when Strauss took too much rehearsal time on Liszt's *A Faust Symphony* in Düsseldorf. But after the success of the second performance of *The Dream of Gerontius* in Düsseldorf, and Strauss's toast to 'the welfare and success of the first English progressivist, Meister Edward Elgar', all would have been forgiven. On 4 June 1902 Elgar met Strauss in London and heard him conduct three of his symphonic poems. On 5 December 1902 the Elgars dined with Strauss at Edgar Speyer's in London, and the next evening heard Strauss conduct the English premiere of *Ein Heldenleben*, whose final rehearsal Elgar had also attended that day. Alice Elgar described this in her diary as 'Very astonishing'. On 6 December 1902 Strauss presented Elgar with a full score of *Ein Heldenleben* and Elgar studied it thoroughly. Where Strauss quoted themes from his earlier works, Elgar noted 'Don Juan', 'Tod und Verklärung' and 'Till Eulenspiegel' on the score; each of these he had heard at least twice that year. In the course of an interview given on 7 April 1907 during an American trip, Elgar affirmed that:

Strauss is the greatest [musical] genius of the age, and his later works I like best of all ... His 'Don Juan' is the greatest masterpiece of the present, and his 'Heldenleben' and 'Zarathustra' I find almost as inspiring.[33]

When he was conducting the LSO in the season 1911–12, Elgar programmed *Tod und Verklärung* and *Also sprach Zarathustra*, but in the event neither was performed.

In the 1880s Elgar was strongly attracted to the music of Berlioz and lesser French composers of the day which he heard principally at the Crystal Palace Saturday Concerts. During his trip to Paris in August 1880, he bought a piano score of Delibes's *Sylvia*, a work he was to hear, play and conduct at regular intervals. In its thematic table he particularly marked Prelude, Les Chasseresses (Delibes's response to Wagner's Ride of the Valkyries), Intermezzo, Scène Finale, Marche, Scène and Divertissement. In these years, prior to his closer attraction to the music of Wagner, Elgar was drawn to distinctively French styles of orchestral scoring. For a concert by the Worcester Festival Choral Society 24 November 1891, he wrote a detailed programme note on Massenet's *Scènes-pittoresques* which tells almost more of Elgar than it does of Massenet or of the German school to which he alluded. The brilliant orchestration of the French, Elgar wrote:

all other nations may well envy; Berlioz, Gounod, Saint-Saëns, Massenet and Delibes, to say nothing of hosts of lesser lights, have a command over orchestral effect never approached by the composers of other countries; the secret lying in the fact that polyphony (as practised by the German school) is incompatible with orchestration in the French sense of the word, the best effects being always gained where the music is practically only treble and bass (the inner parts unimportant), the result being that one, or at most two, instruments stand out alone. The Suite now under notice illustrates this principle on every page.

Elgar returned to two of these composers in his lecture on orchestration at Birmingham in November 1906. Implying that the genius of Berlioz was misunderstood, he referred to him as 'accused of inventing effects and then composing music to exploit them', while of Delibes as orchestrator he noted succinctly 'wastes nothing'.[34] Elgar made himself thoroughly familiar with as much of Berlioz's music as was then accessible, and even prepared a performance of the *Symphonie Roméo et Juliette* with the Worcestershire Philharmonic Society in April 1904.

In the last two decades of the nineteenth century Elgar's tastes were eclectic. In the circles of near-domestic music-making of his earliest Worcester days the repertory relied heavily on arrangements of Italian music dating from earlier in the nineteenth century. Elgar remained true to this music defending it in a note on an excerpt from Bellini's *Norma* included in a concert of Worcestershire Philharmonic Society on 5 May 1900.

It has been the fashion of late years to decry, without discrimination, the
works of the Italian school of the first half of this century. It does not
follow that music which gave pleasure to our grand-fathers and fathers
must necessarily be trivial, weak and vapid.

At the same concert he conducted 'The Dance of the Hours' from
Ponchielli's *La Gioconda* which he described as 'a good sample of modern
brilliant Italian music'. The modern brilliant Italian music which exerted the
most powerful influence on his own music however was Verdi's *Requiem.*
As late as 1931, he described this as a 'work I have always worshipped'.[35]
Except for his seeking out productions of Wagner, Elgar was not an avid
opera-goer, and that may have been something of the penalty of his English
environment. Elgar would have seen a number of more established operas
by composers such as Mozart and Verdi for their unquestioned musical
quality while others by Humperdinck, Mancinelli and Mascagni, were either
first London performances or very recent music.

The most striking aspect of Elgar's apprenticeship is his resolution to gain
a knowledge of the widest possible repertory, and to learn about the most
advanced styles and techniques practised in the wider European domain.
This began as an intuition but was sustained by the growing certainty
that only thus would he find his own distinctive artistic voice. From the
widest sources he distilled what his creativity needed and what English
circumstances dictated, and thus he became an heir of the richest musical
continuity. Such a resolution was not easy in a country that was proud
of its political and religious insularity and its industrial, commercial and
maritime superiority, but Elgar the artist realized that no man, least of all
an Englishman, could afford to be an island.

Notes

1. de Cordova, Rudolph, 'Illustrated Interviews: LXXXI – Dr. Edward Elgar',
   Strand Magazine, 27 (May 1904), 538–9.
2. I am indebted to the Elgar Foundation, its Chairman, E Wulstan Atkins, and the
   then Curator Jack McKenzie and his wife Vivienne, for access to the holdings
   of the Birthplace, and for every kindness and assistance that they so willingly
   gave in the course of these researches.
3. These tables are derived from Elgar's extant programmes, letters, diary entries
   and newspapers, but documentation of some significant concerts, particularly
   from Elgar's earliest years, has demonstrably not survived. In his programme
   for the Wagner Memorial Concert at the Crystal Palace on 3 March 1883, for
   example, Elgar wrote beside the *Kaisermarsch* 'I do not care a lot for this: have
   heard it often.' This is the first of only three occasions when Elgar is known to
   have heard this work, and even allowing for some exaggeration, it would seem
   that he had heard it a number of times prior to March 1883.

4. Housed at the Hereford and Worcester County Record Office, St Helen's Church Worcester.
5. These are all published in Young, Percy M (ed.), *Letters of Edward Elgar* (London: Bles, 1956), unless otherwise located.
6. 'Edward Elgar', *The Musical Times*, 41, (October 1900), 643.
7. Reed W H, *Elgar as I knew him* (London: Gollancz, 1973), p.85.
8. BBC radio talk, August 1960.
9. Reed, p.85.
10. Burley, Rosa and Carruthers, Frank C, *Edward Elgar: the record of a friendship* (London: Barrie and Jenkins, 1972), pp.33–5.
11. Laurence, Dan H (ed.), *Shaw's Music* (London: Bodley Head, 1981), 1, p.56.
12. Young, Percy M (ed.), *A Future for English Music* (London: Dobson, 1968), pp.248–9.
13. This manuscript is a draft for a speech made on 16 November 1927. It is headed 'H. M. V.', and is housed without classification at Elgar's Birthplace. See also Moore, Jerrold N, *Elgar on Record* (London: EMI/OUP, 1974), p.78.
14. de Cordova, 539.
15. de Cordova, 539. *GB-Lbl* Add. 63147, f.13. The first page of another source of this exercise is reproduced in *A Future for English Music* ed. Young, facing p.45, but no location of this source is specified.
16. *A Future for English Music*, p.273.
17. de Cordova, 540.
18. *GB-Lbl* Add. 49973A, f.68v. Elgar later headed this manuscript 'Memento May 1879–83'.
19. Reed, p.83.
20. *A Future for English Music*, p.251.
21. Dennison, Peter, 'Elgar, Brahms and Schumann: A Case of Romantic Continuity', to be published.
22. Quoted in Moore, Jerrold N, *Edward Elgar: a Creative Life* (Oxford: OUP, 1984), p.117.
23. See also Dennison, Peter, 'Elgar and Wagner', *Music & Letters*, 66 (April, 1985), 93–109.
24. *GB-Lbl* Add. 49973A, f.67v. See n.18 above.
25. Date confirmed by Alice Elgar's diary, 2 June 1893.
26. Burley and Carruthers, pp.67–70.
27. Burley and Carruthers, p.56.
28. Young, Percy M (ed.), *Letters to Nimrod* (London: Dobson, 1965), p.4.
29. *The Musical Times*, 41 (October, 1900), 647.
30. Maine, Basil, *Elgar: his Life and Works* (London: Bell, 1933), p.280.
31. *Letters of Edward Elgar*, pp.294–5.
32. *The Musical Times*, 41 (October, 1900), 647.
33. Quoted in *Edward Elgar: a Creative Life*, p.511.
34. *A Future for English Music*, p. 253.
35. *Elgar on Record*, pp. 127–8.

In the following Appendices, **4.84** means the fourth month, that is April, of 1884. Entries in **bold** type signify that on this occasion, Elgar was a performer. On most of these prior to 1897 he performed as a violinist, but from that year he conducted the work in question.

Appendix 1   British music

Armes, Philip
Hezekiah **9.78**

Barnett, John Francis
The Building of the Ship, cantata **9.81**

Bennett, Sterndale
Caprice in E, pf and orch op 22 **4.83**
The May Queen, pastoral op 39 **9.78; 2.86**
The Naiads, overture **4.87; 5.87**; 2.98
Paradise and the Peri, overture **4.83; 4.03**
Parisina, overture op 3 **11.89**
Piano concerto no 4 in F **9.78; 5.87**
Symphony in G op 43 **4.93(iii)**
The Wood-nymphs, overture 10.89; **11.91**

Blair, Hugh
Blessed are they who watch **12.94**; 9.96
Magnificat and Nunc Dimittis in B 9.87
Ode on Death 1.89

Brewer, Herbert
Emmaus (scored by Elgar) 9.01
O sing unto the Lord 9.98

Bridge, Frederick
The Repentence of Ninevah **9.90**
Rock of Ages **10.85**

Coleridge-Taylor, Samuel
Ballade in A op 33 9.98
Solemn Prelude op 40 9.99

Cowen, Frederic
The Rose Maiden, cantata **2.78**
Ruth **9.87**
The Sleeping Beauty, cantata, selections **12.85**
Symphony no 3 in C **4.83; 9.87**
Symphony no 6 in E **1.01**

Händel
Concerto Grosso in D op 6 no 5 **6.11**
Esther, overture **9.84**
Israel in Egypt **4.92; 9.93**
Jephtha (edited by Sullivan) **9.81**
Judas Maccabaeus (abridged version) **2.85; 2.86; 3.87**; 9.98
Messiah (scoring by Mozart) **9.78; 9.81; 9.84; 9.87; 9.90; 9.93**; 9.96; 9.97;
    9.98; 9.99; 9.00
Occasional Oratorio, overture **4.93**
O praise the Lord with one consent **11.90**
Samson (abridged by Prout) 9.96
Serse, Largo (Ombra mai fù) **5.86**
Zadok the priest **5.87**; 9.97

Lloyd, Charles H.
Festival Overture 9.98
Hero and Leander, cantata **9.84; 11.87; 12.92**
Hymn of Thanksgiving, cantata 9.97

Macfarren, George
Hero and Leander, overture **9.81**
Violin concerto in G **12.85**

MacCunn, Hamish
Bonny Kilmeny, cantata op 2 3.90
Land of the Mountain and the Flood, overture op 3 3.90
Lord Ullin's Daughter, cantata op 4 4.93
The Ship o'the Fiend, orchestral ballade op 5 11.89

Mackenzie, Alexander
La belle dame sans merci, orchestral ballad op 29 5.84
The Bride, cantata op 25 **9.81**
Britannia, overture op 52 **4.95**; 9.99
Colomba, ballet music op 28 **10.85**
The Dream of Jubal, cantata op 41 1.98; **5.99**
Rhapsodie Ecossaise op 21 **11.83**
Scottish Rhapsody no 3 op 74 **12.11**
Twelfth Night, overture op 40 6.88

Parry, Hubert
Blessed Pair of Sirens, cantata **12.94**; 9.99
Job, oratorio **9.93**
Judith, oratorio **12.88; 4.91**
The Lotus Eaters, cantata **5.02**
Magnificat in F 9.97

Ode to Music **10.13**
A Song of Darkness and Light, cantata 9.98
St Cecilia's Day **9.90**
Symphonic Variations 1.00
Symphony no 4 in E 7.89
Thanksgiving Te Deum 9.00

Prout, Ebenezer
Organ concerto in E 7.90; 9.98
Symphony no 4 in D, first and fourth movements **5.87**
Symphony in F **2.86**

Stainer, John
The Daughter of Jairus **9.78; 4.89**

Stanford, Charles
The Battle of the Baltic, ballad op 41 **11.91**
By the waters of Babylon **10.87**
The Last Post, cantata op 75 9.00; **1.01**
The Revenge, cantata op 24 **9.87**
Shamus O'Brien 11.96
Symphony no 2 in D, the Elegiac **2.87**
Symphony no 3 in F op 28 **10.87**; 5.88
Symphony no 5 in D op 56, Adagio and Finale 9.98
The Three Holy Children, cantata op 22 **10.85; 12.94**

Sullivan, Arthur
The Golden Legend, cantata **5.87; 9.87; 11.92**; 9.98
Henry VIII, incidental music **4.83 (i)**; 9.96
In memoriam, overture **4.85; 4.95**
Iolanthe 2.02
The Light of the World, oratorio **10.86**
Overture di ballo **10.85; 2.89**; 2.90
The Prodigal Son, oratorio **3.94**
The Sorcerer 10.98
The Tempest, incidental music op 1 **2.84; 9.93; 3.94; 4.95**
Trial by Jury 10.98
Yeomen of the Guard 5.89

Williams, C. Lee
The Last Night at Bethany **9.90**

Appendix 2   European Music

Bach, J. S.
   Christmas Oratorio, parts 1 and 2 9.96; 9.98
     Pastoral Symphony **9.90;** 3.97
   God goeth up, Cantata 43 9.00
   God so loved the world, Cantata 68 **9.84**
   God's time is best, Cantata 106 9.99
   Mass in B **9.93;** 3.95; 5.02
   St Matthew Passion 3.95
   A stronghold sure, Cantata 80 **9.90;** 9.97

Beethoven
   Ah! perfido op 65 **11.83;** 4.94
   Choral Fantasia **12.92**
   Christ on the Mount of Olives (Egendi) **9.81; 9.90**
   The Consecration of the House, overture **12.85**
   Coriolan, overture 10.89; 10.01; **12.02; 6.11; 2.12**
   Egmont, incidental music 3.87
     overture **9.78; 11.83;** 5.84; **11.89;** 4.93; **4.96; 5.98; 2.01**
   Leonore, overture no 2 3.97
   Leonore, overture no 3 **1.83;** 4.90; 4.97; 1.98; 9.00; **10.13**
   Mass in C **5.86**
   Missa Solemnis 9.97
   Namensfeier 6.88
   Piano concerto no 3 **12.83**
   Piano concerto no 4 2.98; **5.00**
   Piano concerto no 5 **10.85;** 3.99; 5.99; 5.02; **2.12**
   Piano sonata in D op 28 2.79
   Prometheus, overture **9.87; 12.94;** 1.98
   Romance in F op 50 1.83; 9.00; 10.01
   Septet op 20 2.88
   String quartet op 18 no 1 2.79
   String quartet op 18 no 3 11.78
   String quartet op 18 no 4 9.00
   String quartet op 59 no 3 3.01
   String quartet op 74 4.02
   String quartet op 130 3.03
   String quartet op 131 3.99
   String quartet op 135 12.87
   String trio op 9 no 1 1.83
   Symphony no 2 3.90; **4.94**
   Symphony no 3 **12.83;** 4.84; 9.98; 10.98; 2.00; 5.01; 5.02; 12.02

Symphony no 4 6.88; 2.90; **11.93;** 11.96
Symphony no 5 **9.81; 4.87;** 10.89; **9.90;** 9.97; 3.99; 10.01
Symphony no 6 **11.83;** 4.90; **4.91;** 2.98; 4.99; 4.99
Symphony no 7 **12.85;** 11.89; **9.93;** 4.94; 2.00; 11.01; 10.02; **11.11**
Symphony no 8 **4.85;** 7.89
Symphony no 9 10.81; 12.95; 10.96; 6.98; 9.00; 9.11
Violin concerto **9.78 (i); 9.84 (i); 6.11**
Violin sonatas, complete **12.92**

Bellini
Norma, overture and selections **2.77; 5.86**
  Act I, 'Haste ye Druids', cavatina with men's chorus **5.00**

Berger, William
Der Totentanz op 86 **4.04***

Berlioz
Carnival romain 2.90; 6.98
The Childhood of Christ **12.99**
  The Shepherds' Farewell **12.02**
Le corsaire **6.11**
The Damnation of Faust 7.89
  Danse des Sylphes, Marche Hongroise **9.84; 5.86 (ii);** 4.97 (ii); 9.97;
  9.00
Les francs-juges, overture 2.81
Grande messe des morts 5.83; 10.02
Invitation to the Dance (Weber) **9.84**
Lélio 10.81
Les nuits d'été 10.81; **9.84 (iv)**
Rob Roy 2.00
Roi Lear 10.97; **11.11**
Symphonie fantastique 10.81 (v); 8.83 (ii, iv, v); 11.02
Symphony Romeo and Juliet **4.04***
Zaïde, boléro op 19 no 1 **9.84; 9.87**

Bizet
Carmen 7.89

Brahms
Academic Festival, overture 5.87
Alto Rhapsody 6.90; **10.13**

* Rehearsed but not conducted by Elgar

Clarinet Quintet 1.99
Double Concerto op 102 3.90
A German Requiem **9.93**; 9.99
Die Mainacht op 43 no 2 6.89; 1.99; 12.99
Partsongs, three, from op 44 **1.99**; **5.00**
Piano concerto no 2 **11.11**
Schicksalslied op 54 **5.00**
String quartet in C op 51 no 1 1.87; 4.02
String quartet in B flat op 67 3.99
String quintet in F op 88 1.83
String quintet in G op 111 3.91
Symphony no 1 9.01
Symphony no 2 10.89; 10.89; 2.98; 11.99; 9.00
Symphony no 3 5.84; 6.89; 10.01; 11.02; **11.05**; **5.11**; **10.11**; **10.13**
Symphony no 4 12.04
Tragic Overture **12.11**; **2.12**
Variations on a Theme by Haydn 9.98; 5.01; **6.11**
Violin concerto 10.04
Violin sonata in A op 100 **4.92**
Violin sonata in D op 108 **4.92**
Violin sonata in G op 78 2.81
Von ewige liebe op 43 no 1 9.00

Bruch
Lay of the Bell, cantata op 45 **12.03**
Violin concerto no 1 in G op 26 6.88; 10.98
Violin concerto no 3 in D op 58 1.98

Bruckner
Symphony no 7 5.87

Cherubini
Abencérages, overture **10.80**; **11.91**
Anacréon, overture **10.87**; 2.00
Les deux journées, overture **2.87**
Mass in D **9.81**; **9.84**

Chopin
Piano concerto no 2 5.99

Cornelius
Die Vätergruft 9.99

Delibes
Le Roi s'amuse, suite **11.81**; **5.02**
Sylvia, suite **11.82**; 8.83; **12.85**; 2.98; **5.99**

Dvorak
Andante for string orchestra **12.98**
Carnival, overture op 92 6.99
Cello concerto **11.12**
Husitskà, overture op 67 **11.11**
In Nature's Realm, overture op 91 4.94
Nocturne for strings op 40 3.90
Piano quintet in A op 81 9.97
Slavonic dances op 46 **1.99 (ii, viii)**; 10.00 (iv); **11.05 (ii, v)**; **12.11 (i, ii)**
Slavonic dances, unspecified 7.91; 9.93; 6.94
The Spectre's Bride op 69 **1.96**
Stabat mater **9.84**; 9.98
Symphonic Variations op 78 6.89; 10.97
Symphony no 6 op 60 **9.84**; **10.86**
Symphony no 8 op 88 7.90
Te Deum op 103 9.99

Franck
Symphony **11.12**

Gade
Christmas Eve op 40 **11.83**
Spring's Message op 35 **4.85**; **4.96**
Symphony no 1 **11.91**

Glazunov
Symphony no 5 1.00

Gluck
Orfeo 11.90; 12.91

Gounod
Faust 11.90; 5.94; 1.98
Funeral march of a marionette **2.85**
Gallia **5.98**
Hymne à Saint-Cécile 4.97
Marche militaire 8.83
Mireille, overture **2.89**; **4.91**
Redemption **9.84**; **9.87**; **1.94**; 9.97
La reine de Saba, pageant march **10.85**
Roméo et Juliette 6.89

Grieg
Länderkennung 1.01; 5.02
Piano concerto 3.90; 9.97; 9.00; **11.02**

Peer Gynt, suite no 1 **9.90**; 9.00

Guilmant
Symphony in D with organ **5.86**; **4.96**

Haydn
Creation **4.92**
   part 1 **9.78**; **4.91**; 9.97; 9.98; 9.00
   parts 1 and 2 **9.81**; **12.86**; **9.90**; 9.99
Mass in C, Paukenmesse 6.89
String quartet op 20 no 4 4.02
String quartet op 54 no 2 3.99
String quartet op 71 no 3 2.88
String quartet op 76 no 2 3.79; 2.81
Symphony no 92 **11.11**
Symphony no 94 1.83
Symphony no 96 **4.89**
Symphony no 97 6.88
Symphony no 99 3.90
Symphony no 102 1.98; **5.11**

Herold
Zampa, overture **5.78**

Hummel
Mass in B flat op 77 **12.91**

Humperdinck
Das Glück von Edenhall **4.03**
Hänsel und Gretel 3.95
Die Wallfahrt nach Kevelaar **5.98**

Leoncavallo
I Pagliacci, Prologue **5.97**

Liszt
A Faust Symphony 5.02
Festklänge 11.89
Hungarian Rhapsody no 1 in F 4.84; 2.00; 11.01
Hungarian Rhapsody no 2 in G 9.00
Hungarian Rhapsody no 4 in D 4.86
Die Ideale **10.11**
Mazeppa 4.86
Orpheus **4.03**
Piano concerto no 1 4.86; 7.90; **12.11**
Piano concerto no 2 11.99

Les Préludes 4.86; 6.98
Ràkòczy March 8.83; 4.86
Totentanz 2.90

Mancinelli
Ero e Leandro 6.99

Mascagni
Cavalleria Rusticana 12.91; 12.92
  Intermezzo **11.92**

Massenet
Le Cid, March 4.97; **5.98;** 9.00
Esclarmonde, Interlude 10.89
Scènes-pittoresques **1.83; 10.86; 12.86; 11.91**

Mendelssohn
Athalie, overture **1.83**
  War March of the Priests **11.86**
Calm Sea and Prosperous Voyage 10.89
Capriccio brillant op 22 **4.93**
Come let us sing **4.93**
Elijah **5.76; 9.78; 9.81; 10.82; 9.84; 1.87; 9.87; 9.90; 9.93;** 9.96; 9.97;
  9.98; 9.99; 9.00
Fair Melusine **4.88;** 1.98
The First Walpurgis Night **4.85; 4.95**
Hear my prayer **9.78; 9.87**
Hebrides Overture 2.81; **2.84; 5.86;** 2.89
Hymn of Praise **9.78; 9.81; 10.82; 2.87; 9.87; 9.93; 5.95;** 9.97; 9.98;
  9.99; 9.00
A Midsummer Night's Dream, overture **9.81**
  overture and incidental music 10.81; **10.84**
Praise Jehova (Lauda Sion) **4.82; 12.88**
Ruy Blas, overture 1.83; **2.85; 12.85; 10.87; 5.99; 10.11**
Son and stranger, overture **3.94**
St Paul **9.84; 12.87; 9.90;** 9.96
String quartet in E op 44 no 2 2.81
Symphony no 1 **10.80**
Symphony no 3 **11.81; 11.83; 10.85;** 2.90; 11.02
Symphony no 4 **1.83; 5.86; 4.88; 12.93;** 10.97
Violin concerto **2.84;** 11.89; 4.93; 10.01; **12.10**
When Israel came out **11.90**

Meyerbeer
Festmarsch, 'Schiller' **11.89**
Le prophète 1.83; 6.90

Coronation march **4.85**

Mozart
Don Giovanni 6.89; 9.97; 7.02
 overture 11.96; **1.99**
Idomeneo, overture 3.90; **5.02**
King Thamos, selections **4.94**
Eine kleine Nachtmusik **12.88**
The Magic Flute, overture **9.81; 9.84**; 4.93; 9.00
The Marriage of Figaro, overture **10.84; 9.93; 11.05**
Piano concerto K 482 **10.84**
Requiem **9.78; 9.90**
Sinfonia concertante K 364 3.03
String quartet in C K 465 **1.94**; 9.97
Symphony in D K 385 6.98
Symphony in C K 425 6.90
Symphony in D K 504 6.99
Symphony in G K 550 **9.78; 9.87**; 9.98; **10.11; 1.12; 10.13**
Symphony in C K 551 **4.82; 4.88; 12.91**
Wind quintet in E flat K 452 1.83

Nicolai
The Merry Wives of Windsor, overture **5.78; 9.78; 11.82; 4.88**

Ponchielli
La Gioconda, Dance of the hours 8.83; **11.83; 5.00**

Raff
Italian Suite, 'In the South' **2.85; 2.86; 2.89**
Symphony no 5, second and third movements **12.94**

Rimsky-Korsakov
Fantasia on Serbian Themes op 6 1.99
The Snowmaiden, suite 6.99

Rossini
The Barber of Seville, overture **4.95**
Otello, overture **2.77; 11.89**
Semiramide, overture **5.78; 12.83; 11.86**
The Thieving Magpie, overture **11.93**
William Tell 6.89
 overture **2.77; 5.78; 9.78; 9.81; 4.82; 4.88**; 2.90; 11.94

Rubinstein, Anton
Feramors, ballet music **2.87; 4.93**
Die Makkabäer 1.83

Piano concerto no 4 in D 2.00
Symphony no 2, 'The Ocean' 1.83

Saint-Saens
  Cello concerto no 1 in A **11.11**
  Danse macabre 1.98; 9.00
  Fantasia Africa op 89 4.94
  The heavens declare 9.97
  Introduction and Rondo capriccioso op 28 10.98; **2.01; 12.10; 6.11**
  Jota aragonese op 64 3.90
  Piano concerto no 2 in G 10.89; **6.11; 11.11; 2.12**
  Piano concerto no 4 in C 4.90
  Le rouet d'Omphale op 31 **2.85;** 6.88; 4.97; **12.11**
  Suite algérienne, Marche militaire française 3.90; 1.99
  Violin concerto no 1 in A 11.89
  Violin concerto no 3 in B 10.97; 5.02

Schubert
  Alfonso und Estrella, overture **1.83**
  Great is Jehova 9.96
  Mass in E flat D 950 **9.87**
  Mass in G D 167 **5.88**
  Overture in C in the Italian style D 591 **4.88**
  Rosamunde, overture **9.87**
     incidental music **6.80;** 4.90
  Song of Miriam D 942 **9.84**
  String quartet in D, Death and the Maiden D 810 2.79; 3.01
  String quintet in C D 956 **3.95**
  Symphony no 4 2.81; **4.92; 11.92**
  Symphony no 5 **5.02**
  Symphony no 8 **11.86;** 3.90; 4.93; **9.93; 1.96;** 9.97; 5.99; 5.02
  Symphony no 9 6.89; 10.97

Schumann
  Die Braut von Messina, overture 2.98
  Etudes symphoniques op 13 2.81
  Fantasy in C for piano op 17 11.78
  Genoveva, overture **3.94;** 1.00
  Gipsy Life, chorus and orchestra 4.82; **4.93**
  Manfred, overture 6.89
  Overture, Scherzo and Finale 1.83
  Piano concerto 1.83; **10.86;** 10.89; 4.90; 1.00
  Piano quintet in E flat op 44 12.87; 3.91; 9.00

Piano sonata no 2 in G op 22 2.88
Song for the New Year op 144 **11.93**
String quartet in A op 41 no 1 3.79
Symphony no 1 1.83; 11.89; 1.98; 11.99
Symphony no 2 **2.84;** 2.90; **3.05; 11.05; 2.12**
Symphony no 3 5.84; 9.96
Symphony no 4 6.88; **4.93**

Spohr
  Christians Prayer **9.84**
  God thou art great **9.90; 4.94;** 9.96
  How lovely are thy dwellings **4.88**
  Jessonda, overture **9.87; 10.87;** 4.90; **4.92**
  The Last Judgement **9.78; 9.87; 9.93;** 9.97; 9.99
  Symphony no 4 op 86 **11.82; 11.86; 12.87**
  Violin concerto no 8 in A op 47 **2.85;** 2.90; 4.94

Strauss
  Also sprach Zarathustra **2.12**†
  Don Juan 5.02; 6.02; 12.04
  Don Quixote 6.03
  Elektra 3.10
  Feuersnot
     Love scene **11.02**
  Ein Heldenleben 12.02; 12.04
  Till Eulenspiegel 6.02; 11.02
  Tod und Verklärung 6.02; 9.02; 10.02; 12.04; **12.11**†
  Violin concerto in D op 8 12.04

Tchaikovsky
  Capriccio italien 3.90; 1.98
  1812 Overture 9.00
  Elegy for strings in G **5.98**
  Nutcracker, suite 9.00
  Piano concerto no 1 5.01; 12.02
  Piano concerto no 2 4.90
  Romeo and Juliet 1.98; **1.12**
  Serenade for strings op 48, waltz 1.98
  Symphony no 4 2.00; 6.00; **11.11**
  Symphony no 5 1.98; 9.00; 8.03

† **Programmed and probably rehearsed, but not performed, by Elgar.**

Symphony no 6 9.97; 6.98; 10.99; 9.00; **11.11**
Variations on a rococo theme 1.98; 9.00
Violin concerto 1.98

Thomas
Hamlet 7.90
Mignon 5.02

Verdi
Aïda 6.01
Four sacred pieces, Stabat mater and Te Deum 9.98
Otello, Acts 1 and 2 7.89
 Canzone ed Ave Maria 2.00
Requiem **2.87**; 9.96; 9.00
Rigoletto, Caro nome **11.89**
La Traviata, Ah fors'è lui 4.97
Il Trovatore, Tacea la notte **11.82**

Wagner
A Faust Overture 4.84; 11.01
Die Feen 8.93
Der fliegende Holländer 9.95; 9.97; 7.02
 Overture **10.76**; 11.89; 9.97; 10.97; 2.00; 9.00;
 Introduction to Act II and Spinning Chorus 3.95
Götterdämmerung 8.93; 9.94; 6.00
 Siegfried's Journey to the Rhine 11.99
 Act II, sc. 3 6.90
 Siegfried's Funeral March 3.83; 3.95
 Act III, sc. 3, conclusion from 'Schweigt eures Jammers' 5.88; 7.89; 6.99; 9.99
Huldigungsmarsch 4.84; 6.89; **11.11**
Kaisermarsch 3.83; 6.89; **2.01**
Lohengrin 1.83; 4.91; 5.02
 Act I Prelude 8.83; 3.95; 10.01
 Act III Prelude 3.83; **4.87**; **9.90**; 4.97
 Act III 'In fernem Land' 6.89
Die Meistersinger 7.89; 7.89; 7.89; 6.90; 7.90; 7.92; 8.93; 9.94; 7.96; 6.02
 Act I Prelude 10.81; 5.84; **11.92**; 3.95; 9.96; 3.99; 10.99; 6.00; 5.01; **5.01**; 11.01; 10.02; **10.11**; **11.11**
 Act I Trial Song, 'Am stillen Herd' 5.84; 6.88
 Act II 'Was duftet doch' 6.89; 7.90; 3.95
 Act III Prelude 6.88; 9.97
 Act III 'Wahn, wahn' 6.89; 10.01
 Act III Prize Song, 'Morgenlich leuchtend' **1.83**; 6.88; **9.93**; 9.00

Act III Sachs's final address and chorus 6.89; 3.90

Act III Prelude, Dance of the Apprentices and Procession 3.83; 11.89; 4.94; 9.99

Parsifal 7.92; 8.92; 7.02; 3.07

Act I Prelude 1.83; 4.84; 6.88; **4.91;** 3.95

Act I Transformation and Grail-Feier 6.89; 9.97

Act III Good Friday Music 3.83; **6.94;** 9.97; 10.01; 11.01

Das Rheingold 8.93; 7.02; 1.09

Rienzi, overture 6.89; 3.95; **5.00;** 9.00; 10.01

Act V 'O Heavenly Father' **11.83;** 10.89

Ring, Der Siegfried's Journey to Brünnhilde's Rock, Day Greeting, and Siegfried's Journey to the Rhine 6.88; 6.89; 7.90; 11.01

Siegfried 8.93; 7.02; 5.10

Act I Forging Song 6.89

Act III, sc. 1 6.90; 11.02

Siegfried Idyll 3.83; 5.84; 6.00; 9.00

Tannhäuser 1.83; 9.93

Act I Overture 3.83; 8.83; 6.89; 10.89; 4.93; 6.98; 9.99; 9.00; **11.11**

Act I Overture and Venusberg Music 4.99; 6.00; 10.01

Act II Elisabeth's Greeting 3.95

Act II March and Chorus, 'Hail bright abode' **9.81; 10.86; 9.90**

Act III Introduction 3.95; 1.98

Act III Elisabeth's Prayer 3.83

Act III 'O du mein holder Abendstern' 9.97; **1.99;** 9.99

Tristan und Isolde 7.92; 6.93; 8.93; 8.97; 6.98

Prelude and Liebestod 3.83; 5.88; 3.95; 3.97; 9.97; 6.98; 6.00; 10.01; 10.01

Walküre, Die 8.93; 7.02

Act I Love duet from 'Ein Schwert' 5.87

Act III Ride of the Valkyries 3.83; 5.87; 5.88; 3.95; 4.97; 9.97; 4.99; 10.01

Act III Wotan's Farewell and Magic Fire 6.89; 10.98; 10.01

Wesendonck Lieder **11.89 (v); 11.11 (iv and v)**

Weber

Clarinet concerto no 1 **11.82**

Euryanthe, overture **9.78; 2.84; 2.87;** 6.89; 11.89; **11.02; 4.03; 10.11; 11.11**

Der Freischütz 1.83

overture **9.84; 11.89;** 4.90; 3.97; 11.02

Jubilee overture **4.87**

Oberon, overture 10.81; 1.83; 8.83; 5.84; **10.84; 10.86;** 4.90; 11.96; 10.01

Ocean thou mighty monster **9.81**; 9.00; 5.02
Preciosa, overture **4.85**

Wolf
Prometheus, song with orchestra **4.04***

Wolfrum
Weihnachts-mysterium **12.01**

---

*   Rehearsed but not conducted by Elgar

Appendix 3   Books on music surviving from Elgar's library

Berlioz, Hector. *A Treatise on Modern Instrumentation and Orchestration to which is appended The Chef d'Orchestre*. London: Novello, 1882. Inscribed by Elgar 'May 27. 1882'.

Catel, Charles Simon. *A Treatise on Harmony*. London: Novello, 1854.

Cherubini, Luigi. *Counterpoint and Fugue*.

Crotch, William. *Elements of Musical Composition*. London: Novello, 1856.

Grove, George. *A Dictionary of Music and Musicians*. First edition, London: Macmillan, 1878, 1880, 1883 and 1890.

Mozart, W A *Succinct Thorough-Bass School*. London: Novello, 1854.

Pauer, Ernst. *The Elements of the Beautiful in Music*. London: Novello, Ewer, n. d. [Author's Preface, 1877].

Musical Forms. London: Novello, Ewer, n. d. [Author's 'Introductory Remarks' dated 1878].

Prout, Ebenezer. *Instrumentation*. London: Novello, Ewer, 1876. Inscribed by Elgar 'October:7:1878'.

Reicha, Anton. *Orchestral Primer*. Inscribed by Elgar 'E W Elgar March 9th 1867', and annotated with Elgar's corrections.

Schweitzer, Albert, translated by Ernest Newman. *J S Bach*. Leipzig: Breitkopf & Härtel, 1911, 2 vols. Given to Elgar by Newman November 1911. Peppered with comments by Elgar critical of Schweitzer's opinions.

Stainer, John. *Composition*. London: Novello, Ewer, n. d. [c. 1878].

A Treatise on Harmony. London: Novello, Ewer, n. d., (5th edition). Annotated with corrections by Elgar, and signed 'Edward Wm Elgar/ April 14. 1883.

Stainer, John, and W A Barrett. *Dictionary of Musical Terms*. London: Novello, Ewer, 1898.

Stone, W H *The Scientific Basis of Music*. London: Novello, Ewer, n.d. [Author's Preface dated 1878].

Appendix 4   Scores and parts surviving from Elgar's library

Armes, Philip. *Hezekiah*. Vocal score. Signed 'E. E. Second violin'.

Bach, J S. Forty-eight Preludes and Fugues. Two volumes bound into one. Undated by Elgar, but acquired through Elgar Bros.

Two volumes of organ music, Peters edition, bound into one. Contains trio sonatas, preludes and fugues including Fantasia and Fugue in C minor. No annotations.

Beethoven. Complete string quartets in Eulenburg miniature score. No annotations.

Berlioz. Seven overtures in Eulenburg miniature score, bound. Waverley, Corsaire, Benvenuto Cellini, Carnaval romain, King Lear, Francs-juges and Beatrice et Benedict. Occasional pencilled phrase marks in Francs-juges.

Bruch, Max. *Romanze for violin and orchestra* op 42 arranged for violin and piano. Given by Elgar to his wife in 1891.

Concerti for Violin. Eulenburg miniature scores bound together. Spohr no 8 in A, Beethoven in D, Mendelssohn in E minor, Bruch in G minor, Brahms in D, Tchaikovsky in D. Elgar's annotations in Brahms's concerto: 'heard' and 'not heard' sporadically over the solo line; in the first movement: 'dull stuff' bar 419, 'lovely' bar 445; in the second movement: 'cor too high' bar 91.

Delibes, Leo. *Sylvia*. Piano score. Inscribed by Elgar: 'Août 1880 Paris', and in the thematic table Elgar has marked with a cross Prelude, No 3 Les Chasseresses, 4 Intermezzo, 13 Scène Finale, 14 Marche, 15 Scène 'good', and 16 Divertissement.

Haydn. 83 String Quartets. Eulenburg miniature scores with occasional corrections by Elgar.

Liszt. Twelve Symphonic Poems in three volumes Breitkopf edition octavo size. Unsigned and undated. Only annotations by Elgar are a few markings on cor anglais phrases in *Orpheus*.

Mozart. Twenty-seven string quartets in four part books. K 387 in G major to K 465 in C major have been played.

10 string quartets, six string quintets, Clarinet quintet in Eulenburg miniature scores. Elgar has corrected one mistake in the Clarinet quintet.

Schubert. Chamber music in miniature score, unannotated. Includes string quartets in A minor, E flat, E, G, B flat, D minor, G minor, D, and C minor, Piano trios in B flat and E flat, String quintet, Piano quintet, and Octet.

Schumann. Octavo volume of piano music unsigned and undated. Contains Abegg variations, Papillons, Paganini studies, Six Intermezzi, Impromprus on an Air of Clara Wieck, Die Davidsbündlertänze,

Toccata, Allegro, Carnaval, Six Studies after Paganini, Sonata in F sharp minor, Fantasiestücke.

Kammermusik. Leipzig: Eulenburg miniature scores bound together. String Quarters op 41, 1–3, Piano Trios, op 63, 80, 110 and 88, Piano Quartet op 47, Piano Quintet op 44.

Spohr. *Complete Duets for Two Violins*, op 3, 9, 39, 67, 148, 150, 153. Dated by Elgar '1876'.

Strauss. Ein *Heldenleben*. Full score presented to Elgar by Strauss. Inscribed by Strauss 'Meinem hochvercherben Freunde E. Elgar Richard Strauss London, 6. December 1902'. Elgar marks where violin 2 tunes down to G flat, and notes the quotes from *Don Juan, Tod und Verklärung*, and *Till Eulenspiegel*.

Wagner. *Die Meistersinger von Nürnberg*. Schott vocal score undated but with a leaf of a German desk calendar stuck in the front bearing the date 6 April 1899. On p. 96, over the last two bars (Act I, bars 1496-8), Elgar has written 'schön'. This appears to be a companion, and is identical in condition to the vocal score of *Tristan und Isolde* (next entry) which Elgar acquired on 1 June 1893.

Tristan und Isolde. Schott vocal score undated, but from Alice Elgar's diary known to have been acquired on 1 June 1893. Only annotation is on the blank page facing the Prelude in Elgar's hand: 'This Book contains the Height, – the Depth, – the Breadth, – the Sweetness, – the Sorrow, – the Best and the whole of the Best of / This world and the Next./ Edward Elgar:'

Appendix 5   Opera librettos surviving from Elgar's library

Bianchi. *Fausta*. Milan. In Italian only, and no annotation.

Bizet. *Carmen*. London. In Italian and English. Inscribed by Elgar '23 July 1889', and Elgar listed the names of the singers of the production he attended that month. He wrote on the front 'Jowsy'.

Donizetti. *Anna Bolena*. London. No date or annotation.

Humperdinck. *Hänsel und Gretel*. London. No date or annotation.

Jacobi, Georg. *Babil and Bijou*. In English only and undated. Annotated by Elgar with comments, mostly derisory of a production and the music.

Mascagni. *Cavalleria Rusticana*. Milan. In Italian and English. No annotation.

Meyerbeer. *Les Huguenots*. London. No annotation.

Le Prophète. London. Inscribed by Elgar 1883 'in Leipzig'.

Mozart. *Don Giovanni*. Munich. German programme and text for an undated production under Hermann Levi. No annotation.

Offenbach. *The Grand Duchess of Gerolstein*. English libretto dated 1897. No annotation.

Madame Favant. London. In English only. Signed by Elgar, but no annotation.

Sullivan. *Iolanthe*. London. No date or annotation.

Ivanhoe. London. Undated, but Elgar has marked three numbers with a vertical line.

The Sorcerer and Trial by Jury. London. Two bound into one volume. No date or annotation.

Verdi. *Aïda*. London. Undated by Elgar, but he has marked some numbers with vertical pencil lines, and beside Amonasro's 'Su dunque', Act III sc. 2 Elgar has written 'good'.

Rigoletto. London. Undated. Only annotation is a tune Elgar jotted down at the end of the libretto.

Otello. London. Inscribed by Elgar '20 July 1889'. No other annotation.

Wagner. *Die Meistersinger*. London. In Italian and English. No date or annotation other than the monogram.

2 Elgar's harmonic language

Ian Parrott

Introduction

'Melody speaks your joy while harmony shows your mind', wrote Sir Walford Davies near the end of his life. It is my belief that the unmistakable personal stamp found on Elgar's greatest works comes to the listener through his special harmony. Derivations from a large number of models (for Elgar was a true eclectic) will have been dealt with by others, so I will concentrate on the emerging genius shown mostly in the 'second' period from the *Enigma Variations* to the Violin Concerto and in the 'third' period of the late chamber works and the Cello Concerto. While mentioning the *Variations*, I might say that Colin Watt, ex-Hereford choirboy, told me in 1986 that he remembered G R Sinclair as an impeccable pedaller, confirming my long-held belief that that variation was first inspired by an organist and not by a dog. 'Elgar was never averse', wrote Simon Mundy,[1] 'to hiding behind shields when it seemed that questions about his emotions were probing rather deeper than he liked.' Unfortunately Mr Mundy applied this to the Lady Mary Lygon variation and not to the G R S. My views on this are found in *An Elgar Companion*,[2] but we must now return to our present theme.

When I boldly wrote *Escape to Outer Darkness*[3] in 1956, Elgar was compared both to Richard Strauss, with his intrusion of onomatopoeia and to Mahler, with his deliberately placed 'vulgarity'. Elgar's music (so it seemed) represented 'a quiet inward exploration which could not be measured. His orchestration was at least the equal of Strauss's and the structures were at least as well planned as Mahler's; but there was in addition a quality which has given his music lasting power ...' It eludes musicologists because it is not 'written in the score'. And then, disconcertingly, after the barbaric harmonic glitter of Judas' suicide in *The Apostles* (1903), Elgar used less and less the 'modern' harmonies of the day, until by the time of the Piano Quintet (1918–19) and the Cello Concerto (1919), he was apparently using a language that Schumann (his 'ideal' in 1883) would not have found amiss. The musical personality is powerfully individual: gone are the 'wrong-note' chords, prophetic of Prokofiev, which he used in the 'march' part (fig.59) of the second movement of Symphony No.1 (1907–8) and gone also are the lush unrelated chords to the words 'impossible seeming' in *The Music Makers* (1912), new-sounding though they seemed at the time.

Wales

To get closer to this strange mind, we might make a visit to the wild west coast of Wales as it was in 1901. From the nearest railway station the last 15 miles had to be undertaken by ox-cart but this did not deter Edward Elgar, nor Rosa Burley, headmistress of 'The Mount', where his daughter went to school. Indeed his daughter Carice broke up for the holidays on 26 July that year. Interestingly the *Welsh Gazette* of 25 July gives an account of a young lady and a gentleman at Tresaith cut off by the incoming tide and unable to climb the cliffs. A pleasure boat from Aberporth, 'upon hearing cries . . . rescued the unhappy pair from their perilous position'. Although Rosa and Edward might well have walked on the seashore three miles south of Llangranog, it seems that this event is at least a week too soon, unless they had got away before the end of term. Geoffrey Hodgkins[4] says that Miss Burley gives the impression that Elgar had been there for some time, but officially he arrived as late as 15 August. So we must, I think, drop our fanciful thoughts of a possible romantic weekend! Much more important, of course, is what they heard by way of distant singing. Where the singing actually was in relation to the listeners has never been quite clear, since Rosa Burley wrote two versions of events. With its frequent drop of a third, it 'had a strangely ethereal beauty which deeply impressed us both and which remained in Edward's mind for many years . . .'

In spite of being told that hymns would be the most likely items, I persisted in reading the local newspapers of that patriotic time and found that the Welsh and English national anthems might have been sung out in the open air: particularly by the 10,000 miners who, with their families, had been entertained with bountiful hospitality by Mr David Davies (later Lord Davies) of Llandinam;[5] and who might have gone to the seaside before returning to the South Wales pits. I make this point since I feel I must accept Alan Webb's suggestion that the most likely music, with dropping thirds, to have influenced the 'Welsh' theme in the *Introduction & Allegro* is the second half of *Hen Wlad fy Nhadau*:

Ex.1 From Welsh National Anthem

Although I do not share Diana McVeagh's enthusiasm for *Moriah*[6] or for any other Welsh hymns, I feel sure we may agree at least on the existence of stodgy hymn-tune harmony (which I give in Example 1). Elgar would have encountered plenty of musical stodge in Victorian England with no need to explore Wales. This sort of harmony is just what Elgar *avoided*. This may well have been due to an instinct to go against the dos and don'ts of the harmony primer, which often stimulated the proudly self-taught composer; and which we will return to later. Let us now, however, examine his treatments of the resulting melody. Following Mendelssohn, he seems to have contemplated a 'Welsh' overture — but similarly didn't complete it. Then he made a half-hearted attempt at setting his wife's words for a song[7] but left it unfinished. The song in question might perhaps have been intended for a part of Alice's poem 'Reconciliation' of 1901, which the notes fit:

> Come back, and lay thy hand,
> As thou wast wont — just so,
> Within mine own; then stand
> And smile, and whisper, 'Lo'.[8]

It was three and a half years later when the 'Welsh' theme appeared in his masterpiece, the *Introduction & Allegro*. And what a transformation! The plodding root position chords (if they were ever there) have given way to slide-slipping inversions, with passing dissonances, and we notice the sequential rise and fall.

Ex.2 From *Introduction & Allegro*

I have fitted Alice's words to this passage as they enhance the profound personal melancholy of the music. All Elgarians will know the bars which follow my quotation, marked 'largamente', 'molto espress' and 'ff', as an agonized outburst. Like the wringing of hands, what do they mean specifically? Perhaps we need not delve.

Musically, for certain, here is some of the finest Elgar, in which it can be seen that the 'notorious' sequences are not confined only to the melody. You remember that Walton joked[9] that Elgar wrote the first phrase and then went for a walk, leaving Lady Elgar to complete the descending sequences (see, for example, at fig.66 in Symphony No.2 (1910)). But, of course, the whole harmony moves, the parts twisting and crossing.

Theory books

What applies to J S Bach might also apply to Elgar; the three s's: sequences, suspensions and secondary sevenths. The sevenths (also noticeable in his melodic lines) will be a part of most descending sequences in any case, so we may turn now to Elgar's idiomatic use of suspensions, many unprepared and so technically named appoggiaturas. Shall we consider one of those dreary theory books, which the composer came to loathe or deride, setting forth the 9–8, the 7–6 and the 4–3 suspensions? The last of these would be on a root position, as in (a), not as in (b) (see Ex.3 below):

Ex.3

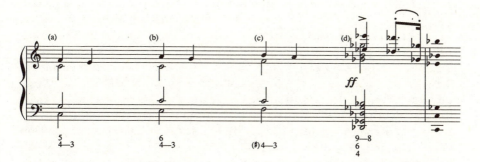

Indeed (b), on a first inversion, would be considered 'weak'. Pearce, for example, says 'The 4–3 can only be used over a note which is the root of a consonant triad'.[10] A strange thing then, is it not, that Elgar should make it into one of his 'strengths'? I have already pointed out the Wagnerian 'weak' movement in *Gerontius* (after fig.115);[11] and the influence of Wagner in other places.[12] Although many people would associate Wagner with chromaticism, it is sometimes the diatonic writing which has rubbed off on the younger man. For example, the passage, starting with boys' voices near the end of Act I of *Parsifal*, is mostly diatonic. So is the short sequence[13] in Act III, where Kundry washes Parsifal's feet, quoted in my letter to the Elgar Society Newsletter in May 1978.

In Ex.3 above, it is but a short step to (c), which, with its dreaded tritone, *diabolus in musica*, appealed even more strongly to Elgar, since the academic finger might wag even more ominously. 'Thou shalt not suspend the tritone', he might have heard; and he loved demons . . . And what about (d) on a *6/4*, i.e. a banned second inversion (Violin Concerto, fig.56)?

Did Elgar read the textbooks of the day? Most certainly he did. During his teens and into his twenties, in fact, he carefully read a number of books some of which are to be seen now at the Birthplace. With the kind help of the present curator, Mr Jim Bennett, I have looked through them, noting especially Elgar's pencil annotations and comments. We might remember that he did not make his first impressionable visit to Germany until 1883.

Much later in life[14] he referred to the books as 'repellant. But I read them and I still exist.' The first, he said, were Catel and Cherubini. *A Treatise on Harmony* by the former (member of the Paris Conservatoire), was translated and published by Novello in 1854. The Biographical Notice starts with 'Charles Simon Catel, born at l'Aigle, in the month of June, 1773, repaired, when quite young, to Paris . . .' Elgar has pencilled after 'born': 'Alas!' On the further reference to the book being that on which Catel's reputation will chiefly rest Elgar is even ruder. He writes, 'No wonder the other things failed'.

A Treatise on Harmony by Stainer,[15] signed Edward Wm Elgar, April 14th, 1883, contains one thing which meets with the owner's approval: the idea that a clef should show exact pitch and not that of an octave lower. However, he clashes strongly with the author on the various forms of the minor scale demonstrated. When Stainer calls the harmonic minor 'beautiful', Elgar crosses out the word; and when Stainer writes that it 'has the advantage of having its ascent and descent exactly similar', Elgar changes 'advantage' to 'disadvantage'. Here, maybe, is an early clue to Elgar's idiomatic writing in the minor – what Percy Young calls his whimsical treatment of minor tonality.[16] Surely there is no more aggressive expression of his defiance than the opening bass note of the Violin Concerto, which is 'incorrect' according to all the rules. There are many other examples of Elgar's writing in the minor: not modal, not harmonic minor and not melodic minor (the three forms presented by Stainer[17]) culminating in the so-called plain-song melody in the Piano Quintet (1919), where the theme is never fully modal (see fig.9). The 'Spanish' theme just before it, however (fig.5), does suggest a touch of Andalusia.[18]

Also in the volume by Stainer Elgar marked all the consecutive fifths, pp.130–33, in pencil; and after the footnote, p.23, 'The student will do well to collect and arrange other examples,' he appears to add: 'I won't'. Later, he works on the first and one other out of 60 exercises, after which he is obviously bored. When in 1909 a rash Novello proof-reader for some *New Cathedral Psalter Chants* marked some consecutive fifths '? intended', Elgar responded, 'Yes! if you don't like them leave the chant out. E.E.'[19] So it cannot have been merely coincidental that the motive for Mary Magdalene, a 'wicked' woman, is a series of blatant consecutive fifths (see fig.75 in *The Apostles*), calculated, thought Buckley, to make the old theorists uneasy in their graves.[20] 'The worst of the old textbooks,' said Elgar, 'was that they teach building but not architecture.[21] They were not entitled to lay down hard and fast rules for all composers to the end of time.'[22]

Buckley noted (p.13) that Elgar 'eagerly devoured' Cherubini on Counterpoint.[23] If this is not an exaggeration, he will also have noted that Rockstro (1823–95), in the first edition of *Grove*,[24] said that Cherubini persisted in condemning the false relation of the tritone. We know that Elgar also read Grove so this will be interesting when we come now to the consideration of modulation.

The second volume by Stainer called *Composition* is bound together with *Musical Forms* by Ernst Pauer, 1878, of which Elgar is sometimes critical; *The Scientific Basis of Music* by W H Stone, again carefully scrutinized; and *The Elements of the Beautiful in Music* by Pauer, 1877. In this last short book Elgar read that Beethoven was censured for passing, in the scherzo of the 'Pastoral' Symphony, from the key of F major into that of D major. He will also have noticed Pauer's subjective opinions on keys, D minor, for

example, expressing a subdued feeling of melancholy, grief, anxiety, and solemnity while A flat major 'is full of feeling, and replete with dreamy expression'. Elgar was all the time having the real experience of studying scores and playing music. Of course he preferred Beethoven to Catel, who had said that 'in order to render modulation pleasing, the common chord of the key quitted should carry into the key entered, at least one note belonging equally to the two chords'. Trivial though it may seem, it was evidently defiance of such dogmatism which acted as a catalyst, so that Symphony No.1 is not just in A flat major. It is in *both* A flat major and in D minor!

Conclusions

By looking at these early textbooks I have tried to show a powerful negative effect on the self-taught rebel's harmonic writing. There is one more thing: his orchestration.

Most people know in a general way that Elgar was phenomenally skilful, but may not realise how early he acquired his uncanny knack. Two other books can be seen in his collection. Reicha's *Orchestral Primer*[25] appears to have the composer's juvenile signature, E W Elgar, March 1867 rubbed out and that of his brother, Francis T Elgar, May 1878, substituted. It looks, therefore, as if Elgar read the book first at the age of 10, when he had started to browse in his father's shop. Even if he made his annotations and emendations at a later date, they are quite astonishingly authoritative. Indeed the reader knows more than the author; he corrects the bottom note of the oboe, he considers the tone of the top notes of the clarinet, he shows up the writer for not knowing how to write open notes for the horn, he points out that cor anglais is *not* a translation of Basset horn, he crosses out 'English flageolet' and 'Kent bugle' as unworthy of inclusion; and he corrects other misprints or faults. Then, like a master, he disapproves of certain woodwind doublings, he finds a melody too low on the bassoon, he adds colour with violin open string tremolando and says 'Why not' give the melody to the first horn, and so on. In the small Prout volume,[26] signed Edward Wm Elgar, Oct 7th, 1878, he shows interest in the 'best effect' of having an equal proportion in the orchestra of 3-string and 4-string double-basses, adding 'as at Crystal Palace'. He also marks the basset horn in a part of *La Clemenza di Tito* as 'silly and ineffective'. Generally he seemed somewhat kinder about writers on orchestration. On 14 February 1899 (just after Quinquagesima) he wrote to his violin pupil, Edgar Baldwyn, 'You cannot learn much orchestration from books: the new book by Prout [*The Orchestra*, 1897] pubd. by Augener is a practical treatise and his smaller primer [i.e. the one in his collection referred to above] pubd.

by Novello is useful – larger works such as Berlioz are useful for advanced students. You had better try Prout. Sincerely Edward Elgar'.[27]

A great creator of melodies and a superb orchestrator, Elgar had something more: a very personal way of thinking out his harmonies. Many of these ideas are in less than four parts, another dig at the conventional textbooks. And some centre round two chords. The following from four bars after fig.55 in the Violin Concerto demonstrates many of the points made, not least the noble combination with the melodic falling seventh (which the composer oddly and scrupulously denies to the soloist, who has to be content throughout the slow movement with a counter-melody). Note the 'irregular' resolution of the dissonance.

Ex.4 From Violin Concerto

Perhaps, however, we need not look much further than the *Introduction & Allegro* for those wonderful gliding first inversions, with their deliberate collisions. A similar passage in the slow movement of Symphony No 2 might have gone on with its dissonance much longer, if the composer's sketches are to be believed with his remarks, 'clashes', 'later' and 'together'. As it is, we have these similar first inversions for strings (with violas first at the top on an Elgarian 'minor' melody), only twice: at the beginning and at the end. And the 'clash' chord has lost its insistence but none of its impact. 'English' reticence?

Ex.5

(a) Elgar

(b) Bach

If some of this comes from Bach, it is not entirely from that composer at his most harmonic nor indeed at his most contrapuntal. It is a sort of ebb-and-flow music hitting occasional rocks (as in Cantata No 21). Bach also was sorrowful but here he expressed the consolation of the Christian message. Elgar, perhaps wistfully, was remembering not so much the funereal splendour of a monarch in imperial London but 'something we hear down by the river' or, who knows, wafted on the air from his memories of West Wales.

Notes

1. Mundy, Simon (1980). *Elgar.* Omnibus Press: London, p.46.
2. Redwood, Christopher, ed. (1982). *An Elgar Companion.* Moorland: Ashbourne, Part II, Chap. 5, by I.P., pp.82–90.
3. Parrott, Ian (June 1956). 'Escape to Outer Darkness'. *Musical Times.*
4. Hodgkins, Geoffrey (1975). 'Elgar's Visit to Llangranog'. *Elgar Society Newsletter.*
5. See *Cardiganshire County Times,* 27 July 1901.
6. See *Elgar Society Journal* (January 1986), pp.23 & 24.
7. Young, Percy M (1978). *Alice Elgar.* Dobson: London, p.151.
8. Parrott, Ian (1984). 'Some Notes on Elgar and Wales'. *Welsh Music,* Vol.7, No.7, pp.36–43.
9. Cohen, Harriet (1969). *A Bundle of Time.* London, p.149.
10. Pearce, Charles W. (1911). *Students Counterpoint.* Vincent Music Co.: London, p.34.
11. Parrott, Ian (1971). *Elgar.* Dent, p.86.
12. *op. cit.,* pp.61, 69.
13. Parrott, Ian (1978). *Elgar Society Newsletter,* pp.27, 28.
14. *Strand Magazine* (1904). Interview, p.539.
15. Stainer, John. *A Treatise on Harmony.* Novello, 5th edition.
16. Young, Percy M. (1955). *Elgar O.M..* Collins, p.277.
17. See also my *Elgar,* p.83.
18. Foreword by Michael Pope to 'Piano Quintet' by Elgar (1971). Eulenberg Miniature Score.
19. Chambers, H A (1957). 'Publishing House Memories', in *Edward Elgar Centenary Sketches.* Novello, p.14.

20. Buckley, Robert J. (1904). *Sir Edward Elgar,* Introduction. John Lane.
21. *op.cit.,* p.13.
22. *op.cit.,* p.32.
23. Cherubini, L. *A Treatise on Counterpoint & Fugue.* Translated Mrs Cowden Clarke, Novello 1854. He uses the words 'harsh' and 'very great licence'.
24. Editor, George Grove, D.C.L. *A Dictionary of Music & Musicians* (A.D. 1450–1880) by Eminent Writers, English and Foreign. 2 Vols, Macmillan & Co., 1879.
25. Reicha, A. *Orchestral Primer.* D'Almaine & Co.: 20 Soho Square, London.
26. Prout, Ebenezer (1876). *Instrumentation.* Novello.
27. Letter from Elgar to Edgar Baldwyn by kind permission of Dr Rodney Baldwyn. Edgar was Rodney's paternal grandfather's younger brother.

3   *King Olaf* and the English choral tradition

Michael Pope

King Olaf is at the present time one of the least familiar of Elgar's principal works, and yet many people have considered it a fine one.[1] The purpose of this essay is to question some of the premises of past critical censure, and to look afresh at the place the work occupies in the English choral tradition.

Before proceeding further, let us take note of a type of view which was widely accepted until quite recently, and is still encountered from time to time. According to this, all the choral works Elgar composed before *The Dream of Gerontius* are precluded from recognition as significant works of art, since they fall within a period described as his apprenticeship, a stage which allegedly lasted until 1898, when he was forty-one years of age. What are we to say of a supposition which would relegate *The Black Knight, The Light of Life, King Olaf, The Banner of Saint George,* and *Caractacus* to virtual oblivion?[2] I venture to suggest that such a view appears insufficient to account for the facts, as provided by practical performance of the music.

But this is not all, for the English choral tradition itself was represented some years ago as having a bogus reputation; and it is still sometimes said that there was no English music for two centuries after Purcell, a period of our history which has been described as one of almost complete musical sterility.

I propose now to discuss some of these wider issues, before turning to a closer examination of *King Olaf.*

I

Let us first consider the position at the beginning of 1951, when the Elgar Society was founded. It was the general tendency at that time to place British music into watertight compartments, a situation which may roughly be described thus. (1) Any music from the Tudor period had an automatic passport to acceptance. (2) Our attitude to the greatest English master of the late seventeenth century was expressed by Ralph Vaughan Williams: 'We all pay lip service to Henry Purcell, but what do we really know of him? . . . In this country we have too long allowed one of the greatest geniuses of music to languish unwept, unhonoured and almost unsung'.[3] (3) The patronage accorded to German and Italian musicians during the first half of the eighteenth century had ensured a prolonged period of neglect for composers of the distinction of Greene, Arne, Boyce, and Stanley. (4) It was then the established view that the achievements of British composers throughout the Classical and Romantic periods up to 1899 were, with only a few exceptions, unfit to be represented in public concerts as a viable part of our musical heritage.

Many unfamiliar treasures were revealed in the Festival of Britain later in 1951. Two notable series were presented by the Arts Council of Great Britain, each consisting of eight concerts. The first, in association with the Purcell Society, was devoted to a wide-ranging survey of Purcell's works; the second, comprising music by other English composers from around 1300 up to 1750, brought to performance many unfamiliar medieval and early eighteenth century works, as well as music by Byrd, Dowland, and other representative composers of the sixteenth and seventeenth centuries. These series, with a further historical series of English Song presented by the BBC and many more enterprising promotions throughout the country, did much to extend the knowledge of British musical achievement through the centuries. There still remained, however, the general underlying assumption that our native genius for music departed in the eighteenth century, and did not reappear until 19 June 1899, when Edward Elgar, so we were told, made a sudden leap from a state of prolonged apprenticeship to one of international excellence, with his Variations on an Original Theme, op.36.[4] It follows that almost all the music Elgar wrote before the appearance of the 'Enigma', with the conspicuous exception of the Serenade in E minor, op.20, was confined to a limbo. It was one which inevitably confined, in addition, such distinguished figures as Shield, Linley, and Storace, Samuel Wesley, Crotch, Field, and Potter, Macfarren, Pierson, and Bennett, Mackenzie and Parry, Cowen, Stanford, and Smyth, and many more fine composers who still await due reappraisal. Apart from those works which were heard in Cathedrals and Collegiate churches and chapels, almost all this music, which in some other European countries would long have been held in honour, was enveloped in obscurity.

II

Before we look further at the wider scene, let us first take note of Lady Elgar's pertinent comment after a memorable performance of *The Apostles* given by the North Staffordshire Choral Society at Hanley in 1905. She was reported as saying that they always kept a warm corner in their hearts for North Staffordshire, 'since it was here that Sir Edward, through the birth of *King Olaf,* first had that attention drawn to him which we all know has never since been relaxed'.[5] The point is an important one. *King Olaf* was a landmark in Elgar's career: it may well be regarded as a landmark in English music.

In *Music in the Five Towns,* published in 1944, Reginald Nettel recorded the impressions of some of those present at the first performance of the cantata, which Elgar conducted at Hanley on 30 October 1896. Having stated that *King Olaf* removed any doubt that may have lingered that the composer was to be passed over lightly, Nettel continued:

> By the time the opening chorus was over the audience was in a state of high expectation, and when the second chorus burst upon them, 'The Challenge of Thor', they knew that they were on the verge of a new age in music – that this young man who had fiddled among them had now found his true vocation. Men who are now hardened veterans of the orchestra speak of the tensity of the atmosphere at that concert as an unforgettable experience.[6]

Now that is quite remarkable. How does it happen that a work which made such a deep impression at its first performance should later be dismissed, as it still is, not infrequently, today?

As Parry observed, 'all things that have any value in life are not isolated but inherently connected';[7] and we have to try to connect English music of the nineteenth century with that which preceded it, and to reject the long-standing dichotomy in our musical heritage, which suggests that anything written by a Tudor composer is a work of high quality, whereas almost everything composed between the time of Purcell and Elgar's Variations is, allegedly, of little or no account.

III

In addition to the general neglect of this whole period, and the widely received view that Elgar produced no choral works of note before *The Dream of Gerontius,* some of the art-forms in which he worked have been dismissed. For a long time, and until quite recently, the partsong was dismissed. Whereas madrigal singing was taken seriously, the singing of partsongs, strangely enough, was thought to be *de trop.* Unaccompanied choral music has a long and distinguished history, and the partsong, to which Elgar made an outstanding contribution, is simply the term used in England since the middle of the last century to describe the secular Romantic form. We may, in fact, trace a continuing tradition from the Renaissance madrigal, through the Baroque catch and the Classical glee, to the Romantic partsong. The view that partsongs are ephemeral as a genre, whereas madrigals can be taken, *en bloc,* as classics of the art, is one which the test of performance does not support.

Turning now to the accompanied field, a similar divergence of view may be found regarding the two principal genres of music for chorus and orchestra in England, the oratorio and the cantata. Why is it that the oratorio has been acknowledged as a great art-form, yet the cantata, as a general rule, has not?[8] The remarkable impact made by the oratorios of Handel, and the larger scale of that form, may perhaps have contributed to such a view; yet these seem inadequate grounds on which to base the almost complete neglect, in recent times, of the Romantic cantata.[9] There seems no more reason to disparage a secular cantata, *per se,* in relation to a sacred oratorio, than there is to belittle a madrigal of Wilbye in relation to a motet of Byrd; and so far as musical value is concerned, is it not time we recognized that the Age of Elgar was itself a Golden Age, comparable in beauty and variety of expression to the Age of Byrd?

Elgar's first choral-orchestral work, *The Black Knight*, op.25, which appeared in 1893 as a cantata, was actually designed by the composer as a symphony for chorus and orchestra, in four divisions founded upon the poem, and 'different to anything, in structure, ever done before'. The orchestra played a particularly important role, and the setting of the poem was for chorus alone, there being no soloists. It was followed three years later by *Scenes from the Saga of King Olaf*, op.30, a setting for soprano, tenor, and bass soli, chorus, and orchestra, of the poem by Longfellow, adapted for the purpose by Harry Arbuthnot Acworth. *King Olaf* is, of course, a cantata proper.

The cantata has a historic lineage, which may be traced back to the time of Byrd. To look on the Romantic cantata as something which simply sprang into being in the nineteenth century, occupied a transient position as a junior partner of the long-established oratorio, and left posterity with little or no music of lasting significance, is a hasty generalization. It is not substantiated by practical performance of representative works, and it fails to take account of the gradual elaboration of the choral cantata from various earlier sources reaching back to the late Renaissance.

Although the term 'cantata' was for long used in a solo context, rather than a choral one, the typical characteristics of the choral cantata, a setting for one or more soloists, chorus, and instrumental accompaniment, were manifested in Elizabethan and Jacobean times, both in the verse anthem and in its secular counterpart, the consort song with chorus.[10] In these fields, as in others, Byrd was a notable pioneer, and his *Songs of Sundry Natures* of 1589 include examples of settings for one or two solo voices, chorus, and viols.[11] Gibbons, who in some respects forms a link between Byrd and Purcell, continued this pioneering work.[12] Not only are two-thirds of his anthems in the new 'verse' style, but several of his *Madrigals and Motets* of 1612 seem to be consort songs, including the great 'What is our life?', which may have been composed originally for soprano solo, chorus, and viols.[13]

The name 'cantata' was introduced no later than 1620, the year which saw the publication of the second edition of *Cantade et Arie* by Alessandro Grandi, principal assistant of Monteverdi at St Mark's, Venice.[14] These compositions were set for solo voice and continuo; and in due course the solo cantata developed into one of the most important vocal forms of the Baroque period. Although the chamber cantata, even when set for two or more voices, might seem somewhat distantly related to the Romantic choral cantata, it is relevant to note the following points which became apparent during the course of its development: (1) it was often dramatic in character; (2) the accompaniment grew, until it sometimes comprised an orchestra with obbligato instruments; (3) a composite structure evolved, with independent movements.

Let us now turn to Purcell, whose beautiful setting of Psalm 3, the motet 'Jehova, quam multi sunt hostes', was orchestrated by Elgar, at the request of Sir Ivor Atkins, for the 1929 Worcester Festival.[15] Purcell wrote a number of chamber cantatas (though not so called).[16] But he also composed more than twenty odes and welcome songs for soloists, chorus, and orchestra, and a similar number of verse anthems with string orchestra for the Chapel Royal; and these, leaving aside textual aspects, are akin to choral cantatas.[17] In this connection we should also note that it was Purcell in the 1680s, a generation before the appearance of Handel, who, in the words of A K Holland, 'brought into English music the type of broad and massive choral effect'.[18]

It was some time before the term 'cantata' was used in a choral context; but the tendencies which contributed to the form are further demonstrated during the first half of the eighteenth century. The next stage of the developing English choral tradition owed much to the patronage of James Brydges, a native of Herefordshire. He was Member of Parliament for Hereford from 1698 to 1714, when he succeeded to the barony of Chandos of Sudeley, becoming Earl of Carnarvon on the eve of the coronation of George I, a few days later. In 1717 he invited Handel to be resident composer at Cannons, his mansion at Little Stanmore in Middlesex; and it was for Carnarvon, who became Duke of Chandos in 1719, that Handel composed his Chandos anthems, the overture to the second of the series, 'In the Lord put I my trust', being the Overture in D minor which Elgar orchestrated for the 1923 Worcester Festival. These extended anthems were themselves tantamount to short sacred cantatas; but Handel also composed two masques during this phase which later exercised a significant influence on choral composition in England: *Acis and Galatea*, in May 1718, and *Esther*, probably in the same year.[19] In May 1732 *Esther* was performed under Handel's direction without action, in a revised version given at the King's Theatre in the Haymarket,[20] an event which has long been acknowledged as laying the foundations of English oratorio.[21] In the following month *Acis and Galatea* was also performed without action under the composer's direction, in a new version at the same theatre, when it was described as a serenata. The many subsequent performances of *Acis* in the concert hall, together with its suitability for such presentation, give this parallel event a similar claim to laying the foundations of the large-scale choral cantata in this country.[22]

The influence on the English choral tradition of the Saxon-born Georg Friederich Händel is as evident as that exercised on the French operatic tradition by the Tuscan-born Giovanni Battista Lulli: what can no longer be accepted is the widely received view regarding the consequence of his domicile in London. Let us acknowledge that Handel dominated the early Georgian musical scene; but, as Dr H Diack Johnstone has observed, 'the notion that he, by some mysterious alchemy, effectively stifled the creative talents of his English contemporaries, or that they, poor things, were incapable of producing anything other than a pallid reflection of the master's style, is absurd.'[23]

The idea that any English-born masters could have emerged during the time of Handel's residence in London is still sometimes looked on as a heresy; yet we have only to listen to some representative works by two of Elgar's predecessors as Master of the King's Musick, Greene and Boyce, to appreciate the high quality of their contribution to our musical heritage. Boyce's serenata *Solomon*, which was completed in 1742,[24] is of particular relevance in the present context. The theme of the libretto is wholly secular like that of Handel's *Acis and Galatea*, with which it shares a pastoral character; in addition, it is a true concert work[25] and was from the outset designated as a serenata.

The terms used to describe such works were admittedly somewhat variable in the eighteenth century; and although this is not the place to dwell on questions of nomenclature, it is appropriate to look forward for a moment to the nineteenth century and to reflect on the fundamental nature of those two great choral art-forms, Oratorio and Cantata. The usual practice at the Three Choirs and other Festivals, and of Novello, the chief publisher of choral music and of Elgar's works, indicates the following broad classifications. (1) The term Oratorio was normally reserved for full-length works founded on sacred themes. (2) A sacred work of less than full length was generally described either as a 'sacred cantata' (as in Bennett's *The*

Woman of Samaria of 1867), a 'sacred musical drama' (as in Sullivan's *The Martyr of Antioch* of 1880), or a 'short oratorio' (as in Elgar's *The Light of Life* of 1896). (3) With certain exceptions, such as the special case of Bach, the unqualified term Cantata, or sometimes Dramatic Cantata, was generally used as the secular counterpart of Oratorio (though such works were at first on a smaller scale than the average oratorio). This is in full accord with Renaissance practice regarding the Madrigal, where only the sacred form required qualification, as in the *Madrigali spirituali* of Palestrina and other composers. With these classifications in mind, as well as the points of difference from the kindred form the Ode, Boyce's *Solomon*, related as it is to Handel's *Acis and Galatea*, has a good claim to be regarded as the first large-scale choral Cantata by a native English composer. It may also be observed that the historical line from *Solomon* to *King Olaf* corresponds to that from Boyce's Eight Symphonies, which were published in 1760,[26] to those of Elgar, one and a half centuries later.

IV

It is clearly beyond the scope of the present essay to recount the development of the choral Cantata from Georgian to late Victorian times; yet it may be worth while to touch on a few further points concerning the intervening period.

For a long time it was the general tendency to assume that the second half of the eighteenth century, together with the first three-quarters of the nineteenth, represented a waste period of our musical history unredeemed by any compositions rising above the mediocre. It is good to know that recent scholarship, coupled with practical performance, is step by step showing such a view to be mistaken. Fellowes has amply demonstrated the close relationship between the 'Cathedral Anthem' and 'short cantata' form;[27] and in 1755 Boyce composed one of his finest and most extended anthems, 'Lord, thou hast been our refuge', for the Corporation of the Sons of the Clergy, for whose Festival in 1914 Elgar wrote his setting of Psalm 29, 'Give unto the Lord'. Boyce's work is an outstanding example of this form; and after it was published in 1802, his pupil Charles Wesley described it as 'a most excellent composition', which was, in his view, not inferior to Handel or Purcell.[28] Apart from the verse anthem, we may observe that the English choral tradition was further enriched by fine examples of the full anthem, such as Battishill's 'O Lord, look down from heaven' of 1765, which Elgar orchestrated for the 1923 Worcester Festival.

If we turn now to secular examples of the choral cantata form we shall find that, in addition to the annual Court Odes which were composed by the Master of the King's Musick,[29] and Odes to St Cecilia, various odes were written for other occasions, sometimes (as in the later case of Elgar's *Coronation Ode*) resulting in works of high quality. One such is the *Shakespeare Ode* of 1776 by Linley,[30] who was also a pupil of Boyce. Both this work and Linley's short oratorio of 1777, *The Song of Moses*, have been described by Dr Roger Fiske as masterpieces,[31] a thought which should prompt increased exploration of this neglected period of our musical history

The adverse views which have sometimes been expressed about the choral Cantata impel one to point out that, quite apart from its cultivation in England, it has been widely cultivated abroad, and by some of the greatest composers in the history of the art. The many examples by Bach form, as it were, a link between the seventeenth century solo cantata and the Romantic choral cantata. This becomes more apparent when we recall that, in addition to some two hundred surviving Church cantatas, Bach wrote a number of secular cantatas, a significant example being *Phoebus and Pan*, which was probably composed in 1729.[32]

Only a small number of Bach's cantatas were described thus by the composer;[33] but during the Classical era, when interest in the solo cantata was declining, more general use was made of the term for choral works. Haydn, Mozart, and Beethoven all produced examples of the Cantata; so, too, did Schubert: and it is to the nineteenth century, when the choral Cantata really came into its own, that we must now turn.

V

The new century was heralded by an important choral work of Haydn, *The Seasons*, which, though described as an oratorio, might have been designated later as a large-scale cantata in view of its essentially secular character. It has been suggested that this work may have influenced Mendelssohn when he composed the overture to *The First Walpurgis Night*.[34] In 1831, when Mendelssohn began writing this 'ballade', as he called it, he was aware that it could become 'a new sort of cantata.'[35] He revised it in 1842 and it was performed at Leipzig in the following year. Mendelssohn conducted the first performance in England at a Philharmonic concert in July 1844, and it soon became a classic of the genre.

The fuller development of the Cantata in England sprang from the results of industrialization. The increasing number of people changing from a rural to an urban life, and their desire to sing with others as a means of expression and recreation, led to the formation of many new choral societies.[36] The Sight-Singing movement of the 1840s, in which a distinguished Worcester-born musician, Dr John Hullah, played an important role, enabled thousands of singers to learn their part in choral music by reading rather than by ear. More concert halls were built, more public concerts were given, and less expensive editions of music began to be published. One consequence was the growth of the partsong; and on a larger scale, as Sir Anthony Lewis observed, 'the spread of public concert-giving opened up new prospects for the secular choral cantata which had hitherto enjoyed little scope'.[37]

The first English Romantic Cantata to take a place comparable with that of Mendelssohn's *Walpurgis Night* was Bennett's *The May Queen* which was produced at the inaugural Leeds Musical Festival in 1858. This work, which is for four soloists, chorus and orchestra, was published as a 'pastoral', and it has a clear affinity with those exemplars remarked upon earlier, *Acis* and *Solomon*.

During this period the 'short cantata' form of the Cathedral Anthem was being developed further by Sebastian Wesley. Fellowes has drawn attention to the individuality, beauty, and dramatic feeling of his writing for the solo voice.[38] In 1853 he published a volume of *Twelve Anthems*, which included such well-known classics as 'The Wilderness' and 'Ascribe unto the Lord', together with others of a larger scale which have a claim to concert performance, such as 'O Lord, thou art my God' and 'Let us lift up our heart', the last of which was orchestrated by Elgar for the 1923 Worcester Festival.

The high quality of some of the choral music which followed *Walpurgis Night* and *The May Queen*, as demonstrated by the test of performance, makes it hard to understand the current tendency in the English-speaking world to dismiss the Romantic Cantata from serious consideration. In Germany, by contrast, so fine an instrumental composer as Max Bruch has been judged by critics to excel in his choral works, such as the cantata *Odysseus* of 1872.[39] Bruch himself, we are told by Colles, 'expressed a belief that in the dramatic cantata lay the hope for the future of the art'.[40]

It was a dramatic cantata by Parry, a former pupil of Bennett, which initiated what may fairly be called a new epoch in British music. His setting of Scenes from Shelley's *Prometheus Unbound*, which was produced at the Gloucester Festival on 7 September 1880, was the first in an outstanding series of works for chorus and orchestra, of which the ode *Blest Pair of Sirens* is the most familiar and the reflective cantata *The Vision of Life* perhaps the greatest: both were much admired by Elgar.[41]

The distinction of many of the vocal works written by British composers in the 1880s requires emphasis, in order to dispose of any suggestion that Elgar's cantatas were created in some kind of cultural desert. It was in connection with Sullivan's oratorio *The Light of the World*, first heard at the Birmingham Festival of 1873, that Davison expressed the opinion that musical life in England was on the eve of a revival in all its forms.[42] In 1886, when that prediction had come true, Sullivan made his chief contribution to secular choral music with a splendid cantata, the setting of Longfellow's *The Golden Legend*, so reaching, in Tovey's view, the highest point of his achievement.

In 1884 Mackenzie followed Boyce in producing a notable choral work founded on the Song of Solomon, *The Rose of Sharon*. In writing this, one of the most important compositions of his Tuscan period, Mackenzie was drawn primarily to the literal rather than the allegorical interpretation of the text, and this led him later to prepare a revised version in which any suggestion of a religious basis disappeared.[43] Though described as a dramatic oratorio the work could well be regarded as a large-scale cantata, akin in its warmth of expression and oriental feeling to Bantock's great trilogy of cantatas, *Omar Khayyám*. The first performance of *The Rose*, Mackenzie's *magnum opus* in the choral field, took place at the 1884 Norwich Festival, and it was welcomed as the most remarkable British work of modern times.

But that was not all: as Mackenzie wrote later, 'Stanford's beautiful *Elegiac Ode* was first heard in this Festival'.[44] This Whitman setting was the first of a number of odes by Stanford, who, like Byrd three hundred years earlier, produced music of distinction in a wide range of forms, both secular and sacred. The first secular choral form to attract his interest was the dramatic cantata, his chosen poet, Longfellow; and by January 1875 he had completed the first part of a setting of *The Golden Legend*. In addition to his odes, and various other cantatas of a non-dramatic cast, some of his finest music appeared in the form of the 'choral ballad'. His celebrated setting of Tennyson's *The Revenge*, which was produced in 1886, became a classic of the choral ballad, the form to which Elgar turned in 1897 for *The Banner of Saint George*. It is worth remarking that Stanford's choral masterpiece, the *Stabat mater* of 1906, was designed as a symphonic cantata, a concept analogous to Elgar's design for *The Black Knight*. As Porte discerned so truly in 1921: 'The creative spirit of Stanford in its maturity has much that is akin to Elgar'.[45]

In a valuable *Summary of Musical History* first published in 1893, Parry wrote of the 'richness and variety, the poetry and masterly craftsmanship' of recent choral works by Mackenzie and Stanford, and pointed out that they were very worthily supplemented by numerous works by their fellow composers, 'many of very high excellence'.[46] The significance of Parry's own works, and his influence on Elgar, are implicit in a comment by Godfrey made from the viewpoint of 1924: 'Save for Elgar, no one seems able to follow, much less develop, the glorious choral tradition of Hubert Parry ...'.[47] We are surely entitled, therefore, to propose that the misleading legend of the 'Pre-Enigma Limbo' should be abandoned. In particular, it is high time that the first-fruits of this Second Golden Age were more widely enjoyed. Until this happens, neither Elgar's Cantatas nor the fine music of his distinguished contemporaries can be truly appraised as an important part of the national heritage.

And this brings us to the final points in our consideration of the Cantata form, and its place in the English choral tradition. (1) When *Prometheus Unbound* burst upon the scene in 1880 the oratorio was regarded as being the highest art-form to which the British composer could aspire.[48] (2) By 1893 Parry had himself composed two oratorios, *Judith* and *Job;* nevertheless, in his account of modern tendencies which appeared in *The Art of Music* that year, he observed that 'the forms of secular choral music, such as odes and cantatas, which are cast on the same general lines as oratorios, and are controlled by absolutely the same conditions of presentation, tend to become even more important and comprehensive than oratorio itself.[49] (3) With the composition of *King Olaf*, between 1894 and 1896, Elgar raised the choral cantata to fresh heights; and by extending the size and scope to the fullest extent he created a secular work on the scale of his last oratorio, *The Kingdom*. (4) If we consider the splendid flowering of the Cantata in England between 1880 and 1914, we find that it is broadly comparable with that of the Elizabethan and Jacobean Madrigal three hundred years earlier. Weelkes reached out in 1600 to a 'dramatic treatment and force of emotional expression' characteristic of the approaching seventeenth century,[50] with his *Madrigals of 5 and 6 parts*, 'apt for the viols and voices', and especially with the remarkable double madrigal 'O Care/Hence Care'. In similar manner, Elgar, employing the most developed harmonic and textural means at his disposal, heralded with *King Olaf* the striking musical achievements of the coming Edwardian era.

VI

'A new light of exceptional brilliancy came rapidly to the forefront in the last five years of the century in the person of Edward Elgar (born 1857), whose fine cantatas *King Olaf* and *Caractacus* came out respectively at Hanley in 1896 and at Leeds in 1898': so wrote Parry in the new edition of his *Summary of Musical History* which appeared in 1904.[51] Let us now turn to Mackenzie: 'The publication of *King Olaf* brought Edward Elgar's name into sudden prominence by immediately stamping him as an exceedingly accomplished musician who quickly secured unanimous recognition. It was Stanford who enthusiastically drew my attention to the almost unknown new-comer's splendid gifts, upon which it would be an impertinence to dwell here and now'.[52] It is important to quote these views in order to make it clear that Mackenzie, Parry, and Stanford were united in their warm appreciation of Elgar's outstanding gifts, and especially of *King Olaf*.

What was it that drew Elgar to write a work based upon a Norse Saga? Let us recall Buckley's words in the first biography of the composer, which was completed in 1904: 'His surname, of Scandinavian origin, is a modernised form of Aelfgar, or "fairy spear"'.[53] In 1932 Brian followed this up with some interesting comments on the possibility of a Scandinavian influence in Elgar's music.[54] It should be mentioned here that in October 1900 an article on Elgar appeared in the *Musical Times*, which stated unequivocally: 'His patronymic is of Saxon origin . . .';[55] and in 1940 Colles cited the view of St Clair Baddeley that 'the name Elgar is one of pure Anglo-Saxon origin'.[56] The point is one which bears closer examination.

The name Elgar is found in Kent, the county of the composer's forbears, as early as 1317, and the derivation in this case comes from the Old English Æthelgar, 'noble spear': how that conjures up *Froissart*, and evokes those later *nobilmente* passages where the music soars to the Empyrean! This form of the name can be traced prior to 988, the year Æthelgar, a former monk of Glastonbury, became 25th Archbishop of Canterbury. He succeeded Dunstan, who had influenced him when abbot of Glastonbury, and who, in Hadow's words, 'bears the name of the greatest English musician before the Conquest'.

It seems that the earliest record of the name Elgar, in the same spelling as the composer's family, occurs in Suffolk in 1234. Its derivation could be from the Old English Ælfgar, 'elf-spear', which can also be traced back to the tenth century, or from the Old English Ealdgar, 'old spear', or even from Æthelgar. There are, however, various other related forms which derive from the Old Norse Alfgeirr or the Old Danish Alger; some of these may be from Old English forms such as Ælfgar, 'but all', says Reaney, 'are from counties where Scandinavian influence was strong'.[57] Dr Basil Cottle has summed the matter up thus: the 'noble spear' and 'old spear' forms are both Old English; the 'elf-spear' form is either Old English or, if the family 'originated in a county with Scandinavian traditions', Old Norse.[58]

Taking into account the published statements of Buckley, Brian, and Reed,[59] it would seem that Elgar at some time believed his name to be of Scandinavian origin;[60] and that would in turn conduce to a special sense of identity with a theme such as 'The Saga of King Olaf'.

This brings us to the author of the poem on which Elgar's cantata is based, the Romantic poet who touched the hearts of a countless number of English-speaking people and whose influence on Elgar was greater than that of any comparable figure, Henry Longfellow. Not only was he the most admired American poet of the nineteenth century, but his reputation in England rivalled that of Alfred Tennyson; and, as with

Tennyson, long-sustained appreciation was followed by a long period of reaction.

The deeper values of poetry, as of music, may well become more manifest in time of crisis. Let us recall some lines from one of the great wartime broadcasts of Winston Churchill:

> Sail on, O Ship of State!
> Sail on, O Union, strong and great!
> Humanity with all its fears,
> With all the hopes of future years,
> Is hanging breathless on thy fate.

These lines were contained in a letter sent to Churchill by President Roosevelt during the year when Britain and the Commonwealth stood alone. He was deeply moved, and included the quotation in a speech broadcast world-wide on 9 February 1941. Some years later he wrote: 'These splendid lines from Longfellow's "Building of the Ship" were an inspiration'.[61]

If we consider this example alone, does it not appear that we should call into question the sweeping criticisms which have been levelled at Longfellow's poetry? As with most creative artists, his work went through an unfashionable period for a considerable time after his death; but he could never have become the household poet of America and, to a large extent, of England unless he had 'reached the hearts of the people', as Parry said of Elgar.[62] We should also remember that, apart from Sullivan, Stanford, and Elgar, Longfellow's poetry has inspired many other composers, ranging from Dvorak, in the beautiful Largo of his Symphony 'From the New World',[63] to Coleridge-Taylor, in his fine cantata trilogy, *The Song of Hiawatha*.

The fact remains, however, that a certain amount of critical comment on *King Olaf* has been based on the premise that the libretto is defective, not only in structure but also in literary merit. For instance, few of those who appreciate Elgar are likely to dissent from Newman's comment on the musical treatment of the text, at the close of his discussion of the cantata: 'There is rare beauty and consummate power in much of the writing'.[64] But when he refers at the outset to 'the tepid muse of Longfellow',[65] we are entitled to reply that the poet can now be regarded as a 'Classic Romantic', somewhat like Mendelssohn, with whom he had a good deal in common: and it was natural for such an artist to couch this tale of medieval adventure in the restrained style of classical models.

Professor Woodberry, a colleague of MacDowell at Columbia University, when writing of the refinement and simplicity of Longfellow's art, described it as being 'so limpid as to deceive the reader into an oblivion of its quality and sometimes into an unwitting disparagement ...'.[66] Further light has recently been shed on the real nature of the poet by a scholar who is also an authority on Whitman, Mr Lawrence Buell. After drawing attention to the 'often restless, melancholy spirit' of Longfellow, he points out how easy it is to mistake the surface for the totality of his mind. He suggests that the present orthodox version of American poetic history, that the comparatively radical poets such as Whitman constitute the mainstream, needs to be tested by more attentive reading of Longfellow. The tendency to concentrate on 'the aesthetics of visionary romanticism' and to dismiss the 'aesthetics of restraint' has created a 'powerful but reductive critical myth', which might prove of limited validity.[67]

So far as England is concerned, Longfellow was held in such esteem that in 1884, two years after his death, a bust to his memory was placed in the Poet's Corner of Westminster Abbey, next to Chaucer, the only occasion on which an American subject has been honoured in this manner. It is not difficult, therefore, to understand why he was a favourite poet of Ann Elgar, the composer's mother; nor need we feel any surprise that she inspired her son Edward with a love for Longfellow's writings, both poetry and prose.

During the 1890s Longfellow was the source of inspiration for no less than four of Elgar's compositions: (1) the serenade 'Stars of the summer night!', from Act I of the play *The Spanish Student*, which he set for chorus and orchestra in 1892 as *Spanish Serenade*, op.23; (2) the translation of Uhland's 'Der schwarze Ritter' from the semi-autobiographical story *Hyperion*, which appeared in 1893 as *The Black Knight*, op.25; (3) the translation of lines from a rondel by Froissart, 'Love, love, what wilt thou with this heart of mine?', which was set as a song for voice and piano in 1894, and appeared two years later as 'Rondel', op.16 no.3; (4) the Musician's Tale, 'The Saga of King Olaf', from *Tales of a Wayside Inn*, which, with the Interludes on either side of it, provided the major part of the libretto for the Cantata under discussion.

But that is not all, for in 1902 Longfellow's verse drama *The Divine Tragedy* was an important influence in the shaping of Elgar's libretto for the most extended work he ever composed, the great oratorio *The Apostles*, op.49, which he completed in the following year.[68]

A comparison of the two reveals various examples of this, one of the most striking being Longfellow's scene 'The Tower of Magdala' from 'The First Passover', which prefigures the opening scene in the oratorio's third section, 'By the Sea of Galilee'. As Jaeger wrote before the first performance: 'The scene, "In the tower of Magdala", is perhaps the most original thing which we owe to the composer's genius'.[69] In 1973, in an essay on '*The Apostles* reconsidered', Mr Michael Kennedy observed that 'Elgar produced something far ahead of its time – Hardy's *The Dynasts* had not appeared – almost a film scenario ... tempting the thought today that a wonderful film could be made of the work ... by a musically sensitive and imaginative director'.[70] He then gave examples of how cinematic (or televisual) the work is, one of them being the scene of 'Peter's attempt to walk on the sea watched by Mary Magdalene from the tower'.[71] As Elgar acknowledged, the source of this inspiration was Henry Longfellow.[72]

If we consider these matters afresh does it not seem that a reappraisal of Longfellow's contribution to Elgar's works is overdue? In any event one conclusion seems clear: Longfellow possessed the imponderable spiritual qualities required to fire Elgar's imagination.

VII

Let us turn now to the libretto itself, and consider some further points which have given rise to critical discussion. Before doing so we should observe that there seems to be a certain discrepancy between the criteria applied to librettos for cantatas and those for Opera; for when the music of an opera is of a quality which offsets any alleged deficiencies in the libretto, the work not infrequently receives both critical approval and regular public performance. Is it not reasonable that similar criteria should apply to the Cantata, and indeed to the Oratorio?

So far as the libretto of *King Olaf* is concerned, the main points we have to consider are the structure and organic unity of the plot, and the motivation and consistency of character of Olaf; and in this regard, I suggest that some of the adverse views propounded in the past appear to rest on insufficient grounds.

In recent years, more and more evidence has accumulated to show that Elgar, like Wagner, had 'a brain of the rarest and subtlest composition', as Newman wrote of the latter; and we should surely give him credit for thinking carefully about these matters. He was scarcely going to accept a libretto for a full-length work, requiring at least one and a half hours of music, unless the result was going to be in his opinion a viable work of art. It is then of paramount importance to give the cantata the attention it deserves; and, as with *The Ring*, this means getting to grips with the story.

'The Saga of King Olaf' is the fifth story in Part I of Longfellow's *Tales of a Wayside Inn*, an extended sequence which follows the model of Chaucer's *Canterbury Tales*. The stories are told by a group of friends of the poet, who used to meet 'At the Red Horse in Sudbury'. The Saga is the first of three tales told by the Musician, who was in reality the Norwegian violinist Ole Bull. The imagination of this remarkable virtuoso had been stirred since childhood by 'the weird poetry of the Sagas of the North', and his powers in relating such tales were by all accounts irresistible, their effect being 'not unlike that of his violin-playing'.[73] The Musician's first Tale is of considerable length, being in twenty-two sections, and it therefore required adaptation to fit it for setting as a cantata.

Elgar was assisted in this task by Harry Arbuthnot Acworth, who also rewrote several scenes for the purpose of the libretto and contributed the stanzas for the solo recitatives, and who later became the librettist for *Caractacus*, op.35. Acworth, who was born in 1849 and educated at Worcester College, Oxford, had recently returned from India. In 1891 he had published *Ballads of the Marathas*, and his own English version appeared in 1894. His contribution to the success of *King Olaf* was acknowledged by Buckley. After pointing out that Longfellow's words had been cleverly connected and reinforced by Acworth, Buckley continued: 'So far Elgar has fared well with the librettists. Fastidious as Mendelssohn, he is more fortunate'.[74]

The test of practical performance demonstrates that each of Elgar's choral works 'sings well' and gives the sympathetic listener a deeply moving experience. Is it not time that we considered this matter afresh and reappraised the qualities of his librettos from a practical standpoint?

One who was better fitted than most to take a well-informed view was Joseph Bennett, chief music critic of the *Daily Telegraph* and also one of the foremost librettists in the country. His experience in this field had included the selection of the words for Mackenzie's *Rose of Sharon* and the adaptation of Longfellow's verse drama for Sullivan's *Golden Legend*. A few years later he supplied Mackenzie with a poem which was, in the opinion of that widely experienced musician, 'the best cantata libretto ever handed to a composer', *The Dream of Jubal*.[75] After the first performance of *King Olaf*, Bennett wrote a detailed review of the work in which he expressed the opinion that Elgar had exercised 'wise discretion' in asking Acworth to supplement Longfellow's poetry, adding that he had 'generally well discharged a task by no means easy'.[76]

Acworth's contribution to *King Olaf* was, in fact, a considerable one. The 'Conversion' and 'Sigrid' scenes, and 'The Death of Olaf', are entirely his work, as are the duet between Thryi and Olaf, 'The gray land breaks to lively green', and the six linking recitatives for the bass soloist.

With regard to the shaping of the libretto, Acworth helped Elgar in the reduction of Longfellow's twenty-two sections to eight, together with an Introduction and an Epilogue. In addition, the sequence of the scenes from 'The Conversion' to 'Sigrid' represents a modification of that in Longfellow's Saga, where the order is as follows: 'Queen Sigrid the Haughty' (iv); 'The Wraith of Odin' (vi); 'Iron-Beard' (vii) (which becomes 'The Conversion'); and 'Gudrun' (viii). This follows the sequence of *Heimskringla*, in which 'King Olaf Trygvesson's Saga' has a hundred and twenty-three chapters. It is known, however, that, with a view to achieving a stronger dramatic impact, the chapters are not always laid out in exact chronological order;[77] and there are cogent reasons, both dramatic and musical, why these scenes in the cantata, with its reduced number of sections, should have been arranged thus: 'The Conversion' (iii); 'Gudrun' (iv); 'The Wraith of Odin' (v); and 'Sigrid' (vi).

When Newman declares that the libretto of the cantata has 'a series of flaws in the structure', we are entitled to respond at the outset with the following points, which indicate the care taken in adapting Longfellow's poem for a semi-dramatic choral work. (1) The meeting of King Olaf and Queen Sigrid, which took place at Konghelle in the spring of 998, half-way through Olaf's reign, marked a critical point in the growth of the conflict. It is therefore placed later, immediately before the scene in which Queen Thyri asks Olaf to rescue her domains from King Burislaf, the ruler of Vendland (vii), an expedition which resulted in the catastrophe set forth in 'The Death of Olaf' (viii). (2) The appearance of the wraith of Odin is interpreted by Olaf as signifying 'the downfall of Odin the Great, and the effectual triumph of the Christian faith'.[78] It therefore follows logically after 'The Conversion' and 'Gudrun'. (3) The shattering of the image of Thor, the death of Ironbeard, and the Conversion which results, are the direct consequence of the challenge of Thor (i) and Olaf's acceptance of that challenge. They therefore follow on naturally from 'King Olaf's Return' (ii). The 'Gudrun' scene does, of course, necessarily follow the death of Ironbeard in all three texts.

From the point of view of musical structure, 'The Conversion' scene brings Part I of the cantata to a conclusion which is both deeply moving and artistically satisfying.

VIII

Now that we have touched on the historical meeting of Olaf and Sigrid in the year 998, we should observe that the action of all Elgar's cantatas of the 1890s takes place before 1300, two being set in the Middle Ages and two in Antiquity. His final work in this genre, *Caractacus*, is set in Britain and Rome around AD 50; its predecessor, *The Banner of St George*, is according to legend located in the Middle East during the time of the Emperor Diocletian, around 300; *King Olaf* is, of course, set in and around Norway between 995 and 1000; and *The Black Knight* appears to originate in Scotland in 1285.[79]

A sense of historical perspective is particularly necessary in the case of *King Olaf* since we have sometimes been told that the principal character lacks consistency. Bearing in mind, however, that we are dealing with a hero of the late tenth century, is it reasonable to judge his character according to standards which only really developed in the late eighteenth century?[80]

Let us turn to the Introduction of the cantata, where the assembled company of Skalds,[81] or Bards, having described 'a wondrous book' of Legends in the old Norse tongue, sing:

> Heimskringla is the volume called;
> And he who looks may find therein
> The story that we now begin.

It may here be observed that those who look in *Heimskringla* will also find ample support for the characterization of Olaf in Elgar's cantata.[82]

The author of *Heimskringla*, the renowned Icelandic historian Snorri Sturluson, lived from 1178 to 1241; and it is thought that he completed this work, a survey of Norwegian history up to 1177, before his second journey to Norway in 1235.[83] The two Olaf Sagas in *Heimskringla* concern King Olaf Trygvesson (Olaf I) and his kinsman King Olaf Haraldsson (Olaf II). Olaf Haraldsson was declared a saint and became the patron saint of Norway; but it is, of course, Olaf Trygvesson who is the subject of Elgar's cantata. It is appropriate to recall that he was also the subject of Grieg's choral work *Landkjenning* (Land-sighting) of 1872 and of his unfinished opera *Olav Trygvason* of the following year, which was later arranged for concert performance as *Scenes from Olav Trygvason* and was first performed at Christiania in 1889.[84]

The English translation of *Heimskringla* by Samuel Laing was brought out in London in 1844; and in the Introduction to a revised edition of *The Olaf Sagas* published in 1964, Dr Jacqueline Simpson observed that Snorri had a threefold aim in the Saga under discussion: 'to reconstruct as truthful a picture of the past as the best sources available to him will allow; to enrich that picture by the interpretations which his experience and clear insight may suggest; and to present it lucidly, powerfully and with all the resources of his artistry'.[85] Bearing this in mind let us now consider some further points which call for comment.

Elgar's cantata, like Shakespeare's plays, has incurred censure on grounds which suggest that the libretto is in conflict with the 'rules' of the drama. Let us turn for guidance on this issue to one of the leading men of letters in the late Victorian period, Professor A W Ward, whose standard *History of English Dramatic Literature to the Age of Queen Anne* was first published in 1875.

Commenting elsewhere on the law of 'completeness of action', Ward points out that it is the dramatist's fault 'if in the action of his drama anything is left unaccounted for – not *motivé*'.[86] Olaf had spent almost his whole life up to the age of about twenty-seven in exile, and his motivation for sailing back to Norway was, it appears, cumulative. In Longfellow's poem the motives are threefold, and may be stated thus: the resolve to establish Christianity in the kingdom, first expressed in his words, 'I accept thy challenge, Thor!'; the wish 'To avenge his father slain', that is Trygve

Olafsson, who had been treacherously killed by Gudrod, a son of Queen Gunhild, before his mother Astrid gave birth to him; and the inclination to 'reconquer realm and reign', or as Snorri puts it 'to go to the heritage of his ancestors', for he was 'of the udal succession to the kingdom', being a great-grandson of Harald Haarfager (Fairhair), the first king of a united Norway.

Few of those who know and appreciate the cantata's qualities are likely to disagree with Newman's opinion about Elgar's setting of 'King Olaf's Return' (a view expressed, it should be remembered, after the production of the 'Enigma' Variations, *The Dream of Gerontius*, and *The Apostles*): '... music that still remains among the finest Elgar has written, music of a singularly lucid, limpid beauty, full of magical suggestion'.[87] But when he says that 'we naturally expect the action here to hinge upon the strife between the two religions', we may answer that Olaf is sailing 'Northward into Drontheim fiord' during this scene, but that the ensuing scene, 'The Conversion', was specially written by Acworth to highlight that conflict and its successful outcome. When we are then told that the motivation of the story is 'already approaching chaos', we must simply reply that such a view appears mistaken, and for various reasons.

(a) The Synopsis by Burrows, which was incorporated in the vocal score of the cantata following a performance by the Sheffield Musical Union, adds further force to the message expressed in 'The Conversion' and the Epilogue: Olaf's dominant motive is the accomplishment of his mission to establish Christianity in Norway, as 'an alternative to the ever-recurring sacrifices of blood' demanded by the tenets of the old Norse religion.[88]

(b) As Sir Julian Huxley remarked in the course of a memorable address on 'Values in an Age of Scientific Integration', 'you never find a single cause for anything, it is always multi-causal';[89] and it is hard to see any good reason for the exclusion of causes which strengthen the motivation of the principal character.

(c) Whatever view we may take in the twentieth century of the wish 'To avenge his father slain', it should be borne in mind that such a concept was in accordance with the conventional ethics of those times. For instance, two years after King Olaf's reign ended, Gunhild, a sister of King Svend the Dane, was a victim of the massacre of St Brice's day in England, where she was living as a hostage; and it is 'highly probable', says Stenton, 'that the wish to avenge her was a principal motive' for the Danish king's invasion of England in 1003.[90] We should note in passing that Snorri does not seem to ascribe vengeance as a motive for Olaf's return in *Heimskringla*. In fact neither Longfellow nor Acworth mentions such a motive again: it seems clear, therefore, that we should not make overmuch of its significance.

(d) Olaf's inclination to 'reconquer realm and reign' was fired by the information that many of his fellow-countrymen would like to see 'a king of

Harald Haarfager's race come to the kingdom';[91] and in due course, as Snorri wrote, 'Olaf Trygvesson was chosen at Drontheim by the General Thing to be the king over the whole country, as Harald Haarfager had been'.[92] Far from being inconsistent with his resolve to establish Christianity in Norway, it was through his authority as king, helped by the English-born bishop and priests who had sailed with him,[93] that his mission was fulfilled. Nor was that all: for as in the case of King Olaf Haraldsson the Saint, the Christianization of the country had both religious and political aspects, and the two were closely linked.[94]

IX

We come now to the question of Olaf's character. And before discussing this, it will be helpful to refer to Ward's description of the requisites in dramatic characterization: 'A dramatic character must', he says, '... be sufficiently marked by features of its own to interest the imagination; with these features its subsequent conduct must be consistent, and to them its participation in the action must correspond'.[95]

King Olaf Trygvesson was clearly one of the most remarkable figures of his time, not least in the range of qualities he revealed during his northern Odyssey. Bearing in mind Elgar's view that 'Outdoor exercise is absolutely essential to life',[96] let us turn to the chapter on 'King Olaf's feats' in *Heimskringla*: 'King Olaf was more expert in all exercises than any man in Norway whose memory is preserved to us in sagas; and he was stronger and more agile than most men, and many stories are written down about it. ... King Olaf could run across the oars outside of the vessel while his men were rowing the Serpent. He could play with three daggers, so that one was always in the air, and he took the one falling by the handle. He could walk all round upon the ship's rails, could strike and cut equally well with both hands, and could cast two spears at once'.[97]

Snorri's account continues: 'King Olaf was a very merry frolicsome man; gay and social; was most eager in everything; was very generous; stood out clearly among other men; in battle he exceeded all in bravery'. The Saga makes it plain that the young Norse hero was a formidable opponent, fierce when roused and unflinching in resolve. His friends, says Snorri, 'were attached to him warmly, and his enemies feared him greatly'.

We are told in *Heimskringla* that Olaf's exile was spent at first in Sweden at the home of Hakon the Old; then in Estonia, prior to which he was separated from his mother Astrid; and later in Russia, where he was much esteemed by Vladimir the Great. We should observe here that Longfellow's verses relating to Estonia and Russia were included by Elgar in the first version of 'King Olaf's Return'.[98] After nine years in Russia Olaf set out to sea, and eventually sailed to Vendland, the land of the Slavonic people who then occupied the Baltic coast from the Vistula to Holstein. Here he married Geyra, a sister of the future King Burislaf; but in the year 990 she died, and, says the Saga, 'Olaf felt his loss so great that he had no pleasure in Vendland after it'.[99] He provided himself with ships and 'after the manner of his countrymen in those days' set forth on a Viking cruise, sailing to Friesland, Saxony, and Flanders, and then to England.

In August 991 a large Viking force entered the estuary of the Blackwater in Essex. The name of its commander at the ensuing battle of Maldon has given rise to much discussion. In 1976 Mr Eric John, in a paper examining all the facts afresh, was able to state: 'The Viking commander at Maldon was Olaf Tryggvason'.[100] The English commander was a worthy foeman, Byrhtnoth, the ealdorman of Essex; and we may note in passing that the name of his wife's father was Ælfgar, who had been ealdorman of Essex forty years earlier. The action which followed inspired what has been described as 'the greatest battle-poem in the English language',[101] 'The Battle of Maldon'. Towards the close of this epic poem, and after Byrhtnoth has fallen, one of his trusty followers, Byrhtwold, exhorts the survivors to fight on in words which ring through the centuries:[102]

> Thought shall be the harder, heart the keener,
> Courage the greater, as our might lessens.

Such resolution was no less characteristic of Olaf himself, and such was his own heroic courage nine years later when fighting against the odds at the historic sea-battle of Svold, the conflict portrayed so vividly by Elgar in the last scene of the cantata, 'The Death of Olaf'.

We may now picture Olaf as the most brilliant of the young Viking chieftains in the last decade of the tenth century. In September 994 he appeared in England again, this time accompanied by Svend Forkbeard of Denmark, with a combined fleet of ninety-four warships. 'It was', says Stenton, 'the most formidable invasion which England had experienced for half a century'.[103] The Viking forces attacked London where they met with strong resistance and were beaten off. They next engaged in a raid over south-eastern England, entered Hampshire, and then 'took horses and rode whither they would'. King Æthelred II and the Witan now decided to come to terms with them. Three years earlier, after the Maldon campaign, a heavy tax had been raised to buy off the invaders, and this policy of 'paying the Dane-geld', with the ill results which Kipling described,[104] was once more adopted. But other events took place around this time which had a significant effect on Olaf's subsequent actions; and one of them has an important bearing on the characterization of Olaf in Elgar's cantata.

Æthelred made prudent use of the respite to send Bishop Ælfheah of Winchester (later known as St Alphege) and Ealdorman Æthelweard of

Wessex, the chronicler, on an embassy to Olaf at Southampton, where the Vikings had taken up quarters for the winter. The result, Dr William Hunt tells us, was that the alliance between Olaf and Svend was broken,[105] though their sense of conflicting interests may also have contributed to this.[106] Olaf agreed to meet Æthelred and make a lasting peace with him, and they conducted him to the king at Andover.

There has sometimes been confusion as to the nature of the ceremony which now took place, and it will therefore be best to quote Stenton's carefully-worded account of the particular rite which Bishop Ælfheah administered to Olaf: 'Already a baptized Christian, he was confirmed at Andover, with the king as his sponsor, and entered into a solemn undertaking that he would leave England and never return to it in war'.[107] We should note here that the Norwegian kept his word and never came to England as an enemy again.

Let us turn now to the question of Olaf's conversion and 'rites baptismal'. Although the account of Olaf's baptism in the Scilly Isles has sometimes been questioned, it is in accordance with historical possibility, and is moreover true to dramatic probability. Snorri says in *Heimskringla* that 'Olaf Trygvesson had been four years on this cruise from the time he left Vendland till he came to the Scilly Islands', which places his arrival there in 994. He also tells us of Olaf's meeting with the Scillonian hermit, who was a seer, and of his prophetic words: 'Thou wilt become a renowned king, and do celebrated deeds. Many men wilt thou bring to faith and baptism . . .'.[108]

The significance of this event in Olaf's life is graphically conveyed in Thomas Carlyle's essay on 'Early Kings of Norway', an excerpt from which was chosen to preface Bennett's *Analytical Notes on 'King Olaf'*: 'He was told of a wonderful Christian hermit living strangely in these sea-solitudes; had the curiosity to seek him out, examine, question, and discourse with him; and, after some reflection, accepted Christian baptism from the venerable man . . . . The story is involved in miracle, rumour, and fable; but the fact itself seems certain, and is very interesting; the great, wild, noble soul of fierce *Olaf* opening to this wonderful gospel of tidings from beyond the world, tidings which infinitely transcended all else he had ever heard or dreamt of!'.[109]

Although Snorri's account of Olaf's voyages does not refer specifically to the expedition of 994, he does tell us that when Olaf sailed from Scilly to England and put into a harbour, he 'proceeded in a friendly way; for England was Christian, and he himself had become Christian'.[110] It would seem from this that Olaf set out for the Isles of Scilly from Southampton after terms of peace had been agreed upon; that he was deeply impressed by the Scillonian hermit's wisdom and powers of divination, was converted to Christianity, and agreed to let himself be baptized; and that, after sailing back to Southampton, he proceeded in due course to Andover, where he was confirmed by Bishop Ælfheah.

What are we to say, having regard to these circumstances, in answer to Newman's assertion that the character of Olaf in the cantata is 'a mere muddle throughout'? I suggest that it fails to give sufficient weight to the historical principle of viewing a man in the light of the age in which he lived. When we read that 'All through the cantata there is the same alternate presentation of Olaf the pirate and the saint', we must reply that this type of view appears overdrawn and misleading. It seems clear that Olaf ceased his activities as a sea-roving chieftain prior to the Treaty of Andover, many months before his return to Norway and before the action of the cantata commences; and the hero of Elgar's cantata is, as the Prefatory Note to Bennett's analysis points out, King Olaf Trygvesson, 'not to be confounded' with King Olaf Haraldsson the Saint. In any case the suggestion of incongruity is conclusively answered by the description of Olaf Haraldsson in *The Book of Saints*: 'His early youth was spent, after the manner of his countrymen in those days, as a pirate'.[111]

Olaf was, as Newman observed, 'a real creature of his day', and he possessed in full measure the qualities most admired by the Vikings: but he added to them the missionary zeal of the recent convert. It is possible that he hoped to rule 'a united, as well as a Christian, Scandinavia'; and some such ambition would go far to explain his proposal of marriage to Sigrid, the Swedish Queen-mother. The historical writer Robert Bain, a colleague of Colvin and Binyon at the British Museum, when recounting Sigrid's subsequent marriage to King Svend of Denmark, described her thus: 'This lady was a fanatical pagan of a disquieting strength of character. Two viceroys, earlier wooers, were burned to death by her orders for their impertinence ...'.[112] *Heimskringla* adds: 'Sigrid said that she would make these small kings tired of coming to court her. She was afterwards called Sigrid the Haughty'.[113]

It has sometimes been held that the characterization of Olaf in Scene vi, when he meets Sigrid and the sparks fly upward, is inconsistent with that of a convert to Christianity. Yet whatever view we may take of Olaf's response when Sigrid refuses to be baptized, we should surely study his side of the question. The encounter between these two characters, the hero and his most implacable adversary, certainly has an intensity which calls to mind an irresistible force meeting an immovable object; but, leaving aside the fact that conversion to a new faith can scarcely eradicate human nature, the Sagas reveal antecedents which shed fresh light on Olaf's conduct.

(a) We learn from *Heimskringla* that it was during the winter of 997/8 that 'messengers went between King Olaf and Sigrid to propose his courtship to her, and she had no objection; and the matter was fully and fast resolved upon .... The meeting for concluding the business was appointed to be in spring on the frontier, at the Gotha river'.[114] When they met at Konghelle, 'the business was considered about which the winter before they had held communication, namely, their marriage; and the business seemed likely to be concluded'.[115] It seems clear from Snorri's phraseology that Olaf's proposal for this alliance was based on sound political and religious reasons. There is no suggestion of a love-match, unlike his relationships with both Geyra and Thyri. Can we conceive that the matter could have been resolved upon 'fully and fast' (that is, completely and firmly) without reference to King Olaf's stipulation that his future consort should accept Christianity and let herself be baptized? In any case we are told that 'Sigrid was a woman of the greatest understanding, and too clever in many things',[116] and she would surely have apprehended that acceptance of the missionary King Olaf's proposal would involve adopting the Christian faith.

(b) The initial agreement of this essential condition for the alliance would have been a sensible precaution in all the circumstances. Sigrid was portrayed by Bain as 'the most stiff-necked pagan of her day';[117] and one of the earlier wooers killed by her orders was a relation of King Olaf, Harald Graenske, a district king in Norway who was incidentally her foster-brother. Can we imagine Olaf's feelings when, at their spring meeting, Sigrid announced: 'I must not part from the faith which I have held, and my forefathers before me'? And what are we to make of her next remark to the monarch of the neighbouring country who had proposed that she should become his consort: 'and, on the other hand, I shall make no objection to your believing in the god that pleases you best'?[118]

(c) Snorri's description of this dialogue indicates that Sigrid had strained Olaf's patience beyond the limit (in Burke's phrase) 'at which forbearance ceases to be a virtue'. Various references in *Heimskringla* suggest that in his association with women Olaf was habitually courteous and amiable. His demeanour on this occasion represents a departure from his customary behaviour so marked as to suggest severe provocation; and his final words, as recounted by Snorri, suggest that Sigrid's conduct in this matter may have been wily and treacherous.

One of the most remarkable features of Elgar's score is his graphic portrayal of Sigrid's manner as it changes through the stimulus of Olaf's character: first, her outward aspect, expressed by the engaging opening theme which, though light in nature, also hints at the reality which underlies appearances through syncopation and *fp* emphases; then what Newman finely calls 'the spitfire music that is set to Sigrid's angry championship of her old gods'; and lastly, the revelation of her inner nature in her closing soliloquy, and especially in the harmonically striking setting of 'Thou art gone! nay, spur not thro' the gate; I am one that can watch and wait'.

Olaf's closing remarks to Sigrid, which were modified from the original for the cantata, have sometimes been interpreted as indicating that she was plain in appearance and advanced in age. But the 'Sigrid' theme, with which Elgar begins the Scene, suggests neither; indeed, with allowance for the passing of time, it corresponds with Snorri's earlier description of Sigrid as 'both young and handsome'.[119] By the time of her meeting with Olaf, who was then about thirty, it seems likely that Sigrid was still no more than a year or so on either side of forty; and, judging by her zealous though unfortunate suitors of three years previously, she could scarcely have lost her charms. The balance of probability suggests that Olaf's comments arose through sheer exasperation, and points to the breach of a condition, whether expressed or implied, in an agreement 'fully and fast resolved upon'.

In considering the character of Olaf we should bear in mind what Professor Johannes Brønsted described as a fundamental concept in a Viking's behaviour: concern for his own and his family's honour.[120] The principle of family obligation must, says Brønsted, have created 'a check upon any individual's disposition to forgive an affront or wrong';[121] and the fact that Sigrid had been responsible for an act of violence against a relation of Olaf, breaching the bond between foster-children, cannot have made the situation any easier. Equally it is hardly surprising if King Olaf felt affronted when Sigrid, having agreed to become his consort, refused to accept the religion he had proclaimed in his kingdom.

The rapidly increasing tension in this Scene leads to a critical point in the action of the cantata, culminating in the glove incident. Longfellow's treatment of this includes some dramatically colourful features which are not present in *Heimskringla*, and Acworth in turn modifies Longfellow. It is beyond our scope to discuss this matter in detail; but, as it has sometimes been held that Olaf's conduct is inconsistent with that of a convert to Christianity, we should note here a conclusion which has been emphasized by some authorities on the Viking Age. This is (as expressed by Professor Brønsted) that 'it would be relatively easy for Christianity to prevail over Nordic religious beliefs', but much more difficult 'to substitute an ethical formula about loving your neighbours for the Nordic concepts of honour and family'.[122] In Churchill's words, 'It is baffling to reflect that what men call honour does not correspond always to Christian ethics'.[123]

Consistency, says Ward, does not imply uniformity; 'for, as Aristotle observes, there are characters which, to be represented with uniformity, must be presented as uniformly un-uniform'.[124] In the modern drama, Ward continues, Hamlet is the unrivalled exemplar of such 'consistently complex' characters. The 'Sigrid' Scene indicates that what Bradley wrote on the conflict in *Hamlet* and other Shakespearian tragedies also applies, in a certain measure, to Elgar's *King Olaf*: 'There is an outward conflict of persons and groups, there is also a conflict of forces in the hero's soul'.[125]

Newman's espousal of a 'pirate-saint' dichotomy led him to declare that it was a mistake for a modern composer to make Olaf 'pose as a kind of bulwark of the faith', a misleading remark suggesting that Olaf Trygvesson was simply a Viking chieftain who became the King of Norway, and failing to take sufficient account of his dominant motive in the cantata, the accomplishment of his mission. We can best reply to this with some words of Dr Jacqueline Simpson: 'Although he had not been declared a saint, he was yet honoured as a hero of Christendom, the driving force in a movement which brought about the conversion not only of Norway but of Iceland and other Scandinavian settlements'.[126] In sum, King Olaf, like his saintly namesake, was 'a missionary Viking'.

X

In drawing these remarks to a close, I propose to confine them to some observations on the organic unity of *King Olaf*, including Elgar's characteristic use of the Epilogue.

From time to time we have been told that the cantata is not an organic whole, a view which was sometimes expressed about such outstanding works as *The Apostles* and *The Kingdom*, until the increasing number of fine performances, live and recorded, called it in question. In this context 'organic' means, of course, the systematic connection and co-ordination of parts in one whole; and we may refer to Professor Ward for further insight into the laws of drama relating to unity and completeness of action: (a) 'Within the limits of a dramatic action all its parts should ... flow into its current like tributaries to a single stream'; (b) 'every drama should represent in organic sequence the several stages of which a complete action consists, and which are essential to it'.[127]

The more *King Olaf* is studied, the more its dramatic and musical unity become manifest. Each Scene forms 'a link in a single chain of cause and effect', if one allows that the 'Gudrun' Scene is a subsidiary one which completes the story of Ironbeard. Yet that is not all; for the voice which Gudrun seems to hear at midnight, that of her dead father, the leading upholder of Paganism in the Drontheim district, foreshadows 'The voice of Saint John', which Astrid, mother of Olaf, and now Abbess of Drontheim, hears in the convent at midnight, in the Epilogue. The action has its causes, growth, climax, consequences and close; and once the essential facts of the story are grasped, the onward flow of events lives in one's mind in organic sequence.

Now it is right to recall at this point that Elgar's original vocal score, which he took to the publishers in March 1896, contained a considerable amount of linking music between the Scenes, quite apart from two more bass recitatives, before 'King Olaf's Return' and the Duet with Thyri, and a tenor solo for the voice of St John in the Epilogue.[128] The composer was then asked to shorten the work and divide it into separate numbers which could later be issued individually; and the revised version, which was dispatched from Malvern on 8 April, was shorter by about thirty pages.[129] Although one may regret that the continuity of Elgar's original structure had to be modified, this did not impair the organic unity of the cantata, as several fine performances in recent years have demonstrated.

Elgar's use of 'representative themes' undoubtedly contributes to the feeling of unity in *King Olaf*. Macfarren had adopted this device for the concert-hall as early as 1877 in his oratorio *Joseph*,[130] but it was a relatively new technique for a British composer to employ systematically throughout a full-length choral work. Bennett went so far as to affirm that, 'apart from certain operas', it had rarely been made 'so conspicuous, and so closely interwoven with the texture of the music, as here'.[131] Whilst thematic references to the characters in the cantata are easily identifiable, the relationships between them and other persons mentioned in the libretto are less readily grasped, and the genealogical table in the Appendix has been prepared in order to clarify these matters.

Finally, let us note a structural feature common to *King Olaf, St George*, and *Caractacus*: the Epilogue, standing outside the action, like the Prologue of *The Apostles*. *Caractacus* ends with a Choral Epilogue as Thompson's analysis makes clear,[132] and *St George* concludes with a well-known Epilogue, 'It comes from the misty ages'. The Epilogue of *King Olaf* is particularly beautiful, and is notable ior the way the 'Thor' motive from Scene i becomes metamorphosed into the solo trio, 'It is accepted', and then into the chorus, 'Patience is powerful', which leads into the moving setting for unaccompanied chorus of 'As torrents in summer'. Criticism has sometimes been passed on the cantata taking this more serious turn after all the stirring scenes of action. Let us see, then, what happened to King Olaf when, through the treachery of Earl Sigvald of Jomsburg, he was waylaid and defeated at the battle of Svold in September 1000.

We learn from *Heimskringla* that Olaf sprang overboard, threw his shield over his head, and sank beneath the waters. Ten ships which had accompanied him from Vendland, under Sigvald, now rowed towards the battle; but the eleventh ship, which was manned with the men of Astrid, sister of King Burislaf, rowed back to Vendland. Astrid was a friend of Olaf, since he had formerly been married to her sister Geyra; 'and the report went immediately abroad', says Snorri, 'and was told by many, that Olaf had cast off his coat of mail under the water, and swam, diving under the long-ships, until he came to the Vendland cutter, and that Astrid's men had conveyed him to Vendland; and many tales have been made since about the adventures of Olaf the king'.[133] One said that Olaf went on pilgrimage to the Holy Land and lived there for many years as a monk; another, that he became a monk in Greece or Syria. Thus the Epilogue is not only in harmony with the dominant motive of the principal character, but draws a moral fully consistent with other tales of the hero's life.

Apart from this, the Cantata as a form was undergoing modification at this time, as a result of a change in the orientation of large-scale choral music from the old type of oratorio to something 'much more conscious and individual', as Walker put it,[134] a tendency which developed after the publication of Darwin's *The Origin of Species* in 1859. British composers were putting more of their noblest thoughts into secular choral works, as well as the Symphony; and it is therefore not surprising that Elgar decided to end this cantata in a more serious and reflective manner.

In April 1924 the composer wrote to his friend Troyte Griffith that if he had to set *King Olaf* again he would do it 'just in the same way'.[135] He added that he had never done anything like 'Dead rides Sir Morten of Fogelsang'. Indeed, the magnificent music which Elgar composed for this cantata has a quality which made it much more than a turning-point in his career: as well as being a landmark in the English choral tradition, it is a very notable example of his genius; and, beyond cavil, it shows him as a master.

This chapter is an expanded and revised version of the Second A.T. Shaw Memorial Lecture given at the Annual Meeting of the Elgar Society in Worcester on 1 June 1985.

Examples from the following parts of *King Olaf* were played on gramophone records during the course of the lecture:

'And King Olaf heard the cry' ('King Olaf's Return'): Tudor Davies (tenor) with Symphony Orchestra, conducted by Eugene Goossens (abridged version recorded 1923) (ELG 001).

Ballad: 'A little bird in the air' ('Thyri'): Royal Albert Hall Orchestra, conducted by Sir Edward Elgar (abridged orchestral version recorded 1921) (GEM 114).

'As torrents in summer' (Epilogue): Louis Halsey Singers, conducted by Louis Halsey (ZRG 607).

Acknowledgements

The author wishes to acknowledge with gratitude the help of Mr Spencer Noble, Mr Dallas Bower, Mr Christopher Bornet, Professor Alan G Hill, Dr Christopher Kent, Mr Richard Hamer, the staff of the Mayfair Library, and the editor, Mr Raymond Monk.

Appendix: The relationships between the characters in *King Olaf*

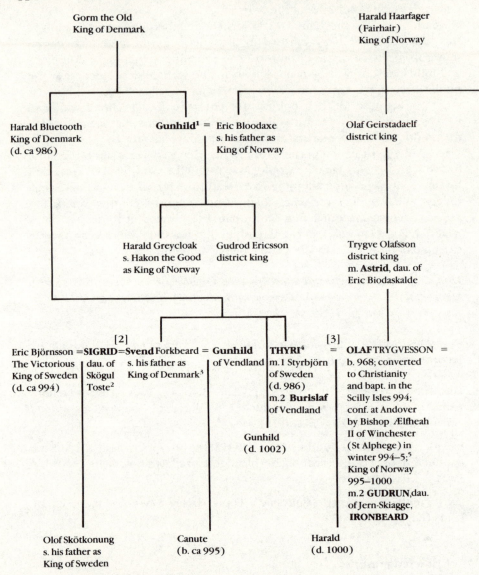

[1]   'King Olaf's Return', vocal score p. 22; see Foote, Appendix I, *Sagas of the Norse Kings*, 425 (note to p. 75).

[2]   On the relation between Sigrid and the legend of Brynhild and Sigurd see Simpson, ed., 'King Olaf Trygvesson's Saga', 80 n. 2.

[3]   See 'The Anglo-Danish Kings of England', *Burke's Guide to the Royal Family* (Burke's Peerage Limited: London, 1973), 192.

[4]   Thyri is said to have died of grief for Olaf's fall a few days after the Battle of Svold: see J.H.S. Birch, *Denmark in History* (Murray: London, 1938) 37–8.

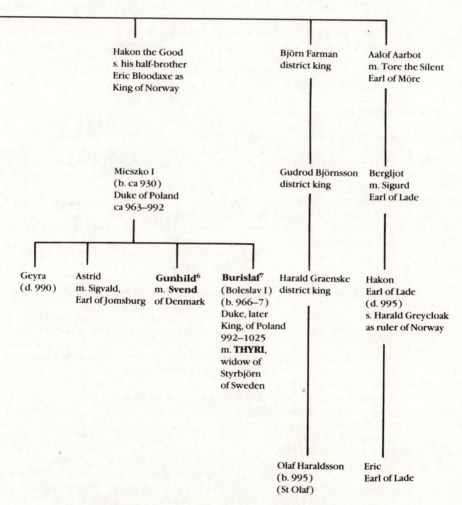

Hakon the Good
s. his half-brother
Eric Bloodaxe as
King of Norway

Björn Farman
district king

Aalof Aarbot
m. Tore the Silent
Earl of Möre

Mieszko I
(b. ca 930)
Duke of Poland
ca 963–992

Gudrod Björnsson
district king

Bergljot
m. Sigurd
Earl of Lade

Geyra
(d. 990)

Astrid
m. Sigvald,
Earl of Jomsburg

Gunhild[6]
m. Svend
of Denmark

Burislaf[7]
(Boleslav I)
(b. 966–7)
Duke, later
King, of Poland
992–1025
m. THYRI,
widow of
Styrbjörn
of Sweden

Harald Graenske
district king

Hakon
Earl of Lade
(d. 995)
s. Harald Greycloak
as ruler of Norway

Olaf Haraldsson
(b. 995)
(St Olaf)

Eric
Earl of Lade

[5] The statement that Olaf, while in England, married Gyda, sister of Olaf Kvaran
Sigtrygsson of Dublin, appears to be unhistoric: see Simpson, op. cit., 31 n.,
32 n. 1.

[6] Choral Recit., vocal score p. 133; see 'The Anglo-Danish Kings of England' above.

[7] On the confusion between Burislaf and his father (e.g. Burislaf was almost an
exact contemporary of Olaf), see Simpson, op. cit., 22 n. 2.

Note: Names appearing in the Cantata (shown in **bold** type) are spelt as in the libretto:
other names are spelt as in *Heimskringla* or according to modern English usage.

Notes

1. The views of Mackenzie, Parry, and Stanford are mentioned in section VI; and in 1932 Brian wrote: '... in my mind [*King Olaf*] stands as the finest secular cantata given to us since Berlioz's *Damnation de Faust*: it has frenzied fire and imaginative choral and orchestral colouring'. See Brian, Havergal, 'Fifty Years of Progress?', *Musical Opinion*, May 1932, pp.667-8, quo. in *Havergal Brian on Music*, ed. Malcolm MacDonald, vol. i, *British Music* (Toccata Press: London, 1986), p.212.

2. It may be suggested that Elgar's Cantatas of the 1890s are no less entitled to recognition than Bach's works prior to the sacred masterpiece of *his* early forties, the St Matthew Passion.

3. Vaughan Williams, Ralph, Foreword to *Eight Concerts of Henry Purcell's Music*: Commemorative Book, ed. Watkins Shaw (Arts Council of Great Britain: London, 1951), p.7.

4. A Beamon may, on rare occasions, shatter the world long jump record with a 'sudden leap'; but it may be questioned whether such a phenomenon in creative work accords with the principle of the Law of Continuity, that all change in nature is continuous, and does not go *per saltum*.

5. Nettel, Reginald, *Music in the Five Towns, 1840–1914* (OUP: London, 1944), p.95.

6. ibid., p.41.

7. Parry, Sir Hubert, 'Routine and understanding' (January 1911), *College Addresses*, ed. H.C. Colles (Macmillan: London, 1920), p.102.

8. A significant example of such acknowledgement is the four-volume *History of the Oratorio* by Professor Howard E. Smither.

9. For example, one standard work of reference lists a number of eminent Romantic composers of cantatas, but says of their contributions that there were 'none of lasting importance'.

10. Fellowes, Edmund H, *English Cathedral Music* (4th edn, Methuen: London, 1948), pp.79–80; Brett, Philip, 'The English Consort Song, 1570–1625', *Proceedings of the Royal Musical Association*, 88 (1962), pp.87–8.

11. Kerman, Joseph, *The English Madrigal* (American Musicological Society: New York, 1962), p.107.

12. See Walker, Ernest, *A History of Music in England* (3rd edn, rev. and enlarged by J A Westrup, OUP: London, 1952), pp.97–8.

13. Kerman, op.cit., pp.123–4.

14. Fortune, Nigel, 'Solo Song and Cantata', *New Oxford History of Music*, iv, *The Age of Humanism (1540–1630)*, ed. Gerald Abraham (OUP: London, 1968), p.172.

15. Atkins, E Wulstan, *The Elgar-Atkins Friendship* (David & Charles: Newton Abbot, 1984), pp.410–14, 419.

16. The term 'cantata' seems to have been introduced to England in 1710 by Pepusch, whose *Six English Cantatas* were published that year. See Spink, Ian, 'England: Cantata and Ballad: 1710-50', *New Oxford History of Music*, vi, *Concert Music (1630–1750)*, ed. Gerald Abraham (OUP: Oxford, 1986), pp.147–8.

17. Westrup, J A, *Purcell* (3rd edn, Dent: London, 1946), pp.173, 207; Fellowes, op.cit., p.163. See also Rosamond McGuinness, 'The Origins and Disappearance of the English Court Ode', *PRMA*, 87 (1961), pp.69–70.

18. Holland A K, *Henry Purcell: The English Musical Tradition* (Penguin Books:

Harmondsworth, 1932), p.132.

19. Dean, Winton, *Handel* (Macmillan: London, 1982), pp.23-4, 125; Anthony Hicks and Gerald Abraham, 'Oratorio and Related Forms', *New Oxford History of Music*, vi (op.cit.), pp.25–6.

20. On the site of the modern Her Majesty's Theatre: see Fiske, Roger, *English Theatre Music in the Eighteenth Century* (2nd edn, OUP: Oxford, 1986), p.xv.

21. Westrup, J A, 'Opera in England and Germany', *New Oxford History of Music*, v, *Opera and Church Music (1630–1750)*, ed. Anthony Lewis and Nigel Fortune (OUP: Oxford, 1975, repr. 1986), p.296.

22. See McNaught, William, 'Handel', *Lives of the Great Composers*, ed. A L Bacharach, i (Gollancz, London, 1935; repr., Penguin Books: West Drayton, 1947), p.85.

23. Johnstone, H Diack, 'Maurice Greene, 1696–1755' (Broadcast talk on Radio 3, 23 May 1974). Script held by the BBC Scripts Registry.

24. Bartlett, Ian and Bruce, Robert J, 'William Boyce's "Solomon"', *Music and Letters*, 61 (January 1980), p.32.

25. See Hicks and Abraham, op.cit., p.81.

26. The Overture to Boyce's *Solomon* became his Symphony No.6, in F.

27. Fellowes, op.cit., p.184.

28. Bevan, Maurice, Editorial Note to vocal score of Boyce's 'Lord, Thou hast been our refuge' (OUP: London, 1977).

29. McGuinness, Rosamond, 'Dialogue and Ode', *New Oxford History of Music*, vi (op.cit.), pp.21–2.

30. See *Musica Britannica*, xxx.

31. Fiske, op.cit., p.420.

32. Boyd, Malcolm, *Bach* (Dent: London, 1983), p.149.

33. ibid., p.117.

34. Radcliffe, Philip, *Mendelssohn* (Dent: London, 1954, rev. 1976), p.138.

35. Einstein, Alfred, *Music in the Romantic Era* (Dent: London, 1947), pp.174–5.

36. Nettel, op.cit., pp.1, 12, 110.

37. Lewis, Anthony, 'Choral Music', *New Oxford History of Music*, viii, *The Age of Beethoven (1790–1830)*, ed. Gerald Abraham (OUP, 1982; repr., Oxford, 1988), p.596.

38. Fellowes, op.cit., pp.205-10; see also Nicholas Temperley, 'Cathedral Music', *Athlone History of Music in Britain*, v, *The Romantic Age (1800-1914)*, ed. Temperley (Athlone Press: London, 1981), pp.193–9.

39. See Sackville-West, Edward, and Shawe-Taylor, Desmond, *The Record Guide* (rev. edn, Collins: London, 1955), p.168.

40. Colles, H C, *Symphony and Drama (1850–1900)*, Oxford History of Music, vii (OUP: London, 1934), p.416.

41. When Elgar spoke on 'A Future for English Music', in his inaugural lecture at Birmingham in 1905, he expressed the hope for 'something that shall grow out of our own soil, something broad, noble, chivalrous, healthy and above all, an out-of-door sort of spirit', words which epitomize the music of Parry, whom Elgar had described earlier as 'the head of our art in this country'. See Young, Percy M, ed., *A Future for English Music* (Dennis Dobson: London, 1968), pp. 48–9, 57.

42. Willeby, Charles, 'Arthur Seymour Sullivan', *Masters of English Music* (Osgood, McIlvaine & Co.: London, 1893), p.37.

43. Mackenzie, Sir Alexander Campbell, *A Musician's Narrative* (Cassell: London,

1927), pp.122, 124.

44. ibid., p.123 n.l.

45. Porte, John F, *Sir Charles V. Stanford* (Kegan Paul: London, 1921), p.3.

46. Parry, C Hubert H, *Summary of the History and Development of Mediaeval and Modern European Music* (Novello: London, 1893; rev. edn, 1904), p.115.

47. Godfrey, Sir Dan, *Memories and Music* (Hutchinson: London, 1924), p.142.

48. Rockstro, William S, 'Oratorio', *A Dictionary of Music and Musicians*, ed. George Grove, ii (Macmillan: London, 1880), p.559.

49. Parry, C Hubert H, *The Art of Music* (Routledge & Kegan Paul: London, 1893; rev. as *The Evolution of the Art of Music*, 1896; 11th impression, 1950), p.284.

50. Fellowes, Edmund Horace, *The English Madrigal Composers* (OUP: London, 1921; 2nd edn, 1948), p.198.

51. Parry, *Summary of Musical History*, p.124.

52. Mackenzie, op.cit., p.205.

53. Buckley, Robert J, *Sir Edward Elgar* (John Lane, The Bodley Head: London, 1905), p.1.

54. Brian, Havergal, Introduction to Sheldon, A J, *Edward Elgar* (Musical Opinion: London, 1932), pp.2–3.

55. Edwards, F G, 'Edward Elgar', *Musical Times*, October 1900, repr. in *An Elgar Companion*, ed. Christopher Redwood (Sequoia Publishing in association with Moorland Publishing: Ashbourne, 1982), p.36.

56. Colles, H C, 'Sir Edward (William) Elgar', *Grove's Dictionary of Music and Musicians*, 4th edn, ed. Colles, Supplementary vol. (Macmillan: London, 1940), p.191.

57. Reaney P H, *A Dictionary of British Surnames* (2nd edn, rev. Wilson, R M, Routledge and Kegan Paul: London, 1976), p.5, s.v. 'Algar . . . Elgar'.

58. Cottle, Basil, *The Penguin Dictionary of Surnames* (2nd edn, Penguin Books: Harmondsworth, 1978), p.35, s.v. 'Algar . . . Elgar'.

59. Reed, W H, *Elgar* (Dent: London, 1939; repr. 1949), p.79.

60. McVeagh, Diana M, *Edward Elgar: His Life and Music* (Dent: London, 1955), p.1.

61. Churchill, Winston S, *The Second World War*, iii, *The Grand Alliance* (Cassell: London, 1950), pp.24–5.

62. Reed, op.cit., p.69.

63. Colles, *Symphony and Drama*, p.260.

64. Newman, Ernest, *Elgar* (John Lane, The Bodley Head: London, 1906), p.34.

65. ibid., p.17.

66. Woodberry, George Edward, 'American Literature', *The Encyclopaedia Britannica*, 11th edn, i (The University Press: Cambridge, 1910), p.837.

67. Buell, Lawrence, Introduction to Henry Wadsworth Longfellow, *Selected Poems* (Penguin Books: London, 1988), pp.viii, ix, xii.

68. Moore, Jerrold Northrop, *Edward Elgar: A Creative Life* (OUP: Oxford, 1984), pp.379–80, 385–6.

69. Jaeger, A J, *Analytical and Descriptive Notes on 'The Apostles'* (Novello: London, 1903), p.26.

70. On the physical freedom of the cinema, and its application to Hardy's *The Dynasts* and musical works of a dramatic cast, see Dallas Bower, *Plan for Cinema* (Dent: London, 1936), pp.69–98, passim.

71. Kennedy, Michael, '"The Apostles" reconsidered': essay in programme book

of Hereford Three Choirs Festival for concert in the Cathedral on 24 August 1973.

72. Moore, op.cit., p.379 n.51.
73. David, Paul, 'Ole Borneman Bull', *A Dictionary of Music and Musicians*, ed. Sir George Grove, iv (Macmillan: London, 1889), Appendix, ed. J A Fuller-Maitland, pp.568–9.
74. Buckley, op.cit., pp.50–1.
75. Mackenzie, op.cit., p.169.
76. Bennett, Joseph, 'King Olaf', *Daily Telegraph*, 31 October 1896, repr. in *An Elgar Companion*, ed. Redwood, p.15.
77. Simpson, Jacqueline, Introduction to *Heimskringla*, Part 1, *The Olaf Sagas* (Dent: London, 1964), vol. i, p.xxxii.
78. Burrows, A S, Synopsis of *King Olaf*, repr. in later edns of the vocal score after the libretto, s.v. 'The Wraith of Odin'.
79. Pope, Michael, Introductory Note for the gramophone recording of *The Black Knight* et al. (1984; addns 1987) (EMI CDC7 47511–2), pp.5–6.
80. Voltaire's intervention in a celebrated cause in 1762 is cited by Parry, in his remarkable unpublished book *Instinct and Character* (1918), as an early example of the 'expansion of sympathy'.
81. A Skald, or Scald, has been described as 'an ancient Scandinavian bard who recited or sang at feasts compositions in honour of chiefs and famous men and their deeds'.
82. Sturluson, Snorri, *Heimskringla*, trans. Laing, Samuel, Part 1, *The Olaf Sagas*, rev. Jacqueline Simpson (Dent: London, 1964), vol. i, 'King Olaf Trygvesson's Saga'. See also Introduction, pp.xxxii–xxxiv.
83. Simpson, Introduction, p.xxxi.
84. Horton, John, *Grieg* (Dent: London, 1974), pp.38, 41, 75–6.
85. Simpson, Introduction, p.xxxv.
86. Ward, Adolphus William, 'Drama', *Encycl. Brit.*, 11th edn, viii (1910), p.476.
87. Newman, op.cit., p.21.
88. Burrows, Synopsis of 'King Olaf', s.v. 'The Conversion'.
89. See Huxley, Sir Julian, 'Values in an Age of Scientific Integration', *The Plain View*, ed H J Blackham, xv, 2 (November 1964), p.55.
90. Stenton, Sir Frank, *Anglo-Saxon England*, 3rd edn (OUP: Oxford, 1971), *Oxford History of England*, vol. ii, p.380.
91. Sturluson, Snorri, 'King Olaf Trygvesson's Saga', p.46.
92. ibid., p.51.
93. Stenton, op.cit., p.462.
94. See Simpson, Introduction, p.xxvii.
95. Ward, op.cit., p.478.
96. Reed, op.cit., p.80.
97. Sturluson, Snorri, op.cit., p.75.
98. British Library, Add. MS 57994/5.
99. Sturluson, Snorri, op.cit., p.28.
100. John, Eric, 'War and Society in the Tenth Century: the Maldon Campaign', *Transactions of the Royal Historical Society*, 5th Series, 27 (1977), pp.173–95.
101. Gordon, E V, *The Battle of Maldon* (Methuen: London, 1937), p.29.
102. Quo. by Johnston, S H F, *British Soldiers* (Collins: London, 1944), in the series *Britain in Pictures*, ed. W J Turner, p.47.
103. Stenton, op.cit., p.378.

104. Kipling, Rudyard, 'Dane-Geld', repr. in *A Choice of Kipling's Verse* made by T S Eliot (Faber and Faber: London, 1941), pp.287-8.
105. Hunt, William, 'Ethelred or Æthelred II', *Dictionary of National Biography*, ed. Leslie Stephen, xviii (Smith, Elder, & Co.: London, 1889), p.29.
106. Stenton, op.cit., p.378.
107. ibid., p.378.
108. Sturluson, Snorri, op.cit., p.30.
109. Carlyle, Thomas, 'Early Kings of Norway', *Fraser's Magazine*, January and March 1875, quo. in Prefatory Note to Joseph Bennett, *Analytical Notes on 'King Olaf'* (see note 131).
110. Sturluson, Snorri, op.cit., p.30.
111. *The Book of Saints*, compiled by the Benedictine Monks of St Augustine's Abbey, Ramsgate (5th edn, A & C Black: London, 1966), s.v. 'Olav of Norway ... 995–1030', p.533.
112. Bain, Robert Nisbet, 'Sweyn I', *Encycl. Brit.*, 11th edn, xxvi (1911), p.224.
113. Sturluson, Snorri, op.cit., p.44.
114. ibid., p.57.
115. ibid., p.58.
116. ibid., p.43.
117. Bain, op.cit., p.224.
118. Sturluson, Snorri, op.cit., p.58.
119. Sturluson, Snorri, *Heimskringla*, trans. Samuel Laing, *Sagas of the Norse Kings*, rev. Peter Foote (Dent: London, 1961), 'Saga of Earl Hakon', p.122.
120. Brøndsted, Johannes, *The Vikings*, trans. Kalle Skov (Penguin Books: London, 1965), pp.244, 316.
121. ibid., p.317.
122. ibid., p.312.
123. Churchill, op.cit., i, *The Gathering Storm* (Cassell: London, 1948), p.288.
124. Ward, op.cit., p.478.
125. Bradley, A C, *Shakespearean Tragedy* (Macmillan: London, 1904; 2nd edn, 1905), p.18.
126. Simpson, Introduction, xxxii.
127. Ward, op.cit., p.476.
128. Moore, op.cit., p.212; BL Add. MS 57994/5.
129. Moore, op.cit., p.212, and *Elgar and his Publishers: Letters of a Creative Life* (Clarendon Press: Oxford, 1987), i., pp.32–3.
130. Scholes, Percy A, *The Mirror of Music* (Novello & OUP: London, 1947), i, p.101.
131. Bennett, *Analytical Notes on 'King Olaf'* (Novello: London, 1900), p.5.
132. Thompson, Herbert, *Analytical Notes on 'Caractacus'* (Novello: London, 1900), p.32. Although not marked thus in the score, Dr Thompson describes the last section of *Caractacus*, from the pause and double bar at fig. 50 to the end, as 'in the nature of a choral epilogue'.
133. Sturluson, Snorri, 'King Olaf Trygvesson's Saga', pp.97–8.
134. Walker, Ernest, 'A Generation of Music' (1919), *Free Thought and the Musician* and Other Essays (OUP: London, 1946), pp.70–3.
135. Young, Percy M, ed., *Letters of Edward Elgar* (Geoffrey Bles: London, 1956), pp.287–8.

4   Friends pictured within

Percy M Young

The *Enigma Variations* is, of course, rather more than a musical work: it is one of the few compositions by an Englishman that is regarded as an essential part of the national heritage. To be precise, Variation IX takes on the virtues of a national hymn, as which it serves on solemn days. But within the work as a whole there is an endemic quality of Englishness that is undeniable at least in its own setting.

On a grand scale, perhaps, one is entitled to believe that Elgar knew his own value when one day he grandly proposed to Troyte Griffith: 'I am folk music'. Folk music is distinguished variously, but fundamentally by its social origins, and by the fact that within national or regional limits its character elicits responses within the appropriate subconscious.

Elgar himself was never clear as to where the border between 'real' and 'ideal' lay, what was absolute and what was programmatic. He was, however, fairly certain that there was (whatever formal conditions might obtain) a considerable degree of 'about-ness' in his works. 'My friends pictured within': it was not possible to be more explicit. And it is when this point is reached that difficulties arise. What did Elgar mean?

Variation form (in music without words) inevitably contains an element of 'about-ness' if only because in its earliest stages variation is appreciated as thematic-rhythmic commentary on a stated motiv. The development of instrumental music, the possibilities offered by contrasting tonalities, timbres, rhythms and sonorities lead through baroque and classical corridors into the broad expanse of nineteenth century expressiveness. Regarding variation form on the main line of development after Beethoven were Schumann, Mendelssohn, Brahms and Dvořák; on the loop line of British music immediately before Elgar entered this field were the Symphonic Variations of Parry (1897) and Granville Bantock's 'Helena' Variations (his wife being, so to speak, pictured within) of 1899.

There is within variation inevitably an element of parody. Behind Elgar is a row of more specific musical parodies put out in the early nineteenth century for the encouragement of a rapidly growing company of amateurs.

In 1822 J B Cramer published *A Parody in form of a Sonata for the Piano Forte*, with a note that 'this Sonata is intended as a Parody of one by a Celebrated Composer and Performer (now on the Continent)'. F T Latour, Pianist to George IV wrote a set of 26 Variations 'in imitation of many of the most Eminent Performers', among whom were Samuel Wesley, J B Cramer, Dussek and Clementi. More significantly Cipriani Potter in 1825 published his 'The Enigma, Variations and Fantasia on a favourite Irish Air ... in the style of five eminent Artists ... dedicated to the Originals'. The originals were Moscheles, Ferdinand Ries, Kalkbrenner, Cramer, Rossini and (possibly) Beethoven.

> In truth, regarded as directions to discover the peculiarities of manner, they are more useful as well as more agreeable than compositions that may be more strictly termed original; and as they imply a patient investigation of the materials wrought upon by eminent men as well as of the way in which they work, as they imply diligent study, acute apprehension, and facility in the adaptation of the ideas thus gleaned, such compositions are honourable to their authors.[1]

In his apprentice days of the late 1870s Elgar had half-heartedly gone into the air and variations territory attempting the kind of Hungarian Rhapsody that later he was so heartily to condemn, and a not totally unpromising beginning to another violin and piano piece based on 'The pretty girl milking her cow', the tune borrowed from Tom Moore. So far as character study through music occurred to Elgar as a possibility the proposed programme symphony centred on the career of General Charles Gordon offered colourful possibilities. The late General had seen service in the Crimea, in China, in the Danube basin and in the Sudan. Since his end was a British disaster the work would have made a stable companion to *Caractacus*. However, it seems that Gordon was pushed out of the way by the more genial company of Elgar's closer friends. On 21 October 1898 he wrote to F G Edwards, 'Anyhow "Gordon" simmereth mighty pleasantly in my (brain) pan & will no doubt boil over one day'.[2] Three days later Elgar wrote to Jaeger that another idea was not only simmering but coming near to boiling point. 'Since I've been back from the Leeds Festival I have sketched a set of Variations (orkestra) on an original theme ...'[3] On 16 February 1899 this idea was in first place; to Edwards again:

> Just completed a set of symphonic variations (theme original) for orchestra – 13 in number but I call the finale the fourteenth because of the ill-luck attaching to the numbers: these will probably be heard at an orchestral concert in London (for the first time) in this spring.
> Other compositions are nebulous at present.
> The symphony for Worcester *is* to be entitled '*Gordon*' affecting the feelings etc. etc.

A marginal note added:

I have in the Variations sketched 'portraits' of my friends – a new idea I think
– that is in each variation I have (looked at) the theme through the personality
(as it were) of another Johnny – ask Jaeger about this. I don't know if 'tis too
'intimate' an idea for print. It's distinctly amusing.[4]

On 21 February Elgar posted a score of the Variations to Richter's agent
(on the same day Lady Mary Lygon and Miss Winifred Norbury called on the
Elgars) and held his breath. He wrote again to Jaeger on 24 February:

You will see my letter to the firm about the Variations I expect; only for
mercy's sake don't tell anyone I pray you about Richter becos' he may
refuse . . .

All went well and on 19 June 1899 the first performance of the Variations
took place at the fifth Richter Concert of the Season at St James's Hall.
C A Baughan's programme note contained Elgar's famous statement –
characteristically mystifying:

It is true that I have sketched, for their amusement anu mine, the
idiosyncracies of fourteen [sic] of my friends, not necessarily musicians;
but this is a personal matter, and need not have been mentioned publicly. The
Variations should stand simply as a 'piece' of music. The Enigma I will not
explain – its 'dark saying'[5] must be left unguessed, and I warn you that
the apparent connection between the Variations and the Theme is often
of the slightest texture; further, through and over the whole set another
and larger theme 'goes', but is not played . . . So the principal Theme
never appears, even as in some late dramas – e.g. Maeterlinck's *L'Intruse*
[1890] and *Les Sept Princesses* [1891] – the chief character is never on
the stage.

The first performance was a success. Some of the notices, from critics
still exercising caution in respect of the appearance of a composer from the
provinces, mitigated praise with a little irritation at the biographic content
of the work. On 24 June the *Athenaeum* reported:

The special novelty of the evening was Mr Elgar's new work, *Variations for
Full Orchestra* (Op. 36). The composer . . . is a man of whom much may be
expected. To write a really original set of variations is no easy matter, but
this Mr Elgar has done. The theme displays dignity and at the same time
simplicity while of the variations we may say there is not one that could
be termed feeble. They were remarkable for charm, variety, character, rather
than for their skill both of structure and orchestration, by which, however,
these qualities are enhanced. We regret that the composer has dedicated his
work 'To my friends pictured within'. There was no harm in his working,
like Beethoven, to pictures in his mind; but it would have been better not
to call attention to the fact. The variations stand in no need of a programme;
as abstract music they fully satisfy. If the friends recognise their portraits it
will, no doubt, please them; but this is altogether a personal matter. It was
no mere succès d'estime; the variations will, we feel sure, be often heard, and
as often admired.

The *Musical News* of the same date presented the matter not dissimilarly:

Miss Marie Brema's magnificent rendering of the closing scene from *Götterdämmerung* was probably the most attractive item to most of the audience at last Monday's concert. A more exciting and satisfying performance of this inspired scene it would be hard to imagine, and the enthusiasm it aroused was not quickly exhausted. After this Mr Elgar's Variations, given for the first time, appeared to have a hard place; but they were received with warm approval, the composer being called to the platform twice at their close. The Variations are fourteen in number, symphonic in character, and often original and piquant in melody and orchestration. That they are severally labelled with the initials of certain friends of the composer, and 'dedicated to my friends within', we hold to be a mistake. Mr Elgar stated to an interviewer, 'It is true I have sketched ... the idiosyncracies of fourteen of my friends ... but this is a personal matter', – these only distract public attention from the work itself by saying, 'I meant something by all this; but you cannot follow my meaning, as you do not know my friends'? To quote Schumann by way of apology is beside the mark, for, with few exceptions, everyone knew the 'friends' he depicted musically.

It was on 8 November 1905 that Elgar tripped over the musical equivalent of Ockham's doctrine of Nominalism (versus Realism), Hanslick's defence of *absolute Tonkunst* against Wagner's *Gesamtkunstwerk*. Music was at its height, protested Elgar in a lecture on Brahms's Third Symphony, when it merely 'calls up a set of emotions in each individual hearer ... when it was simple, without description'. On Elgar's palpable inconsistency in this matter, his faith in the proposition hardly supported by his own works, Ernest Newman waxed indignantly eloquent. In fact in relation to his concept of the Variations Elgar proposed to have it both ways. What could be more absolute than an *ainigma*, a 'riddle', that was never heard and which therefore could not have been supposed ever to have existed.

During the Elgar Festival of 1904 the programme notes for the concert of 16 March were written by Percy Pitt and Alfred Kalisch. It was the latter who looked at the matter of the 'absolute' in his note on the Variations, which, because of the 'other theme', has

> ... a unique place in musical literature as an experiment in form. The [Pictures of Friends] makes them programme music, and renders futile any comparison with the variations of other composers. Indeed, variations which may be called the most absolute form of absolute music would seem, in their very nature, to be incompatible with the idea of a programme, and so it is not surprising that the catalogue of variations with a poetic basis is a short one. The most striking instance of which is, of course, Strauss's *Don Quixote*, and the contrast between it and the present work is interesting, for Strauss's object is rather to show us one character or type modified by, yet persisting through, every change of circumstance. One may also mention Nicode's Symphonic Variations and the last movement of Huber's Symphony, where we find a set of variations each of which is descriptive of a picture by the painter Boechlin.

Hans Huber (1852–1921), a Swiss composer, was one of the most committed programmatic composers of the Elgar period. The Second

Symphony was based on paintings of Arnold Böcklin a painter who also exercised a fascination for Elgar.[6]

If Elgar's statements are followed to their conclusion (provided that they may be taken to represent his views accurately), it must be acceptable that the 'friends pictured within' are in some way reconstituted within the appropriate variations: in 'mood', in the presumed 'portraiture' by 'another Johnny', in 'attitude' (Basil Maine), or in 'idiosyncracy'. By transposition of gesture Elgar appeared in some cases to ride very close to realism by means of such commonplaces that trespass on musical existence as dogs, bicycles, (banging) doors, a ship's engines as well as recognisable reference points within familiar musical patterning. Alas! what seems initially most certain is often wrapped in doubt, in enigmas within the Enigma.

And so the friends; since they must be counted as significant persons, it is hoped that their modest claim on immortality may be enlarged by a better understanding of who they were, what they did, and sometimes what they did, or did not, say. Whatever else the select thirteen of one time, brought together in one place, are a small but significant Victorian constituency whose corporate presence had a good deal to do with the fact that Elgar became a composer and the kind of composer he was.

Malvern

Some places which pass into cultural history achieve a significance over and above what may be merited in the statistical areas of climate, economics, population growth and so on. In respect of music there are happy towns which are apparently enshrined in particular works, Vienna being the prime example, claiming spiritual incorporation within most classical as well as some other symphonic works. It was as a resident of Malvern that Elgar first made his mark in the wider world and it is incontestable that it is the Variations that may be said to enshrine the 'spirit of Malvern'. On a more modest, and more realistic level, it is reasonable to claim that this work could not have been as it was except that it was composed in this place.

One of the most beautifully situated of towns, with its place in history assured both by legend and record, Malvern in the Victorian era was a refuge for the wealthy, the valetudinarian, the retired and the artistic. Among watering-places it was reputed to have the lowest death-rate. It was here, according to Charles Grindrod's often republished *Malvern: what to see and where to go* (1894), that 'Victories of brain and of muscle commonly go together in schools, and the healthy climatic conditions of Malvern conduce to success in both'. In 1883 Jenny Lind came to Malvern to a house built by a Captain Johnson who dramatically 'blasted the rocks, which he hurled down the great gully which forms the south-eastern defence of the great Camp of the Hereford Beacon'.[7] Adjacent to the town were many country estates with anciently settled families. Within the town the well-to-do built houses, no two being alike, in Gothic, Scottish Baronial, Renaissance idioms with individual flourishes in Dutch gables, turrets and oriel windows. The dominant families, the Masons and Foleys, saw to it that such properties were well set off by splendid, wide roads. Lady Foley, a chief benefactor, had the Foley Institute (a Working Man's Club) built and was among those who approved the building of, while deploring the necessity for, the Chapel of the Diocesan Penitentiary for Fallen Women designed by Sir Vivian Comper in 1898. It was Lady Foley who immediately directed the notice of the Chairman of the Great Western Railway to the potentially dangerous development consequent on the introduction of cheap day excursions (three days a week) from the Black Country to Malvern Link.

Churches were abundant, to plans provided by E W Elmslie, G E Street, P C Hardwick, or restored by, or under the influence of, Gilbert Scott. Culture was served by Church Institute, Naturalists's Club and Subscription Library; for out-of-doors pursuits there were Cricket, Tennis, Archery, Croquet, Golf and Cycling Clubs; and a multiplicity of bodies provided opportunity for amateur musicians and employment for some professionals. The Malvern Vocal and Orchestral Concerts (the orchestra conducted by Ralph E Lyon presented the standard symphonies), the Malvern Choral Society, the North Malvern Choral Society, the Ladies Orchestral Class, the Rhine String and Brass Band were but some of these bodies. All in all it was as good a place as any for a private music teacher to practise. Elgar's status as such in Malvern, as will become apparent, was uncertain, although he was able to shelter behind the social qualifications of his wife. But the circle of acquaintances immortalized by the Variations was a source of assurance not otherwise to have been found.

All within the circle were reasonably protected against the hazards that afflicted the majority of people in late Victorian England. To each is attached a special token of merit, for each was a friend who helped Elgar across the years that followed the despairing return to Malvern in 1891, and persuaded his talent to fructify to the point of genius. But (except for Alice) had it not been for Elgar's recording of their existence as he did their names would have passed into respectable oblivion. As for Alice, none of this would have happened except for her, so, quite apart from any other considerations, it is proper that she should have first place in the scheme.

C.A.E.

Alice, as Mrs Elgar, was conscious of the role she had to play: the honourable one of the protectress of a genius that had extraordinarily asserted its presence in a society unaccustomed to, and generally unappreciative of, the phenomenon. She has popularly come down in caricature (for which she was herself partly to blame) as exemplary helpmeet, hostess, amanuensis and diplomatic mediator. On 8 May 1889 Alice Roberts married Edward Elgar at Brompton Oratory, putting behind her not only her membership of the Church of England but also forty years of a separate life and career; that of the spinster daughter dutiful to her ordained responsibilities to the needs of an ageing and aged parent. Her father, a Major General in the Indian Army, had died when Alice was a small girl.

The family home was Hazeldine near the Gloucestershire village of Redmarley D'Abitot. Alice's mother was granddaughter to Robert Raikes, the Gloucester printer; an outstanding pioneer in the field of social reform whose principal monument is the Sunday School movement, the origins of which lay in Raikes's establishment, in 1780, of classes for the roaming street children of the Gloucester slums. There is also a statue of Raikes in the Embankment Gardens in London as well as one in Gloucester.

The one positive cultural influence in Alice's early life was literature, Lady Roberts having been a founder member of the London Library. It was through books, not only in reading but also in writing, that Alice first found release from the undramatic affairs of church and village, from the endless round of visiting, flower-arranging, entertaining, glee-singing (except that it was not glees that were sung), and piano-duet playing. In 1871 she was persuaded by the Rector of Pendock, W S Symonds, to undertake the proof-reading of, and index compilation for, his admirable volume of popular geology, *Records of the Rocks*. Thus disciplined to literature Alice turned her head even in a professional direction. An extended poem, *Isabel Trevithoe*, was published in 1879. This was followed three years later by the novel *Marchcroft Manor*, and many essays and verses, some published, most not. The significance of *Isabel Trevithoe* (from which Elgar set two brief lyrics) and *Marchcroft Manor* lay in their view of another world: of urban poverty and despair, of the realities of rural disability, even of the stirrings of conscience on the one hand and of impatience on the other.

It was after the death of her mother that Alice was able to leave Redmarley for a rented house in Malvern. Modestly musical she became a pupil of Elgar. She knew that she had discovered a talent of a quite other order than she had ever before encountered. She set herself the task of protecting and nurturing it. From that point her feelings ran through her secret writing. It was in *On hearing some orchestral music* (or *On hearing a certain piece of music*), that was, the Three Pieces for String Orchestra played at a Musical Union concert in Worcester on 7 May 1888, that she exposed her emotions in what may well appear significant and symbolic lines:

> And love and pain
> Now mingle in the strain again,

> While mystically the music swells,
> Floats on and on, and ever tells
> Of joy and love, and yearnings past:
> Of hopes divine and longings vast;
> No instrument could breathe it all
> So subtle, strange, the harmonies that fall.[8]

Oxford

The causes of the 'Renaissance of English Music' have been variously determined. The Enigma Variations, of course, have their place in the accumulation of significant events, if only because one may point back through them to circumstances of which account has not always been taken. Parry's *Prometheus Unbound*, performed at the Gloucester Festival of 1880, was subsequently taken as a point of departure for a new attitude to music in England. Immediately after this first performance, suffering under the weight of unfriendly criticism, Parry exposed an attitude which he felt it a duty to depose. What he had to say is, in the long run, to be seen of more importance than the work itself:

> English musicians err on the serious side by mistaking grammar for exalted poetry or serious art, and on the other by mistaking frivolity for freshness or sentimentalism for feeling.
>   One reason why English music is such a conspicuous failure is because the little circle who profess to play at umpire have always made it their most strenuous endeavour and earnest purpose to suppress individuality.[9]

In his own way and in his own time Elgar said much the same thing. That Parry eventually felt his ideas to have been realised he indicated in a letter which he wrote to Elgar one week after the first performance of the Variations:

> I'm behindhand through constant pressure of work, but I won't give up the intention with which your Variations inspired to write and congratulate you upon such an achievement. They are indeed a brilliant success, and will bring the country as well as yourself honour whenever they are heard. I am sincerely glad of such first rate artistic work being done by an Englishman, and to hear that Richter is going to preside over their presentation to the Viennese. It will wake them up and no mistake.[10]

One particular influence on the development of those wider interests that culminated in the recognition of Elgar as a major composer of striking individuality came from the universities, which unhappily he himself held in some disdain. To be more precise the effective influence derived from the activities of the musical societies that came into being during the latter part of the nineteenth century. It is significant that four men associated with the *Enigma* were active members of such bodies in Oxford. Parry (not a 'variation' but one whose beneficence was a singular agent in assisting Elgar's confidence), Hugh Steuart-Powell and Basil Nevinson were undergraduates at Exeter College and Richard Penrose Arnold at Brasenose.

H.D.S.-P.
B.G.N.

Parry matriculated at Exeter College at the beginning of 1867 (almost immediately successfully presenting himself for the degree of Mus.B.). Steuart-Powell, born in Dorset (with Gloucestershire family antecedents) in 1851, entered the College in 1869; Basil Nevinson (1853–1908), of a Leicester family of solicitors joined Steuart-Powell there in 1872. For some years these students were conspicuous in the affairs of the College Musical Society that had been established in 1859. Parry and Powell were lively pianoforte duettists inclined to relish the presentation of duet versions of favourite overtures of Mendelssohn and Rossini. Powell was notable as an exponent of Chopin. After his playing the Prelude no.17 (Op.28) the *Oxford Journal* of 25 June 1870, noticed, 'Of Mr Powell's solos we cannot speak too highly: we only regret that he did not play a somewhat longer piece for his encore'. Nevinson was a more than useful cellist who retained his connection with College music after he had moved to London to study for the Bar.

The Oxford University Musical Club, founded in 1872, had among its aims the intention 'to improve the taste for, and increase the appreciation of good Chamber Music'. At its meetings stress was on the classics but the newer music of Schumann and Brahms (thanks to the influence of Joachim and Clara Schumann and of travel in Germany) engaged much of the interest of forward-looking amateurs. Steuart-Powell and Nevinson were prominent in the affairs of the Musical Club where they were joined by Richard Arnold. For each of this group music was an absorbing interest, and it was because of their wide knowledge and artistic competence that they were in a position to influence and to be recognized, indeed immortalized, by Elgar.

It was important that in due course they all were able to meet together in Malvern, where Steuart-Powell and Nevinson were regular visitors familiar to the music-loving circle to which Alice Roberts belonged before she was married to Elgar. After their marriage she and Edward were frequently present at parties where Steuart-Powell and Nevinson were guests.

Steuart-Powell led a life that was comfortable and undistinguished. In the appropriate variation, however, it is suggested that his pianistic fluency had not deteriorated since his Oxford days though he would seem to have developed his baroque interests. Elgar maintained contact with Steuart-Powell across the years, from time to time staying with him in

London. His character assessment of him is contained in a letter to Percy
Pitt and Alfred Kalisch, written on 24 March 1904, which refers to a misprint
in Kalisch's programme note on the Variations for the Elgar Festival (Covent
Garden) performance of that month:

> ... H.D.J.P. – he (Var:II) is not a JP but a respectable member of a University
> Club[11] & therefore worthy of respect not only in St James's St. & Regent's
> Park but also in Kensington & Earl's Court.[12]

There is a late glimpse of Steuart-Powell on 18 January 1920. Together
with Troyte Griffith, Barclay Squire, Rosa Burley, Laurence Binyon and
some others, he came to talk to Elgar – probably about the scheme for
the establishment of a Garden City at Welwyn, for the committee of which
Elgar 'consented reluctantly' to allow his name to go forward three days
earlier.

Basil Nevinson, who dabbled in entomology and natural history as a
student and became a barrister but never practised, was a born dilettante.
Supported by an inheritance from his mother he dedicated himself seriously
only to music. He was charming, he was generous and he was of great service
to Elgar who was frequently his guest: at home, at the Club and on the
bowling green.

Nevinson was frequently in Malvern on account (it was said) of his health.
There were in the town a brother, Edward Bonney Nevinson, and a cousin,
Edward Nevinson; the former was an architect and a water-colour painter
of the firm of Nevinson and Newton (to which Troyte Griffith was attached),
the latter, 'Ned', was a solicitor. 'Ned', a keen music-lover, frequently used
to arrange chamber music parties to which Elgar was invited. That Elgar was
often ill-at-ease, and indeed resentful of the advantages enjoyed by some
of his acquaintances and of the often implied sense of social superiority of
which he could be made aware, is well-known. His feelings may be well
understood in the light of this communication:

> The Elgars could scarcely be called 'personal friends' of Ned Nev. 'Edou' [*sic*]
> was from a very different social background which *mattered* in those days
> & it was some time before he 'bettered' himself by his marriage. I believe
> his wife was a lady in the old sense of the word, & 'Edou' himself was a
> social climber. The connection apart from what was possibly professional
> was entirely via music, Ned being devoted to music & a decent performer
> himself, enjoying Elgar's company no doubt, but also anxious to be of help
> to him.[13]

When the Elgars decided to move to 'Craeglea' 'Ned' Nevinson was involved
on the legal side of the transaction. Alice's diary note on her interview with
him makes sorry reading: 'A to see Mr Nevinson on 'Forli' ... generally
unpleasant'.

The friendship with Basil, however, was durable and from the eventful
summer of 1904 there survives this note from Elgar:

Plas Gwyn
Hereford

Augt 24:1904
My dear Nevinson:
We were very glad to receive your letters because we were breathing forth
fire & vengeance upon you believing, as we did, that you & Mrs Nevinson
were in Malvern & scorning Hereford & us. We love this place very much
& the country is lovely beyond words: I find the quietest places about the
Wye and amongst other things a Byzantine ch: (new) in red sandstone at a
place called Hoarwithy – it looks fine: you must really come here with your
bike sometime & explore. The Bl[ac]k Mountains are fine & we have had a
day there.
Our love to you both
Yrs ever
Edward Elgar[14]

That was the year of Nevinson's marriage. Unhappily his wife died before
him and he became increasingly dependent on alcohol. He was finally cared
for by a nurse who, alienating him from his family, contrived to have herself
inserted into his will.

R.P.A.

About his subjects Elgar was, on the whole, distinctly gnomic if not
positively enigmatic. In fact he said nothing about any of them. Richard
Penrose Arnold, the greatly loved and hopelessly spoiled son of the great
poet to whose works Elgar occasionally turned for inspiration, may be said
to have wasted his life.

As a boy 'Dicky' enjoyed his schooldays at Harrow so long as he could
fish, look for wild flowers and listen to music. 'I am', wrote his father on 12
December 1871, 'going to Aston Clinton with Dicky ... Mme Neruda, the
violinist, will be there and Dick will so like that as Lady R[othschild] kindly
asked him to go with me'.[15] Matthew Arnold hoped that when Dicky went
to Balliol he would 'work better than he worked at Harrow'. Alas! he failed
to get a degree and left his father with a pile of debts to pay. So far as a career
was concerned Matthew grieved that 'even the very lowest clerkship in the
education office' was 'absolutely out of the question'. In 1878, according to
the custom of the period in respect of the feckless sons of the well-to-do,
Dicky was packed off to Australia where he became a clerk in the Union Bank
of Melbourne. Here he married Ella Ford a doctor's daughter.

Dick and his wife duly returned from Australia and, helped by his name,
he was given an appointment as an inspector of factories. For some years
he worked in Lancashire, from where he eventually moved to Worcester.
During the last years of his life (he died in 1888) Matthew was obliged

to make himself responsible for his son's gambling debts and often even to make monthly payments to Ella. It is small wonder that she was often unwell. In a surviving letter to Elgar of 18 March 1902 Arnold relates the sorry state of his wife's health:

> ... She, poor dear, has been in bed ever since we came to London with the exception of one day, for in addition to all her other illnesses, she has, of course, had influenza while here. The Doctor has ordered us to go to Mentone for a month, and then to Rome ...[16]

Arnold took 'early retirement' in his early forties. He lived on aimlessly until he died in Bath in 1908 aged 48.

A L Rowse's judgement is severe: 'A feeble specimen who achieved nothing in his short life, except the friendship of Elgar'.[17] However, what remains for Richard Arnold are two poems by his father dedicated to him (on the death of his dachshund in 1881, and a sonnet composed on hearing that Dick's ship was at the Cape Verde Islands), and Elgar's somewhat grave variation.

Madresfield and its festival

Ysobel

More important perhaps than any other family association in Malvern was that with the Fittons: father (in the musical connection inconspicuous), mother, five daughters and two sons. According to the expectations of the times the sons became officers in the army, while the girls stayed at home, practising music, engaging in social welfare (particularly when this could be combined with music), and out-of-door activities until such time as they might be married. The mother of this family, Harriet Margaret Fitton, who had studied the pianoforte in Germany and in London with Brinley Richards, encouraged the establishment of choral and instrumental music societies and was an early enthusiast for the competitive festival movement. When the Elgars came to Malvern the Fittons had been living there for twenty-five years.

> As a young man in the eighties and onwards, Sir Edward Elgar was always a welcome and frequent guest at Mrs Fitton's house, where he played the violin delightfully to her accompaniment, either alone or in pianoforte trios with the Rev Father Henry Bellasis of Newman's Oratorian Order or the Rev E Capel Cure ... and other musicians. An intimate and lasting friendship existed between the late Lady Elgar and Mrs Fitton, their unusually cultured minds being in close sympathy with each other.[18]

When the Elgars set up house in Malvern three of the Fitton girls were variously active in musical affairs. Hilda played the violin, Isabel (who celebrated her twenty-first birthday in 1889) the piano, Monica the cello. Hilda and Monica were also vigorous members of the local Archery Club. Hilda was a member of R E Lyon's orchestra, where her colleagues included Elgar's brother, Frank and a number of his Worcester friends. Together with Monica, Hilda took her occasional place in the less ambitious orchestra of the Wyche Musical Society. Isabel, taking lessons from Elgar, graduated from piano to viola. The existence of some of Elgar's early chamber music sketches undoubtedly owed much to the chamber-music parties at the Fittons' house. One relic is the *Pastourelle* for violin and piano, published in 1913, a piece of *salon* music *par excellence* dedicated to Hilda who had married Edward Capel-Cure two years previously. Capel-Cure, a cellist and the author of the libretto of *The Light of Life*, often quietly helped Elgar in regard to other libretti. Monica Fitton married another cellist, Arthur Trew who taught at Charterhouse, in 1914. Isabel remained unmarried. A kindly, handsome woman, in middle age giving the impression of amused detachment, she was said in the significant Malvern years to have known how to handle Elgar in his less amiable moods. Involved in most things that went on in Malvern and neighbourhood, and always intent in keeping her place in its musical life, she sought no credit for nor made any claims in respect of her friendship with Elgar.

* * *

In 1896 the 'Madresfield Musical Competition' was instituted, to become a significant event in the County. The amateur musicians of Malvern gamely entered themselves in the classes adjudicated on (not without some severity) by visiting adjudicators, of whom the most fearsome was William McNaught. Mrs Fitton entered her choir and the girls played in the orchestra for the final concert. The central figure, however, was Lady Mary Lygon, a lively young woman – she was twelve years younger than Elgar – who appears to have inherited musical talent from her father, the sixth Earl Beauchamp, who has his own small niche in the ranks of the glee composers. Mary Lygon was a bundle of energy, conducting school choirs, village choirs and preparing madrigal groups. There was no-one at the turn of the century who contributed more to extending musical opportunity on a broader front than she. The year of the Variations was a significant year for Lady Mary and her brother, who had succeeded his father in 1891. He was appointed Governor-General of New South Wales, and she was to accompany him to act as his hostess. At the time Beauchamp had shown a notable independence of mind. He was a member of the London School Board and in February 1899 he presided over the annual meeting of the Central Poor Law Conference. His speech was notable for its directness: 'in his opinion', it was reported, 'the labourer deserved well from his country, just as the civil servant did'. While he concluded by entreating 'those present to remember that they were guardians of the poor, not guardians of the rates'.

After her marriage in 1902 Lady Mary Trefusis, as she now was, lived in Cornwall, where she continued a more than lively interest in musical activities. In turn she became Secretary of the Church Music Society and President of the English Folk Dance Society. Delightfully unconventional, once when opening a village fete in Cornwall, she surprised her more staid listeners by saying:

... that it was wrong to make dancing a side-show. They ought all to be dancing. She, the Vicar, the Church wardens, and everyone should open the fete by dancing round the streets, and she hoped that if she went there again for a fete they would let her lead the dance.[19]

About the early days Lady Mary's letters give a clear impression of her relationship with Elgar: of warm friendship and with modest recognition of her standing as pupil before a master. About the Madresfield Festival of 1898 she wrote on 4 April:

I should also much like it, if I may, to go over the trios once with you first – so as to know exactly how you wish them sung – & to be able to teach them properly.[20]

On 29 April she wrote again about the Festival and also about the Philharmonic Society concert in which she hoped to take part:

... your help was a great encouragement to the members of the Committee – and especially to me. Thank you also for letting me sing in the Philharmonic Concert for which I have not really qualified by the number of practices.[21]

Returned from Australia in 1903, Lady Mary wrote to Elgar in Elgarian mood. Signing herself 'ever very sincerely', she said that she was 'revelling in the superior beauty of an English spring to everything else in the world'. From 1895 she had been a Woman of the Bedchamber to Queen Alexandra. During one of her duty turns at Marlborough House in 1904 she was considering plans for the music curriculum of Worcestershire schools. Clearly she was in the van of progress as she wrote to Elgar on 7 October:

I have invited 100 school-masters & mistresses near Madresfield & Worcester to come to a lecture on Sat. the 23rd by Mr W H Leslie – on sight reading in school. Acceptances are pouring in – so I very much hope that interest in the school class may be stimulated – and that we shall have better entries next year.[22]

One of the many red herrings thrown across the track of the Variations was an unsubstantiated proposition that Mary Lygon was not entitled to the ascription of the thirteenth movement. There is a letter from Elgar to Jaeger of 2 May 1899 concerning this variation that makes the position quite clear.[23] There is also Elgar's letter of 25 July 1899 concerning a recent performance of the Three Pieces dedicated to Lady Mary which ends:

> The variations (especially *** no.13) have been a great triumph for me under Richter and he is going to play them everywhere including Vienna. People here are preparing for the Three Choirs festival and we shall all miss you very, very much. My wife joins me in sending regards and all good wishes for a safe and speedy return.[24]

W.N.

> The only *Variation* I knew personally was Winnie Norbury 1861–1918. The Norburys lived between Worcester and Malvern and were vaguely musical. I'm afraid I always thought her rather angular and harsh – and her variation is, I think, one of the loveliest.[25]

In Charles Grindrod's *Malvern: what to see and where to go*, a work distinguished by tourist office prose, there is an evocative description of the drive from Malvern by 'Sherridge, Bridge's Stone and Bachelor's Bridge'; a drive 'not favoured by the flymen on account of the hills' but unforgettable through the 'tree embowered lanes of Sherridge'. Elgar represented that the eighth variation was 'about' place rather than person. In so indicating he was making a pertinent observation on the possible potentiality of music as a describing agent. The rhythms, patterns, colours of the scene, being wordless, are more directly transferable to the medium than human characteristics.

The Norbury family had been established in Worcestershire for hundreds of years. The head of the house at the time of the composition of the Variations was Colonel Thomas Coningsby Norbury Norbury (*sic*). By profession a soldier, sometime a Captain in the 6th Dragoon Guards, he married into the Irish aristocracy. His father-in-law, the second Viscount Guillamore, had fought with the 7th Hussars at Waterloo. Norbury died four months after the first performance of the Variations leaving vacancies on the Justices' Benches of two counties (Hereford and Worcester), on the County Council and numerous other bodies. He had been Treasurer of the County Cricket Club for many years, an officer of the Archery Club and the Rifle Club and Honorary Colonel of the Worcestershire Militia. His chief claim to fame is that he was a witness for the claimant in the celebrated Tichbourne case of 1874. There were three sons and five daughters in the Norbury family, and of the daughters Florence (1858–1937) and Winifred (1861–1938) were the musical ones. Their musical interests were balanced by strong athletic proclivities: archery, tennis, and even hockey on ice. There was also beagling: on the day after the score of the Variations was sent to Richter's agent Elgar went with Troyte to a meet at Sherridge.

Winifred Norbury was a singer and an enthusiastic conductor of village choirs. A strong supporter of the Madresfield Festival, she was invaluable to Elgar in the early days with her readiness to spend hours in copying and correcting orchestral parts. Winifred was a firm woman as was shown by her handling of Elgar at a time of much misunderstanding between him and the Worcestershire Philharmonic Society of which she was the joint secretary. Elgar's last dictated note to Florence, however, is most poignant:

> ... I lie here thinking of our beloved Teme – surely the most beautiful river that ever was & it belongs to you too – I love it more than any other – some day we will have a day together there – on it? You shall choose the place – I shall come and see you as soon as possible but it will be sad to return in winter – it would have been nicer to get better in spring.[26]

Hasfield

W.M.B.
R.B.T.
Dorabella

When the parish church of Redmarley d'Abitot was rebuilt in 1856 there was an imposing list of contributors to the Building Fund including members of the Roberts, Parry, Beauchamp and Baker families. The later history of Hasfield Manor in Gloucestershire illustrates how, during the nineteenth century, the squirearchy was being affected by recruitment from outside the circle of 'landed gentry'. Within the *Enigma* the contrast lies in the Norbury and Baker circumstances.

It was only in 1863 that Hasfield Court was purchased by a master potter of Fenton, William Meath Baker, whose occupation was brief. He died in 1865, his property passing to his brother a clergyman whose heir was the second William Meath Baker. Born in 1858 he was educated at Eton and Trinity College, Cambridge. His subsequent life generally conformed to the pattern described in relation to Norbury. He was an ardent climber and a member of the Alpine Club and on the side of music served as a Steward at the Three Choirs Festival in Gloucester in 1898, a fellow Steward being Hubert Parry.

A frequent guest at Hasfield Court was Richard Baxter Townshend (1846–1923). According to the suggestions of the Variations W.M.B. was an exciting person whereas R.B.T. was not. In truth, however, it was otherwise. Townshend, son of an Irish clergyman, was in many ways the most dynamic and original of all the characters in the Enigma gallery. After school at Repton he went as a classical scholar to Trinity College, Cambridge. Soon after graduating he packed his bags and:

... in 1869 I found myself five thousand miles to the westward of old England, in a car on the newly opened Union Pacific Railroad, with a good hope of being safely landed by it in the part of the Far West known as Wyoming Territory U.S.A. I was a tenderfoot ...[27]

Townshend was away from England for eight years, his experiences being graphically recorded in a number of books which portray their author as a young man of abounding energy, bright humour and a sense of compassionate understanding nurtured by his variety of experience. Among the Enigma characters Townshend was the one who saw the world with wide appreciation of the quirkiness of human behaviour. When he was prospecting for gold he got to know and to appreciate the ceremonial dances of the Jemez Indians, writing of their invocation of the Spirits of the Air and of the Earth;[28] on another occasion he wrote of the terrifying snake-dances of the Hopi tribe among the sacred mountains of the Navajo Indians of Arizona. 'How much longer can they last? For our devouring civilization presses hard upon their heels'.[29]

In New Mexico Townshend saw an advertisement for the capture of an outlaw with a reward of 3,000 dollars:

Smooth face, blue eyes, high colour, long curly hair hanging down on his shoulders; wears buckskin; rides with a very long stirrup; looks like a boy on horseback.

'And', commented Townshend, 'every single point ... could be applied to me'.[30]

He met Billy the Kid:

He was quite pathetic in his earnestness over the redeeming virtues of the domestic piano. One could hardly tell him that elementary civilisation demanded that one should refrain from shooting one's daughter's husband even more peremptorily than one should give her a piano.[31]

In 1881 Townshend, now being an assistant classics master at Bath College, married William Meath Baker's sister, Letitia Jane Dorothea the most intellectually gifted of the generation of Bakers. After four years of schoolmastering Townshend settled down to authorship and to live in Oxford. In 1894 he published a lively translation of the *Agricola and Germania* of Tacitus. In 1892, with Dorothea as joint author, he had published *An Officer of the Long Parliament*, a study of one Richard Townsend (*sic*), who had founded the Irish branch of the family. In 1897 Dorothea published a work that was both scholarly and readable, *The Life and Letters of Mr. Endymion Porter*, a Royalist courtier and patron of poets and painters. It was against this background that the battles of the Baker sons, into which Elgar entered with some glee, were originated.[32]

After R.B.T.'s death in 1923 there came a message from the Indian community at Jemez, New Mexico:

... the old men of the Pueblo remember Mr Townshend very well; the Indians thought very highly of him as Mr Townshend was very kind to the Indians. We shall certainly remember the soul of Mr Townshend in our prayers.[33]

On 27 April 1895 the Reverend Alfred Penny was instituted Rector of Wolverhampton. A widower, he had one daughter, Dora who was at the impressionable age of twenty-one. Four months after his institution Penny married again to Mary Frances Baker, eldest sister of William Meath Baker, the wedding ceremony being conducted by the Bishop of Shrewsbury assisted by the Rector of Hasfield. Mary Baker, who had kept her own house near Hasfield prior to her marriage, was a consistent ally of the Elgars and in 1892 was responsible for their Bavarian holiday. Elgar was delighted when she settled in Wolverhampton, of which town he had favourable impressions. His former partner in the orchestra of the Three Choirs Festival, Charles Hayward, was from Wolverhampton and only two months before the Penny wedding the local choral society had given a heart-warming performance of *The Black Knight*.

Like most well-bred girls of the period Dora Penny was musically educated. Clearly she was more than averagely competent and in due course able to conduct a small orchestra of her own. In 1904 Elgar inscribed a score of the Serenade for Strings, 'To the conductress of the "   " with kind regards from Edward Elgar'. It was a month after her father's marriage that Dora Penny first visited the Elgars. From then on there developed a mutual understanding between the eager girl and the rising composer that ensured their meeting as often as opportunity offered. In October 1898 the performance of *Caractacus* at the Leeds Festival was a particularly heartening event, and it was almost immediately afterwards that the shape of the Variations began to be visible. On 1 November Alice wrote in her diary, 'Dorabella came'. Dorabella was one of those who undertook the copying of parts for Elgar and as she did she undoubtedly made her own contribution to his accomplishment. She was able through friendship to escape from the limitations imposed by Rectory life and to enter another, more creative and more secret world. Dorabella told her own story, but the relationship between her and Elgar is most evocatively enshrined in a letter written in old age to Julius Harrison: she refers to 'the wonder of Elgar's understanding of musical sounds', and continues:

The way he could play what we had just seen. I shall never forget it. One day, we had a lovely bicycle ride to Holm Lacey & we left the bicycles under trees & went & sat down by the river, which was moving very swiftly & laden with small fish. The banks were a smother of wild flowers & I remember trying to choose a place with no flowers to sit on. It was a lovely day & I am afraid I dozed – leaning up against Elgar's shoulder. Suddenly I felt a touch on my hand & I tried not to wake jerkily – but there was a Kingfisher, sitting in a bush opposite – looking for something nice for his tea – and 'plop' soon he was down & we saw him no more.

Elgar picked up his bicycle and started for home to Hereford. Dorabella, sensing his desire for solitude, followed. Having arrived at the house,

> ... he went straight to the study & sat down at the piano. What he played was magic – it was a picture of what we had seen & quite lovely.[34]

It was on 29 April 1899 that the *Malvern News* reported the Countess of Dudley having been fined ten shillings, with five shillings costs, for riding a bicycle on the footpath. Bicycle news of whatever kind then made news, and it is fair to say that no machine has ever played so prominent a part in English musical history, and nowhere is its influence more apparent than in respect of the Variations. (There is a chance, perhaps, that it is the bicycle that provides the eternally elusive counter-theme?)

The eldest son of William Meath Baker, Father Vincent Baker, wrote concerning the tenth variation:

> Elgar and Dorabella used to go for long bicycle rides. Perhaps this music represents the wheels going along the roads and the general pleasant and summery feeling.[35]

As for Dorabella's own recorded view of a detail of the 'portraiture' in 'her' variation, she presumed Elgar to have attempted to refer to her one time misfortune of stammering. About this, however, Malcolm Sargent observed:

> I have the impression that Mrs Powell once told me that Elgar had never teased her about her stammering, which actually would be a very unusual and unexpected thing for him to do. Nor had he ever said that the Dorabella variation represented her stuttering. As a matter of fact it is a very poor imitation of stuttering.[36]

For a better example, suggested Sargent, one should turn to the opening of Beethoven's Fifth Symphony 'which could be taken as stuttering from start to finish'.

Regarding his uncle R.B.T., Father Baker noted two theories concerning that variation: one, that 'the bassoon triplets seven bars after figure 10 ... represent the wheels of his tricycle; another, that they refer to the cowboy galloping over the prairie'. In a memorial lecture delivered before the Elgar Society in Malvern on 11 February 1957 Julius Harrison supported the bicycle theory, but obscurely, 'Then the oboe of Var.3; with Richard Baxter Townshend trundling about on his bicycle ...'

It has long been known that there have been various dogmas of a 'real presence' in respect of G.R.S. His organ pedalling is said to be featured by one faction; for another school it is certain that it was the celebrated, but at the time not fully grown, bulldog 'Dan' thrashing about in the River

Wye. But what ought to be the absolute truth is contained in a reproachful letter to me of many years ago. The G.R.S. semiquavers according to 'Elgar's own information to "Dorabella" [was] that they represented Sinclair's walking-stick flying through the air into the River Wye'.

For full measure that correspondent observed that, regarding 'Troyte', 'you omit reference to the turning wheels of his tricycle which used to cause such hilarity among his friends'.[37] In fact the supporting quotation was taken from R.B.T. (bar 27 f.)

Dorabella's recollections of the golden years, as they appeared to her and indeed in retrospect to many Elgarians, were published in 1936 as *Edward Elgar: Memories of a Variation*. A second edition, including matter that discretion had reserved from the first, appeared in 1946. As Mrs Richard Powell, Dorabella became a notable figure on the Elgar circuit, her lectures colourfully carrying images of yesteryear to new colonies of enthusiasts. She developed a special attachment to the Elgar Society of Sheffield through which her valuable collection of papers in due course passed to the Royal College of Music.

The professional element

G.R.S.

In his sermon at the funeral of George Robertson Sinclair (1863–1917) Canon A T Bannister reminded the congregation in Hereford Cathedral:

> We do not sufficiently realise how much the Church owes to its Cathedral organists and its chapel-masters (sic). For near 200 years, amid many difficulties, over-burdened with the toil of teaching, and with little encouragement from the ecclesiastical authorities ... those men have worked with enthusiastic zeal in the service of their Church and of their art.

Elgar's Enigma tribute to Sinclair, couched in the engagingly inappropriate (for a cathedral organist of that time) nature of the variation, is I suppose a way of registering the fact that men like Sinclair were so sadly ignored. Elgar's connections as violinist with Hereford preceded Sinclair's appointment as organist (in 1889), but the coming of Sinclair introduced to him a man of congenial interests. Of Irish parentage, Sinclair was reluctant to subject himself to provincial standards of musical taste. He was all for the moderns: that meant Wagner, who drew him to Bayreuth in 1891, and from whose *Parsifal* a 'selection' was given at the Three Choirs Festival of 1895. Hereford was the first English cathedral to take in Wagner; it was also the first cathedral to allow a performance of Händel's *Messiah*.

Sinclair was a solid professional. A chorister at St. Michael's College, Tenbury, he became a pupil of and assistant to Harford Lloyd at Gloucester, but after only a year was chosen as the first organist of Truro Cathedral. He was then seventeen. The job was challenging. As yet there was neither cathedral nor organ, and the young Sinclair spent much time during his nine years in Cornwall in campaigning for funds for an organ and also travelling the county to encourage village choirs. The new cathedral consecrated, and Father Willis's fine organ installed, Sinclair was appointed to Hereford.

The rather sombre portraits of Sinclair disguise an ebullient spirit that caused many young female hearts to flutter in Hereford after his arrival in 1889. There are recorded numerous parties and frolics in which Sinclair took part in those early days. Dan may have enjoyed playing in the Wye when his turn came. His master clearly delighted in the pleasures of the river. There was a day in 1890 when Sinclair and girl-friend rowing upstream noticed they were being pursued by another young woman. 'He and I', noted his friend in her diary, 'landed and hid till she had passed'.[38] Sinclair certainly had the ability to match Elgar 'jape' for 'jape' in his day.

However, Sinclair matched conscientiousness with ability above the ordinary. Or so it would seem from George Grove's desire in 1894 to promote his interest in respect of the vacant Chair of Music in Trinity College, Dublin (of which Sinclair's father was a graduate). Sinclair's greatest strength was in his direction of choirs, not only the cathedral choir, but societies in town and country alike. He was also a rather more than good organist. That he was not in any real sense a composer was helpful in the Elgar relationship in that he could appreciate Elgar from an independent angle. He was, in a quiet way, a promoter of the present as well as of the past and alert to the promise of the young. Sinclair introduced Delius and Vaughan Williams into Festival programmes. On 5 February 1917, the day before his death, Sinclair wrote to Elgar that he had just 'heard a new and wonderful viola player'. His name was Lionel Tertis. 'It would be splendid if you could write something for him to play – it would be a great chance.'

Troyte

Arthur Troyte Griffith (1864–1942) was happily able to conduct his life midway between being a professional and a dilettante. Gifted artistically he protested his unmusicality. This he did to protect himself against the assaults of the too eager promoters of *soirées musicales*. In the course of time, and after engaging himself in Elgar's thoughts and ideas 'he became not only a music-lover but very knowledgeable'.[39] No-one who was totally unmusical could have been Secretary of the Malvern Concert Club from its foundation by Elgar in 1903 for some thirty years. The surviving correspondence shows that this duty was conducted with diligence and it is clear that the high reputation of this organisation owed a great debt to Griffith.[40]

Griffith's mother, Harriet Dyke Troyte, was a member of a distinguished family. She was the niece of Sir Henry Wentworth Acland, Professor of Medicine at Oxford and of Sir Thomas Dyke Acland, a politician of pronounced liberal tendencies whose views greatly influenced the course of public education. Griffith's father, George Griffith, was the first science master at Harrow School, where Troyte was a pupil, from 1867 to 1893, after which he was Assistant Secretary to the British Association. Troyte read Classics at Oxford but became an architect. He was a cultivated water-colourist and spent much time in France and Spain in search of subjects for his brush. A discriminating collector, he built up a collection of Japanese colour prints. Troyte's interests were wide so that in 1907 he provided sets for the Vedrenne-Barker production of Shaw's *You never can tell* in 1907. Elgar's friendship with Shaw is well known. That Troyte (in his own right) was also a friend of Shaw is less well known. 'He did know Shaw', wrote Troyte's sister, 'and used to go for long walks with him arguing on all kinds of subjects'.[41] It was generally reported of Troyte that he enjoyed argument (perhaps the thrust of the timpani emphasis of the variation?). His interests included chess and, shared with Elgar, crosswords.

'Elgar was always fond of ingenious conceits and mystifications' noted Troyte in his papers. He himself was on one particular day the victim of this fondness:

> One Sunday when I went into the study at Craeglea, the piano was open and stuck on the notes bits of stamp edge with numbers written on them. 'What's this for?', I asked. 'That's for you', said Elgar. 'Learn the numbers by heart and observe carefully that some of the notes have more than one number. When you can remember them hit the notes in order with one finger hard and fast'. After a few shots I got it right. 'That's it', said Elgar, 'Hit 'em harder and keep your finger stiff.' I said, 'I believe it's a tune. What is it?' Elgar laughed and said, 'Oh nothing, we only wanted to hear what it sounded like when you played it.' That tune must have been the theme.[42]

Nimrod

The place in national ceremonial assigned to this variation constitutes a paradox. In the Enigma sense the music is a record of friendship, but stated in allusive terms. It is, in the sense in which Cipriani Potter undertook to display his impressions of artistic character, a more or less direct stylistic reflection. As Elgar admitted the spiritual tone is of Beethoven[43] and the score only lacks the definition *Gesangvoll mit innigster Empfindung* as attached to the theme of the variations of the Op.109 Piano Sonata, or *con amabilita* belonging to the Elgar-shaped contour of the melody at the opening of Op.110. 'Nimrod', as from Beethoven is hymnic, perhaps a hymn to music itself, in temper properly suggesting a quality once described by Elgar as 'reverential, mystical and devotional'.[44]

August Johannes Jaeger (1860–1909) came to England from Düsseldorf in 1878. After employment in a map-printing firm he was introduced to Novello by C L Graves, man of letters and music critic of the *Spectator*. Jaeger joined the editorial department of Novello in 1890 where he remained until his death. The years of Jaeger's service with Novello covered the period of Elgar's rise from obscurity to eminence. That this was in considerable measure due to Jaeger's understanding of the character of the man, to his encouragement and to his critical acumen is made clear in the correspondence which is the record of this association. That Elgar and Jaeger shared similar responses to music is indicated by a note by Jaeger's obituarist: Jaeger, he said, 'was not judicial. Music either left him cold or filled him with ecstacy'.[45] Elgar had not been accustomed to people whom music filled with ecstacy.

Jaeger introduced Elgar's music to influential Germans, in the first place to Julius Buths (who accompanied Jaeger to Malvern in preparation for a translation of *Gerontius* to Germany). It was the first performance of *Gerontius* in Germany that enabled Elgar to feel that he might deserve a place somewhere within the high German tradition of music.

It is insufficiently recognized that during the period of the 'Renaissance of English Music' (overworked term!) it was the help of Germans that was instrumental in bringing an end to isolationism. Elgar understood this more than most, intuitively as well as intellectually. Particularly it was Henry Ettling and Edward Speyer, cultivated amateurs and influential business-men, who promoted Elgar by engaging the interest of Weingartner and Steinbach respectively. It was the latter who took the Variations on tour in the autumn of 1902. It was the critic of the *Meiningen Tageblatt* who, on 11 November 1902, gave the provincial German response to the music, interpreting the work by finding in it country scenes by day and night: with waving trees, a still lake, weeping flowers; by night with heavy clouds from behind which appeared the moon momentarily; and with dancing elves, goblins, sprites and gnomes; and with a proud procession . . .

Shrouded in mystery

At the end of the day, so to speak and in another setting, the answer to the abiding question is (as it may be supposed Elgar intended) what the listener wants it to be. The Variations were first performed in Worcester during the

1899 Festival, the third item in a programme that was 'too long, even for our capacity for music in a Festival week, which is prodigious!'

> Mr Elgar's Variations formed the largest item on the programme. They are literally and designedly shrouded in mystery. If you do not happen to know the gentlemen or ladies who are said to have suggested the variations you will find it difficult to connect 'Nimrod' with 'Moderato 3–4 E flat major', and Mr Elgar seems reluctant to let us into the secret. The 'Enigma' is not to be explained. 'I warn you', says the composer, 'that the apparent connection between the variations and the theme is often of the slightest texture; further, through and over the whole set another and larger theme "goes", but is not played'. The set of variations, therefore, looked at in this way is a kind of series of conundrums. But we are to regard them as 'absolute' music, and as such they are remarkable for originality of design and treatment.[46]

At the same time there were the thirteen 'gentlemen and ladies' whose personalities once flitted across a small area of creative inventiveness. Elgar, as he said, had Maeterlinck in mind as he considered the Variations so that their subjects in such a context may be discovered as agents of a secret power derived from an ambient, unseen, reality. Troyte seems to have had something of this in mind when describing a conversation with Elgar at Marl Bank:

> He or I suggested that the Enigma might be a veiled dancer. But when I said that she would unveil at the end and the orchestra would play the theme, he shook his head.

Notes

1. *Quarterly Musical Magazine*, no.7, 1825, pp.507–509.
2. British Library, Eg. MS 3090.
   cf. Maine, Basil, *Elgar, his Life and Works*, 2 vols, London, 1933, p.101:

   > One evening in the autumn of 1898 after a long and tiresome day's teaching, aided by a cigar, I musingly played on the piano the theme as it now stands. The voice of C.A.E. asked with a sound of approval
   >   'What is that?'
   > I answered 'Nothing – but something might be made of it; Powell would have done this (variation 2) or Nevinson would have looked at it like this (variation 12).

3. Young, *Letters to Nimrod*, p.27.
4. Eg. 3090.
5. Translation of *ainigma*, Liddell and Scott, (abridged) Lexicon, 1909.
6. '... and paints strange symbolical pictures a la Boecklin', *Letters to Nimrod*, p.250.
7. May, Norman, *Guide to Malvern*, 1895, p.99.
8. This is the final stanza of the poem which is to be found in Young, *Alice Elgar*, p.94.

9. Graves, Charles L, *Hubert Parry*, 2 vols, 1926, I, p.214; excerpt from Parry's diary.

10. Letter from the Royal College of Music of 26 June 1899, RCM MS 1150. On 1 February 1900 Parry wrote again:

   I shall indeed very much like to have the copy of your Variations which you so kindly offer me. I have not the luck to possess a copy yet, but it will be extra pleasure to have one from the composer himself. You know how much I admire them, and shall be delighted to revise my impressions of the brilliant orchestration by reading them to myself.

   Hereford and Worcester Record Office 705:445:2791

11. Steuart-Powell became a member of the Oxford and Cambridge Club on 15 March 1877, one of his proposers being a descendant of Dr Charles Burney, also Charles Burney.

12. From a letter of which a copy was furnished to me by the late Sir Adrian Boult.

13. Letter from Bridget Nevinson to John Lea Nevinson, 30 June 1976; copy by courtesy of the late J L Nevinson.

14. The church at Hoarwithy was built by S S Teulon; this letter also belonged to J L Nevinson.

15. *Letters of Matthew Arnold*, collected and arranged by George W E Russell, 2 vols, 1895, II, p.72.

16. Letter in Elgar Birthplace.

17. Rowse, A L, *Matthew Arnold, Poet and Prophet*, 1986, p.154.

18. *The Malvern News*, 26 January 1924, obituary notice of Mrs E B Fitton.

19. *Worcester Daily Times*, 13 September 1927, obituary notice of Lady Mary Trefusis.

20. HWRO 705:445:1912.

21. HWRO 705:445:1923.

22. HWRO 705:445:1920.

23. *Letters to Nimrod*, p.48.

24. Published in *The Packet* (Falmouth).

25. H M Adams to Bridget Nevinson, 20 July 1951; quoted in communication to J L Nevinson, see 13 above.

26. Letter of 15 October 1933, see Young, *Letters of Edward Elgar*, p.320.

27. Townshend, R B, *A Tenderfoot in Colorado*, 1923, Chapter 1; this book has illustrations of the author, 'showing Oxford the Lasso', 'rounding up', and with 'Leonardo Garcia'.

28. *The Tenderfoot in New Mexico*, 1923, Chapter V, 'Pious Orgies', pp.48–65.

29. *Last Memories of a Tenderfoot*, 1926, p.197.

30. *The Tenderfoot in New Mexico*, p.86.

31. ibid., see pp. 227–39.

32. *Letters of Edward Elgar*, p.94f.

33. Related by Dorothea Baker in her Preface to *The Tenderfoot in New Mexico*.

34. Letter to Julius Harrison, March 1961, by courtesy of the late Mrs Julius Harrison.

35. 'Elgar and the Baker Family', Hamilton, Gervase, *Musical Times*, 1979, p.121.

36. Malcolm Sargent to Julius Harrison, 17 January 1961.

37. Letter to the author from Dr T P Fielden, undated, c.1957.

38. Diaries of Margaret DuBuisson, HWRO (Hereford) K51/1–27 and Young, 'George Robertson Sinclair 1863–1917', Hereford Festival Programme Book 1985, p.28f.

39. Letter to author from Miss Lilian Griffith, 15 February 1955.
40. Griffith's Malvern Concert Club correspondence is in the Griffith Collection, Archives Department, Manchester Central Library.
41. Griffith, Lilian, *ibid*.
42. Notes in author's possession.
43. See Elgar's note in *My Friends pictured within* (Novello).
44. See Cumberland, Gerald, *Set down in malice*, 1918, p.83.
45. *The Spectator*, 25 December 1909, quote by M Hurd. *Vincent Novello – and Company*, 1981, p.108.
46. *Gloucester Journal*, 16 September 1899.

5   Elgar the Edwardian

Michael Kennedy

To write of Elgar the Edwardian is to acknowledge that he is regarded as a significant historical figure, quite apart from his music. His 'image' to many of the public is still as the embodiment of certain aspects of the period from 1900 to 1914. He even looked like a soldier or a squire. It was very reassuring to English philistines to have a composer who did not look much like one. Besides, to those who did know of Elgar the musician, he fitted the image they had devised for him: 'Pomp and Circumstance'; 'Imperial March'; 'The Banner of St George'. So we have Elgar the Edwardian or Elgar the Imperialist and for a long time he obscured the real Elgar, who was someone very different. The real Elgar is always there, of course. He is in *The Banner of St George* and all the marches. But it takes attuned ears to hear him, or it did until quite recently. We are told in one history of the period that Elgar 'plunged himself into the popular emotions of the day with a sensual romanticism. He was 40 years old in the year of the Diamond Jubilee and he saw himself then as a musical laureate, summoned by destiny to hymn Britannia's greatness'.[1] It is only non-musicians who write like this. Far from being summoned by destiny, he was commissioned by his publisher to write the *Imperial March* and *The Banner of St George* and he viewed both as jobs of work, though writing them to the best of his ability, and hoped for a commercial success so that he could concentrate on a symphony.

It is this patriotic element that attaches an Edwardian label to Elgar. Who has ever written about Delius the Edwardian or Bantock the Edwardian or even Vaughan Williams the Edwardian? The label is a legacy from the 1920s when Elgar was out of favour and was seen by the new generation as the embodiment of everything against which they reacted. Osbert Sitwell's description of the 70th birthday party in 1927 at Frank Schuster's country home, with its references to 'the plump wraith of Sir Edward Elgar glimpsed through the mists' is well known.[2] It is strange, incidentally, that we have several literary portraits of Elgar from those years, yet there is no painting or drawing by a really front-rank artist. This, I am convinced, reflects the true Edwardian estimate of music and musicians, that a composer was not in the same rank of priority for such attention as actors, poets, playwrights, novelists and even cricketers. Elgar was not, of course, in the front rank of Edwardian society anyway. He was invited to dine with the King occasionally and he had friends at Court such as Lady Maud Warrender and Lady Mary Lygon. He enjoyed Frank Schuster's country-house weekends. But until 1904 he still lived modestly in Malvern, then a little more grandly in Hereford until 1912, and though he had a *pied-à-terre* in London he was by no means a metropolitan figure.

However, it cannot be denied that Edward Elgar's greatest creative period coincided with the reign of his namesake. Appropriately, the first large-scale work he composed in this reign was the *Coronation Ode* (1902), which contains the choral setting of 'Land of Hope and Glory', and begins with the superb exordium *Crown the King!* At once it presents us with the contradictions which are inevitable when we consider this most fascinating of composers. It is proud, confident, assertive music: 'Crown the King with life!' Yet beneath the confidence there is a worm burrowing away to undermine the structure, the worm of discontent, disillusion, pessimism, the self-knowledge that he was out of tune with his times. It is always there in Elgar's music, though the ability to hear it has increased as he has receded from us into history. Only a few of his contemporaries heard it and then only those who knew him best and appreciated the *personal* nature of his music. That worm is even burrowing away in the *Coronation Ode*, in the dramatic coup that takes the unsuspecting listener by surprise in 'Crown the King'! when the tune of 'Land of Hope and Glory' creeps in on the orchestra, but it is a moment of *melancholy*, not triumph.

Here is another contradiction or paradox: neither Edward VII nor Edward Elgar was really an Edwardian. They were Victorians. Elgar was 43 when Queen Victoria died, the King was over 60. The Edwardian age has been much written about and, of course, much generalised about, so that a defective and lopsided image of it is presented to modern minds. It was, we are told, a leisurely, opulent age, with society at its most glittering. It was an age that seems permanently lit by golden sunlight, with glorious days at Ascot and Goodwood, with England's cricket team blessed by players like Fry, MacLaren and Ranjitsinhji, an age of splendid Royal Academy exhibitions, of the Entente Cordiale, of the country-house weekend. The Edwardian age sometimes seems like one long country-house weekend, and no doubt it was for some, especially if you lived at Chatsworth or Blenheim Palace. But the truth is that, like every age, it was a complex, difficult mixture. There was great wealth and also dire poverty. If the King was called the peacemaker, there was plenty of war being prepared. There was industrial strife on a scale that makes today's efforts seem small beer. There was intense political controversy and social change. There was unemployment and trouble in Ireland. There were entrepreneurs on a major

1   The fall of Simon Magus: Pollainolo relief, c.1480 (see page 124)

2   Elgar in 1880 (aged 23)

3   Elgar in 1896

4   Elgar in 1904

5   Elgar at Severn House, Hampstead, 1913

6   Elgar at Severn House, Hampstead, c.1915 (with Anthony Goetz, son of Muriel Foster)

7   Elgar with Algernon Blackwood, London, c.1916

C·A·E: C·Alice Elgar. H·D·S·P: H·D·Steuart Powell. R·B·T: R·B·Townshend. W·M·B: W·M·Baker.

R·P·A: R·P·Arnold. Ysobel: Isabel Fitton. Troyte: Troyte Griffith. W·N: Winifred Norbury.

Nimrod: A·J·Jaeger.

Dorabella· Dora Penny (Powell). G·R·S: G·R·Sinclair. B·G·N: Basil Nevinson.

* * * Lady Mary Lygon. E·D·U: Edward Elgar.

8   Friends pictured within

9 Elgar with John Coates, Gloucester, September 1925

10   Elgar with Bernard Shaw, Malvern, 1932

11   Elgar at Marl Bank, Worcester, 1932

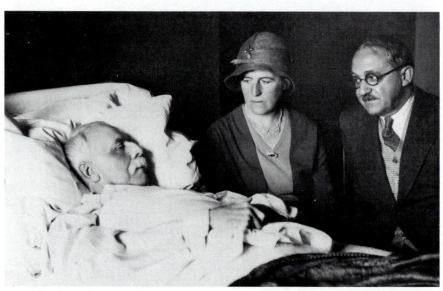

12   The last photograph: Elgar with Carice Elgar Blake and Fred Gaisberg,
Worcester, 12 December 1933

scale, like the King's financial friends, and there were little shopkeepers and commercial quacks like H G Wells's characters. You will find one part of Edwardian England in Arnold Bennett's *The Old Wives' Tale* and *The Grand Babylon Hotel*, another part in Wells's *Kipps* and *Tono Bungay* and *Ann Veronica* (for the Edwardian age was also the age of the New Woman and of the suffragette), and yet another part in Bernard Shaw's *Man and Superman* and *The Doctor's Dilemma*. There was glory in the Edwardian age, in literature, painting, music and on the cricket field; there was shoddiness too, in every walk and branch of life. In other words, men and women were as they always were and always will be, a compound of good and bad, of idealism and selfishness, of greed and generosity. The world does not change much and I do not believe anyone who lived between 1900 and 1914 would recognise those years in the highly coloured and selective portraits which are sometimes drawn of them.

Nevertheless, it would be foolish to deny that life was more leisurely then, the countryside more unspoilt, gardens more scented, most human beings less sophisticated and cynical. There was *style* in that era and most of all a degree of innocence and charm which was to be blasted away for ever by the First World War. Style and the lament for innocence are the qualities which we find in Elgar. They were qualities of the age but they were personal qualities too, and when we talk about the Edwardian Elgar, we are really talking about Edward Elgar himself, not some symbolic figure. If he was in a very real sense the musical laureate of his time, it was not just in occasional works. He had written the *Imperial March*, *The Banner of St George* and the finale of *Caractacus*. He wrote the *Ode* for King Edward and nine years later he dedicated the Second Symphony to his memory. But the *Coronation Ode* was an occasional piece, deliberately designed as such, and a masterpiece as it happened; the Symphony a chapter of autobiography very little related to kingship or the sunset of empire.

The Elgar of the Edwardian era also wrote the *Five Part-Songs from the Greek Anthology*, a title that must have deterred many from discovering the beauties of the music it concealed. The second song begins 'Whether I find thee bright with fair, Or still as bright with raven hair'. In it we hear the innocent Elgar, the boy from Broadheath, the dreamer by the reeds of Severn. It epitomises the charm and lyricism of Elgar, what I would call his Tennysonian element. The frequently-made comparison with Kipling, though obvious, is not really very apt (though Kipling is as complex as Elgar and still as misunderstood as Elgar was until a few years ago) but Tennyson is the Elgar of poetry with the gift for imparting intense lyricism to anything he undertook. You will find in Elgar the musical equivalent of 'Now sleeps the crimson petal'. The parallels between Tennyson and Elgar are striking, both artistically and in relation to their personalities. Both were streaked by a dark strain of utter melancholy, both were supreme lyricists capable of exquisite small gems and especially of pastoral evocation. Both expressed their love of their country through love of its countryside. Not even Wordsworth wrote more beautifully of Nature than Tennyson; no composer distils the essence of English woodland and river into music as Elgar could and did. Both men reached a wide popular audience because they put their art at the service of popular themes and events and both suffered a critical reaction for that very reason. When I was young, Elgar and Tennyson were both spoken of by intellectuals in the most disparaging terms. It was considered almost indecent to admire them. You would have thought that neither had written anything besides *Land of Hope and Glory* and *The Charge of the Light Brigade* (not that I would mind having written either). But it is significant that in 1887, the year of Queen Victoria's golden jubilee, Elgar chose to set these words of Tennyson:

> Low! my lute speak low, my lute, but say the world is nothing
> Low, lute, low.
> Love will hover round the flowers when they first awaken,
> Love will fly the fallen leaf, and not be overtaken.
> Low, my lute! O low my lute! we fade and are forsaken.
> Low, dear lute, low!

There is also a Thomas Hardy strain in Elgar – of pessimism and melancholy and realism. By those comparisons I am ranking him with two other eminent *Victorians*. The very first Elgarian music of the Edwardian age was the Incidental Music for W B Yeats's and George Moore's play *Grania and Diarmuid*, with its Hardyesque spirit of sadness tinged with something almost supernatural. Yeats, when he heard Elgar's Funeral March from *Grania*, described it as 'wonderful in its heroic melancholy', surely a judgement of real poetic insight by one genius on another.

Elgar's first preoccupation in the Edwardian reign was with his vast ambition to compose a trilogy of oratorios on the life and teaching of Christ's Apostles. Only two were completed, *The Apostles* and *The Kingdom*, and opinions differ as to whether they represented an enormous wrong turning, an obeisance to the Anglican church tradition to which he, a Roman Catholic, did not naturally belong, or whether they were a necessary stage through which he had to work in order to achieve the symphonic mastery that followed. Whatever may be felt, the fact remains that he composed them and that they occupied him for most of a decade. Those who were in Worcester Cathedral in August 1984 when Dr Donald Hunt conducted them both in one day will have heard that, flawed though they are and with some *longueurs*, they contain some deeply impressive music. Because he was so fine a composer, Elgar rescued himself from what threatened to become a kind of artistic straitjacket by discovering a new freedom of expression and, in a characteristically British way, he snatched victory from the jaws of defeat. Elgar had a titanic struggle to finish *The Kingdom*. The marvel is that it emerged as a masterpiece, for it was composed amid physical illness and under the constant cloud of a nervous breakdown. The year of 1905 was a watershed in Elgar's emotional life for he seems to have lost his religious beliefs, which must have made his composing of *The Kingdom* almost unbearable; he was in the midst of his Birmingham University lectures and hating the controversy he caused; he was, I suspect, wracked with guilt over his love for Alice Stuart-Wortley; and he was taking on too much work, conducting the London Symphony Orchestra not merely in his own works but in those of others, and for two months he went to America, a country he intensely disliked. It is small wonder that he was weeping when he conducted the first performance in Birmingham, and that in Cambridge 18 months later the nightmare had still not left him when he told A C Benson that it was no sort of pleasure for him to hear *The Kingdom* because it was so far behind what he had dreamed of: it only caused him shame and sorrow. Benson remarked that Elgar 'seemed all strung on wires'. And yet when Elgar went to his desk, when he escaped from the world and its inhabitants and entered the kingdom of his own creative imagination, he composed music which cannot be written off as profitless and pointless or devoted to debatable ends. It is not a debatable end to uplift our hearts and minds with such music as he gave to St Peter in *The Kingdom*.

Nevertheless, for all the loveliness and power of the music in the last of his oratorios, one is bound to salute the perspicacity of Ernest Newman's heretical opinion, expressed in print in 1907, that Elgar should turn his back on oratorio and turn his mind to other themes. Newman was convinced that it was with the orchestra that Elgar's real greatness lay. He must have been strengthened in his opinion when, between the two oratorios in 1905, the *Introduction and Allegro for Strings* was composed.

In 1904, his personal *annus mirabilis*, Elgar might have seemed the musical representative of the age of empire and opulence. In March that year he received the almost unprecedented tribute of a three-day festival of his own music at Covent Garden, with a member of the Royal Family present at each concert. Three months later he was knighted at the age of 47. Seven years earlier he had been almost unknown in London, a struggling provincial musician who was still giving violin lessons to unwilling schoolgirls. If this was the age of opportunity, then Elgar had certainly made full use of it, when the opportunity arose. Although it was to be another 20 years before he actually became Master of the King's Music, Elgar occupied that position in the public's mind after the 1904 festival, or perhaps even earlier after the 1897 jubilee.

This is the point at which I will make a diversion to deal with the allegation which has recently gained wide currency (particularly among Left-wing sympathizers) that Elgar came to 'hate' *Land of Hope and Glory* and to disapprove of its use on national, and especially political, occasions. There are no grounds for this belief. It probably arises from his famous letter to Alice Stuart-Wortley in 1924 about the musical plans for the Wembley Exhibition: 'the K.[ing] insists on Land of Hope & there were some ludicrous suggestions of which I will tell you'. Ken Russell's television portrait of Elgar shows him walking out of Wembley in fury with the strains of *Land of Hope and Glory* mocking him. A marvellous piece of film, but not true! Elgar merely hoped that something perhaps more imaginative and new could have been performed on what he later regarded as a lamentable occasion. He was always proud of *Land of Hope and Glory* ('a damned fine popular tune . . . a tune that will knock 'em flat'). In 1927 he was enthusiastic about writing music for a silent film called *Land of Hope and Glory* and conducted the orchestra at its first showing as Strauss had done for the silent film of *Der Rosenkavalier*. True, a year later, when Boosey sent him words to be fitted to the Trio of the *Pomp and Circumstance* March No 4, he replied: 'I think the pronounced praise of England is not quite so popular as it was; the loyalty remains, but the people seem to be more shy as to singing about it'.[3] He then collaborated on the project with Alfred Noyes. And in 1929, replying to a request from Boosey's about the use of *Land of Hope and Glory*, he said: 'All right about Lady Rodd & the conservatives – don't let any blasted labour rogues or liberals use the tune!'[4]

With *The Kingdom* completed in 1906 Elgar was working towards what had been so long awaited, his First Symphony. Like Brahms before him, he developed almost a mental block about completing a symphony. There had been sketches for years but nothing had materialised. Curiously he found his way to it by a means which certainly was an Edwardian, or again more accurately a Victorian, preoccupation: the idealisation of childhood. He looked out in 1907, at the time of his 50th birthday, some music he had written for a family play when he was 12 years old. He re-orchestrated and perhaps re-composed it as *The Wand of Youth*. If we like to seek a pertinent literary parallel, we need only remind ourselves that, while Elgar was working on *The Wand of Youth*, Kenneth Grahame was completing *The Wind in the Willows*. Elgar knew all about life and inspiration on the river bank and by entering that lost world of innocence and charm and sentiment, just as Grahame had, Elgar unlocked the door that led to a symphonic masterpiece. And he did it with music that was often happy and boisterous, but just as often withdrawn and lonely. Elgar himself supplied the perfect description when, by use of a pun in a letter to Arthur Troyte Griffith in 1914, he wrote of 'boyhood's daze'. 'Fairy Pipers' charmed the characters in the Elgar children's play to sleep, so we must accept that at the age of twelve Elgar imagined going to sleep in the exact musical terms he was later to use for *Gerontius*.

It was no great distance from *The Wand of Youth* to the second movement of the First Symphony, completed in 1908, the music he told orchestras to play 'like something you hear down by the river'. He had made the same point in a different way in one of his Birmingham lectures when he said he wanted English music to have 'a broad, noble, chivalrous, healthy and above all an out-of-door sort of spirit'. Here I should mention another Victorian-Edwardian whose most celebrated work appeared in 1904, another boy from a poor family who became one of the greatest figures of his day, another boy who like Elgar was always seeking the Wand of Youth, the land of lost content, 'the happy highways where I went and cannot come again'. He was James Barrie, the author of *Peter Pan*. If there is an Edwardian characteristic which unites some of the great English writers, poets and musicians of that era, it is not a dream of empire, or jingoism, or call it what you will, but this desire to escape into an idealised childhood as if the real world was too painful. I do not want to exaggerate the comparison with Barrie, but it is there and it emerged most strongly in 1915 when Elgar poured his heart and soul in the midst of war into music for a sub-Barrie play, *The Starlight Express*, adapted from a story by Algernon Blackwood. When Barrie is acted well and sincerely his mawkishness vanishes and what may embarrass us in a lesser performance becomes magical and occasionally sinister. So it is with Elgar in his children's play and it is significant that in the score he quoted several times from *The Wand of Youth*.

The Starlight Express and that underrated and moving cantata *The Spirit of England* are an epilogue to the years of Elgar's high noon and a prologue to the last flare-up of his genius in 1918 and 1919 in Sussex with the chamber music and the Cello Concerto. But the climax of Elgar's Edwardian period is the trilogy of works composed between 1909 and 1912 in which, to quote his own words, 'I have written out my soul, I have really *shewn* myself'. These are the Violin Concerto, the Second Symphony and *The Music Makers*. They have nothing to do with the Edwardian age in its social and historical aspects; they are the music of a private man, deeply divided against himself, his religious beliefs in tatters, his emotions torn between loyalty and devotion to his wife and another kind of love of a highly complex and noble kind for Alice Stuart-Wortley; his personality at once the prey of insecurity and depression or the onrush of sudden high spirits, a man who had a deep grudge against Providence for its failure to recognise him at the first glance, and an equally deep scorn for the ingrained philistinism of the country which had loaded him with more honours than any other musician. Is it any wonder that the central climax of his Second Symphony, when the violent hammering of percussion blots out the rest of the music, took its cue from Tennyson? It is an episode that has rightly been called demonic. It has also been compared with Mahler though it lacks Mahler's ironic tone. We can understand when we hear it why one perceptive and astute contemporary critic wrote of the symphony's 'pessimism and rebellion'. No doubt it can be interpreted as a vision of some dreadful national catastrophe – music is ambivalent – but with Elgar we are dealing, I stress again, with a private person not a public orator. He linked this passage with lines from *Maud*, where the hero sees his own burial after his love has turned him away:

> Dead, long dead,
> Long dead!
> And my heart is a handful of dust,
> And the wheels go over my head,
> And my bones are shaken with pain,
> For into a shallow grave they are thrust,
> Only a yard beneath the street,
> And the hoofs of the horses beat, beat
> The hoofs of the horses beat,
> Beat into my scalp and brain.

Dr Northrop Moore says of this passage: 'The growing tension of pursuing his own heroism through a world that showed itself more and more alien to the real old-world values the more loudly it applauded his music, had exploded in this Rondo with a concentration of all the headaches which had split the composer's brain with ever-increasing relentlessness through these years of his greatest success'. There is another very celebrated passage in this symphony, the coda of the *finale*. Those elegiac and deeply moving closing pages have been seen in retrospect, by those wise after the event, as an epitaph for the age that was to end on 4 August 1914. So great an Elgarian conductor as Sir John Barbirolli heard in that music the death-knell of a civilisation and equated it with the words spoken by the British Foreign Secretary, Sir Edward Grey, in 1914: 'The lamps are going out all over Europe; we shall not see them lit again in our lifetime'. It is a valid reaction to the music, especially by Sir John who spent his boyhood in Edwardian London, and if it inspired his marvellous interpretation, who will complain? But, in a way, to attach this music to so temporal an event is to belittle it and to receive only a tithe of its message. Writing about this passage in 1957, Peter J Pirie was inspired, and what he had to say about it was then novel and daring and so full of insight that one must salute afresh its pioneering thought. He wrote, memorably:

> It is a farewell to a vision that had been glimpsed but never held, to an illusion, stubbornly maintained in the face of overwhelming evidence, that the dignity of 19th century society was real, its values true, its structure stable. The vision was seen by a boy in a candlelit bedroom of a country cottage ... it was the blackcurrant tea that he mourned, and the life of a schoolboy on Malvern slopes.[5]

So if the Second Symphony is in one sense a requiem for Elgar's shattered illusions, *The Music Makers* is a requiem for his creative psyche. O'Shaughnessy's poem is often criticised, but I like it and can easily see why Elgar identified with it and wanted to set it to music. It was the apotheosis of the ideals of the boy who had tried to write down what the reeds were saying and who thereby believed he could sway the hearts and minds of mankind. 'We are the music makers, we are the dreamers of dreams, yet we are the movers and shakers of the world forever it seems'. But Elgar had found that music did not move and shake the world. He was badly treated by publishers and he knew the fickleness of the public response to his and others' work. So *The Music Makers* is suffused with an anguish that is almost unbearable in its poignancy. I do not understand why it was underrated for so long. At last it is being more widely recognised for what it is: one of Elgar's most moving and painful confessions.

In the context of the Edwardian era, against the broken-hearted pessimism of *The Music Makers*, we may set the aspiration of Vaughan Williams's *A Sea Symphony* (1910). But Elgar's nearest English contemporary was Frederick Delius, who did not live in England and was a part of the German and French musical scene. During Elgar's pre-1914 heyday there had been a coolness with Delius. At the 1912 Birmingham Festival they avoided each other. Writing to C W Orr in 1918,[6] Delius said he found Elgar's invention 'weak' and his orchestration 'thick and clumsy'. The Violin Concerto was 'very long & dull' but Elgar 'sometimes gets hold of a good tune – Pomp & Circumstance'. But during Elgar's visit to Delius at Grez-sur-Loing in 1933, the two old men, neither with much longer to live, discovered that they liked each other and, more important, admired each other's music. Nothing would have made Delius like 'those long-winded oratorios' (in any case it was the religion he disliked, so the music stood little chance) but he found the Cello Concerto 'beautiful' and *Falstaff* 'magnificent, so greatly conceived, so full of life and in its changing mood so vigorous and natural. It is the outcome of a rich nature'. Elgar, in a letter to Delius written on Christmas Day 1933, seven weeks before he died, mentioned *A Mass of Life* and added that it was 'a matter of no small amusement to me that, as my name is somewhat unfortunately indissolubly connected with "sacred" music, some of your friends and mine have tried to make me believe that I am ill disposed to the trend and sympathy of your great work. Nothing could be farther from the real state of the case. I admire your work intensely and salute the genius displayed in it'.[7] One further manifestation of how far behind him he had left the religious beliefs of his youth.

Elgar's greatest continental contemporaries were Richard Strauss and Gustav Mahler, two other composers of autobiography. For Elgar belongs not merely to Edwardian England but to a musical world populated by Sibelius, Stravinsky, Ravel, Debussy, Schoenberg, Webern, Berg, Rachmaninov and Puccini and many others. Still the most astonishing fact about him is that a composer of such originality and poetic imagination should have emerged from the provincial milieu of late 19th century England. As Diana McVeagh has pointed out, that year in London in 1889 was not perhaps as barren as it might appear. The music he heard at the concerts he attended was a truly wide and representative selection of what was being written abroad. The language he then absorbed and which he turned into the Elgarian style (because fortunately he had a strong enough individual creative personality to withstand mere influence) was the language of the continent, and it was therefore natural for Richard Strauss to salute it as 'progressive'. Much the same path was trodden by Delius but he achieved his salvation by living amongst it all. Who would have rated Elgar as one of the world's orchestral masters in 1897? Yet after *Enigma* and *Gerontius*, we find the German-born American conductor Theodore Thomas describing him in 1902 as the superior as an orchestral writer of any 'composer living or dead'. What a triumph of creative will we witness there. Strauss, seven years younger than Elgar, was brought up amid the music of Munich and was able at 16 to hear his compositions rehearsed or tried out by the court opera orchestra no less. No quadrille arrangements for a lunatic asylum for him. While Elgar was courting Alice and writing *Salut d'Amour*, Strauss was composing *Don Juan*. It took Elgar 10 years to catch him up, but catch him up he did, in *Cockaigne* and *In the South*.

Mahler too, though from as lowly a background as Elgar, studied and matured in Vienna, a city of conservative outlook but where rebellion and revolution in the arts were part of the climate. His First Symphony, composed before Strauss's *Don Juan*, is an even more remarkable example of a new, freer use of the orchestra. Elgar in 1888 could not have matched it however hard he might have tried. Yet by the time we come to the symphonies, we recognize that Elgar and Mahler are twin souls, allowing for national and psychological differences. The worlds of the first movements of Mahler's Sixth and Elgar's Second Symphonies are not too far apart.

It would be a distortion if I were to suggest that Elgar was not in many ways a representative figure of his time. He was innately conservative and patriotic, he respected and loved tradition and he enjoyed honours. (Although he said he accepted them only 'for Alice's sake', after her death he constantly angled for a peerage.) We forget today what a patriot is. Newspeak and the twisting of language to political ends have equated it with naked militarism and aggression. Elgar loved his country because he loved its rivers and trees and cathedrals and lanes and the pageantry of the streets of London. He loved Shakespeare and the other poets. He loved its prose. He wanted to share his love, through music, with his fellow-countrymen, to give them something *they* might love. As Strauss polarised the popular element of his music with the waltz and Mahler with the *Ländler*, so Elgar did with the march. And what marches! How *nostalgic* they are. That is the clue to them. They also represent aspiration and hope and those are the qualities we hear too in the march-based passages in *The Dream of Gerontius*, the *Enigma Variations* and the symphonies. In his symphonic use of the march-rhythm in his symphonies Elgar can be ranked with Beethoven and Mahler. And if we wish to have Elgar's comment on his own times in an entirely *un*ambiguous way, we should go not to the confessional of the Second Symphony but to the strange, angry, disturbing *Coronation March* he wrote for George V. This is no complacent, imperialistic celebration but an elegy of symphonic proportions and I think I can understand why Elgar suddenly decided not to go to the Coronation itself when the march was performed as the recessional. A *Recessional* indeed to rank with Kipling's.

The *personal* nature of these works has until recent years been misunderstood or overlooked. Or the works have been heard only in the context of spurious extra-musical associations. Of course it does no real harm to hear *Der Rosenkavalier*, Mahler's Ninth and Tenth Symphonies and Elgar's Second Symphony as the swansong of a civilization. But I do not believe that Strauss and Hofmannsthal in *Der Rosenkavalier* consciously anticipated the end of their own era by setting their comedy of love and manners in doomed 18th century Vienna. Mahler's last symphonies predicate the musical death-agonies of tonality, but emotionally they are not 'about' the state of Europe. They are about his daughter's death, his own approaching death and his love for his unfaithful wife. Through a deep *personal* statement he made a great universal statement applicable to almost anything you like to name. So did Elgar in the Second Symphony. From the death of his friend Alfred Rodewald, his love for Alice Stuart-Wortley and his vision of a time now beyond reach, he distilled a narrative of his own times which is for *all* time because he spoke not temporal but eternal truths. At the end of his life he said that the only thing he had really loved was the golden valley of the River Teme. We are back to the river theme again. The Edwardian Elgar *is* Edward Elgar and his age lasts from 1857 to the end of civilisation. If we want to understand his music, we should forget its external trappings and accretions and remember only his descriptions of the Cello Concerto and the Second Symphony: 'a man's attitude to life' and 'the passionate pilgrimage of a soul'. Therein is enshrined the soul of Edward Elgar.

Notes

1. Morris, J, *Pax Britannica* (London, 1968), p.343.
2. Sitwell, O, *Laughter in the Next Room* (London, 1949) pp.196–7.
3. Moore, J N, *Elgar and his Publishers*, Vol.II (London, 1987) p.855
4. *ibid.*, p.860.
5. Pirie, P J, 'World's End' *Music Review* (1957), p.89.
6. Carley, L, *Delius: A Life in Letters 1909–1934* (Scolar Press, 1988), p.189.
7. *ibid.*, pp.430–5.

6 Elgar's magus and projector

Robert Anderson

Among Elgar's sketches for his *magnum opus*, the oratorio trilogy that remained unfinished, is a brief one in pencil headed 'Magus';[1] he later crossed out the word. There are two further pencil pages, set out for voice and keyboard, with fragmentary text underlay hastily written and difficult to decipher.[2] It can be shown that these two were planned for a scene in which Simon Magus, the sorcerer of Samaria, was to confront Peter in the laying on of hands. When writing for his own eyes alone Elgar like the rest of us made little attempt to be intelligible. But the phrase 'baptized in the name of Jesus Christ' is clear enough. This, set to the music so memorable from Scene III of *The Kingdom*[3] and near neighbour to a jotting of the 'New Faith' theme[4] from the same work, leaves no doubt that these sketches were to be part of the oratorio scheme at some point after Peter's sermon. Their exact position can be settled by recourse to Elgar's copious drafts for the libretto. Furthermore one page of these sketches, which found no place in the completed oratorios, was developed at considerable length in the composition drafts Elgar made in his last years for his Ben Jonson opera, *The Spanish Lady*. The heretic Simon Magus, with his legendary ability to assume all shapes, finally took up residence in the 17th Century *projector*, Meercraft.

Elgar's ambitions for his *Apostles* scheme are well known. How far these were abandoned when he came to fulfil the Birmingham commissions for October 1903 and 1906 has also been well charted.[5] *The Apostles* as finally completed represents only half of what was publicly announced in the *Musical Times* as late as April 1903, a Part I to a hardly sketched Part II, which was given up in Elgar's letter of 28 June 1903 to Alfred Littleton, chairman of Novello.[6] It was much the same with *The Kingdom*. The proposal was to end Part I of the new work with the Lord's Prayer, already sketched for *The Apostles*; Part II would continue till the disciples reached Antioch, where for the first time, according to Acts xi.26, they were called Christians. Elgar's lectures as professor of music at Birmingham, his concert engagements, ill-health and discouragement forced a crisis in February 1906 and change of plan; again only Part I was written.

The failure to fulfil his highest ambitions in no way detracts from the achievement of *The Apostles* and *The Kingdom* as finished. The wealth of incident proposed as sequel to the Lord's Prayer would have demanded a whole series of oratorios if handled in the contemplative manner Elgar had hitherto adopted. Stephen was to be stoned, Saul was to persecute and be transformed into Paul, the devout centurion Cornelius was to receive the Holy Ghost amid his gentile followers, the pleasure-loving city of Antioch was to be described as background to the further propagation of the gospel. And above all there was the fascinating figure of Simon Magus.

Twice Elgar made a pencil jotting on the spiritual connection between Judas, Simon Magus and the Antichrist.[7] Judas was to be the great antagonist of the first oratorio, Simon of the second and Antichrist of the third. In December 1902, a year after he received the Birmingham commission for *The Apostles*, he was given for Christmas a copy of the *Encyclopaedia Britannica* (tenth edition), as well as Wagner's prose works in Ellis's eight-volume translation. How far he delved into Wagner's *Jesus of Nazareth*, for instance, is matter for conjecture; but the motives of their two Judases have much in common. His delight in the *Encyclopaedia* is well attested. On 21 December he wrote to 'Dorabella' in gleeful vein: 'Oh! Child, I know things now – 35 volumes' and signed himself 'Isaac Newton Elgar'.[8] The same day he wrote to 'Nimrod' a 'regular Yule-loggy puddingy, Brandy-saucious letter', describing a butterfly in his study:

> ... who is helping the Apostles ... I'm sure the beast is a familiar spirit
> – Angel Gabriel or Simon Magus, or Helen of Tyre or somebody: just
> fancy sitting in this Study surrounded with flowers & a *live* butterfly at Xmas
> – this music's going to be good I can tell you.

He signed himself 'Paracelsus Elgar'.[9]

The article on Simon Magus in the *Encyclopaedia* was lengthy and exhaustive. That Elgar absorbed it thoroughly is clear from jottings he made in connection with the Magus scene, the draft text for which was completed. The hold the Magus had on Elgar is demonstrated also by the fact that he sketched music for this separate scene alone of those ultimately intended for the trilogy but not composed. It is possible he planned to introduce the Magus first in what is now Scene II of *The Kingdom*, along with the Holy Women, as suggested in a brief memorandum for the libretto. But the Magus's function in the ensuing Scene III is clear. After the descent of the Holy Ghost and the gift of tongues the multitude expresses its amazement in the chorus, 'Behold, are not all these which speak Galilaeans?' In a libretto draft the ensuing query is made by Simon Magus (or Simon of Gitta, from the place in Samaria where he is supposed to have been born): 'hear ye every man in your own tongue wherein ye were born?' To accommodate Simon, Elgar has changed the biblical 'we' and 'our' to 'ye' and 'your'. To Simon are also given the lines, 'These men are full of new wine' and 'They drink and forget the law, and pervert the judgment'.[10] From the outset, therefore, Elgar intended to present Simon as incredulous and a negative force.

Elgar carried out extensive research for the Magus scene and made many notes. On a sheet now bound with libretto drafts for the third oratorio he jotted points of interest in the Magus's career: 'meets Philip in Samaria Acts 8.5–24'; 'Hippolytus (vi.20) says S.M. went as far as Rome & was opposed to Peter'; 'The source of all heresy is Simon of Gitta'; 'Simon according to the Legends might appear anywhere'; 'some modern criticism says S.M. is a pseudonym of the apostle Paul'. He also mentioned the name of Simon's companion, the former prostitute Helen of Tyre, and referred to 'Longfellow. 2nd passover'.[11] The Longfellow passage is entitled 'Simon Magus and Helen of Tyre'.[12] The scene is a house-top at Endor (evocative name for any composer). Simon's necromantic powers are demonstrated and there is a sharp exchange with Helen who calls him a juggler and charmer of serpents. Simon denies he is a magician though he has charmed Helen, his 'beautiful asp'; he makes higher claims: 'I am the power of God, and the Beauty of God! / I am the Paraclete, the Comforter!' He pronounces also a superb apostrophe to Helen:

> Thou art Helen of Tyre,
> And hast been Helen of Troy, and hast been Rahab,
> The Queen of Sheba, and Semiramis,
> And Sara of seven husbands and Jezebel,
> And other women of like allurements;
> And now thou art Minerva, the first Aeon,
> The Mother of Angels!

The extravagance of Simon's thought was precisely echoed in Klingsor's evocation of Kundry at the start of *Parsifal* Act 2, a work Elgar had heard at Bayreuth in July 1902. Hence an added fascination in the Magus. Elgar was well aware what Christian tradition had made of Simon. The account in *Acts* is comparatively sober, doubtless intentionally so. Simon was the first sorcerer any of the apostles had met. Philip's arguments and works so impressed the Magus that he was baptized among other Samaritans. It was when Peter and John arrived to administer the gift of the Holy Ghost by laying on of hands that Simon displayed his true colours. He offered money so that he too might have the power to bestow the Holy Ghost. Peter spurned the offer, describing Simon's state as 'in the gall of bitterness, and in the bond of iniquity'. Simon appears contrite and asks for prayers 'that none of *these things which ye* have spoken come upon me'. There the biblical account ends, leaving Elgar in some perplexity what was going to happen to Simon. He had underlined the italicized words and added plaintively in pencil, 'what things?'[13]

There are two accounts of the Magus's death. One is in the passage of Hippolytus referred to by Elgar. His continuous skirmishes with Peter took Simon eventually to Rome. There he affirmed that if he were buried alive, he would rise on the third day. His disciples dug a grave for him and interred him with due ceremony. 'He remains in the grave, however, unto this day', remarks Hippolytus drily, 'for he was not Christ'.[14] The other account, no less sensational, is to be found in the apocryphal *Acts of Peter*. On his arrival in Rome, Simon had astonished the populace by flying. Peter's presence provided its inevitable challenge and Simon proposed a flight over the Roman forum:

> Lo and behold, he was carried up into the air, and everyone saw him all over Rome, passing over its temples and its hills; while the faithful looked towards Peter. And Peter, seeing the incredible sight, cried out to the Lord Jesus.

He prayed that the Magus might fall and break his leg in three places but not die. This is what happened; so that the people stoned Simon and believed in Peter.[15] The scene of Simon's fall was sculpted for the ciborium of Sixtus IV in Old St Peter's (c.1480: see Plate 1). Elgar almost certainly saw it in the Grotte Vaticane when he visited them on 11 March 1908; in her diary Carice Elgar mentions some lovely carvings by Mino da Fiesole, to whom the ciborium was attributed. On 3 December 1907 Elgar informed Alfred Littleton at Novello that he had urged the Birmingham authorities 'definitely & finally to give up the idea' of a third oratorio for the 1909 festival.[16]

Elgar had no doubt that Simon Magus was a fitting antagonist to Peter for his second oratorio. Justin Martyr, writing c.150 affirms that in the reign of Claudius the senate and Roman people were so impressed by the teachings of Simon that they erected a statue in his honour on the island in the Tiber.[17] It so happens that in 1574 a statue with the inscription '*SEMONI SANCO DEO FIDIO*' was excavated on the island. This referred to Semo, a god of oaths perhaps Sabine in origin, nothing to do with Simon but near enough to account for Justin's mistake. Justin was himself a Samaritan and explained that his own people and more besides recognised Simon as a god. Simon, using Christian phraseology, appears to have taught that he 'appeared among the Jews as Son, descended in Samaria as Father, and came among the other nations as Holy Spirit'. Justin is clear in his mind that Simon came from Gitta (he calls it Gitton) rather than heaven.

A fascinating theology grew up around the Magus, justifying the Church in regarding him as 'the first heretic'. The attractive side of Simonism is its emphasis on self-knowledge. This involved freedom from the God of the

Old Testament and his law. In Simon's system a first Power had generated a first Thought, which in turn had produced the angels who created the world. But these angels imprisoned the Thought through jealousy. It was the angels who inspired the Old Testament prophets and dictated its law. It was Simon, a god apparently in human form, who descended to free the Thought and end the power of the Jewish law. He set himself up as a redeemer after the manner of Christ.[18]

Longfellow's powerful description of Helen of Tyre is closely based on Simonian tradition. A pivot of the Magus story is his redemption of the former prostitute, which must have recalled to Elgar the problems he had already had with Mary Magdalene in *The Apostles*. Simon maintained Helen was the divine Thought which had migrated from one human body to another till finally redeemed by him. Irenaeus, writing c.180, preserves the essence of the teaching:

> The Thought was in that Helen on whose account the Trojan war was undertaken . . .
> She passed from body to body,
> Always suffering disgrace from it;
> Last of all
> She was manifest in a prostitute;
> This is the lost sheep.
> For her sake he came,
> To free her from her bonds,
> And to offer men salvation
> Through their recognition of him.[19]

Simon was Peter's opponent in Caesarea, Tyre, Laodicea, Antioch and Rome. There was a late tradition that Simon was one of the 30 disciples of John the Baptist. This was eloquently countered by Origen, who doubted c.245 whether there were 30 Simonians left in the whole world.[20] Simon's reputation as sorcerer and wonder worker preserved his memory long after the Simonians disappeared. His prowess made a contribution to the Faust legends that have played so important a part in European literature. It is a curious coincidence that Sir George Alexander of the St James's Theatre, London, wrote to Elgar on 7 November 1905 with a request that he write music for a *Faust* play, to be based on Goethe, written by Stephen Phillips, and to be performed late in 1906 or early the following year. Elgar received the letter at precisely the time he was trying to order his thoughts for *The Kingdom* amid professorial lectures and a conducting tour.[21]

In the Middle Ages it was the biblical association with 'simony' that kept the Magus's name alive, nowhere more tellingly than in Dante, who begins Canto xix of the *Inferno* with an address to the first heretic:

> O Simon Magus! O wretched and rapacious followers of his, who prostitute for gold and silver the things of God that should be wedded to right-eousness.

Elgar, basing his oratorios on the text of the Bible, was bound to concentrate on Simon's attempt to purchase spiritual power for money. However widely he ranged in the Simonian literature, however conscious he was of the later significance attached to the Magus and his heresy, his own scene must be based primarily on the account in *Acts* viii. For the compilation of his text Elgar followed his usual practice of ranging the Bible and his favourite commentaries, most of which are preserved at the Elgar Birthplace. Among notes for the libretto of *The Apostles* is a list of 'Books referred to'. The third mentioned is *The Apostles* by Ernest Renan.[22] By a double pencil line in the margin Elgar has marked the beginning of the passage on the Magus:

> A certain Simon, of the village of Gitta, or Gitton, who afterwards rose to a great reputation, began about that time to make himself known by his wonderful operations.

Elgar later expressed doubt how to name the Magus in the oratorio: '? Simon Gitton / ? or Simon of Gitta'. Though Renan uses the former, Elgar decided on the latter. Elgar marked other Renan passages about the Magus, notably the fact that 'in the Pseudo-Clementine literature, "Simon the Magician" is often a pseudonym for St Paul', and Peter's forthright reply to Simon's offer: '"Thy money perish with thee, because thou hast thought that the gift of God may be bought!"'[23]

Elgar's linking of Simon first with Judas and then the Antichrist is well borne out in the commentaries he consulted. The horror of the Judas story lay in his betrayal of Christ for 30 pieces of silver. Simon's attempt to traffic financially with spiritual gifts was 'not offensive only but blasphemous'. Thus C J Vaughan in a lecture on 'The Sin of Simon'. He goes on to characterise the Magus:

> Money was his god ... Simon offered money to the Apostles to share their gift with him. He would purchase the Holy Ghost with money. The very idea is blasphemy ... Simon had that mercenary mind which St Paul calls the *root of all evil* [underlined by Elgar]. He thought that money could do anything.[24]

At the Birthplace are two books of particular significance for the connection of Simon Magus with the Antichrist. Renan's *Antichrist* has a number of pencil markings by Elgar. Referring to the 'second beast' in *Revelation* xiii.11–18 and enlarging on the theory that the Antichrist was the emperor Nero, Renan states that:

> The author of the Apocalypse is greatly concerned about a "false prophet", whom he represents as being an instrument of Nero, a thaumaturgist making fire descend from heaven, giving life and speech to statues, branding men with the mark of the Beast ... These characteristics point to a false prophet, an enchanter, in particular to Simon the Magician, an imitator of Christ, who in legend had become the flatterer, the parasite and the wizard of Nero.[25]

Frederic Farrar in *The Early Days of Christianity* spells out the significance of Simon to Elgar yet more clearly. While subscribing also to the theory that by the 'false prophet' and the 'second beast' of the Apocalypse was meant Simon of Gitton, Farrar explicitly calls him an 'antichrist':

> It is clear that Simon Magus was not only a heresiarch, but also a false Christ or antichrist. His notions were partly Jewish and Alexandrian. Philo had spoken of "Powers" of God, of which the greatest was the Logos. According to Jerome, Simon used to say, "I am the word of God, I am beautiful, I am the Paraclete, I am the Almighty"

This utterance was paraphrased by Longfellow.[26]

The making of the Simon libretto can be followed in some detail. At the Birthplace is a Bible dated by Elgar, 'Liverpool / Nov 1902'. It contains an additional note: 'Mem: Bought this in Liverpool with my dear friend Rody: used it for the *Apostles*'. When he came to *Acts* viii, Elgar ringed the first mention of Simon in v.9 and underlined the word 'bewitched'; he also put a pencil mark along the column containing the rest of the story.[27] Elgar's copy of *The Red Letter New Testament*, dated by him 'Smyrna / Oct: 1905', contains further evidence. At the foot of p.162 Elgar has written, 'Simon Magus must have known all this'; the passage referred to is John iv.7–25, in which the Samaritan woman is asked by Jesus to draw water for him. The point of Elgar's note is that Simon Magus was himself a Samaritan and was doubtless familiar with Christ's activities in his district. At the bottom of p.222, containing parts of Acts x and xi, Elgar has made a further reference of interest: 'S Magus 2P2,1,2,3'. This leads to 2 Peter ii, where v.1 mentions 'false prophets' and 'damnable heresies'; Elgar has marked the beginning of v.3 and underlined certain words: 'And through covetousness *shall they with feigned words make merchandise of you*'.[28] Though Elgar did not in the end use this passage, its relevance to his purpose is obvious.

When he came to draft the text for the Magus scene, Elgar headed it 'In Samaria'. He eliminated the biblical Philip altogether, so that the characters in order of appearance are Simon of Gitta, Chorus, John and Peter. The narrative is carried by Acts viii, partly reordered and recast to allow the maximum of direct speech. Simon, for instance, opens the scene with 'To me they all gave heed' instead of the biblical 'To whom'. In his lengthy first speech Simon refers to Jacob's well and the Samaritan woman, quoting from John iv as indicated in *The Red Letter New Testament*; he makes use also of the Psalms and the book of *Wisdom*. The Chorus interposes with a passage from Isaiah xii about 'the wells of salvation'. After Simon has paraphrased Acts viii.13: 'I believe also and wonder, beholding the miracles and the signs', John confirms him in his faith with two extracts from his own gospel. It is then that Simon makes his crucial offer of money. Elgar considered two main passages at this point, Genesis xxiii.13 and 2 Chronicles xvi.3, toying also with the far less suitable Proverbs xx.15. Thenceforward Elgar followed the narrative of Acts for the exchange between Simon and Peter, ending at v.24.[29]

The proposed scene was eventually typed. A number of interesting points now arise. After Simon's paraphrase of Acts viii.12, 'they are baptized in the name of Jesus Christ', Elgar has various suggestions for a brief choral passage. Among the words considered are the approximation to Zechariah xii.10, 'pour upon us the Spirit of grace'; this found its final place at cue 114 in *The Kingdom*. At the Jacob's well reference Elgar has noted in pencil, 'Wayside', presumably signalling his intention of quoting the theme that opens the second number of *The Apostles*. The choral interruption from Isaiah xii.3, is scanned with long and short marks so as to suggest its musical setting: With jōy shăll yĕ drăw wātĕr oŭt ŏf tħe wēlls ŏf sălvātiŏn'. It takes a stretch of the imagination to realise that Elgar had here the *New Faith* theme in mind, as is clear from ex.1.[30] The confirmation of Simon's faith is now performed by both Peter and John and again words familiar from another context were typed out. By the side of a slightly altered Malachi iv.2, 'Unto you that fear His name shall the Sun of righteousness arise' Elgar has noted the fact that this had already been 'used' in the second oratorio, *The Kingdom*, after cue 137. This note must have been written when *The Kingdom* as we know it was already complete and Elgar was surveying his *disjecta membra* for the third oratorio.[31]

Ex.1

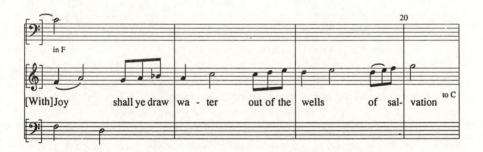

Just as Elgar's libretto notes are dotted with biblical references, all to be considered, some finally to be taken up, so musical references abound too. For these he adopted a shorthand system relating to the sketchbooks he was using at the time. On 6 November 1901 Elgar asked Jaeger to procure him some new sketchbooks. In further correspondence he specified their binding and it was decided they should be eight in number.[32] They are now lodged in the British Library where can be seen the original numbers I–VIII stamped on the front covers.[33] It is in these sketchbooks that the main material for the trilogy is to be found. The music proposed for Simon Magus is in sketchbooks II and III. For his first appearance Elgar has two references, '2/II' and '3/II' in the libretto notes.[34] These lead one to pages 2 and 3 of sketchbook II, where is music eventually used in *The Kingdom* Scene III, after cues 84 and 88.[35] This became the choral movement, 'Behold are not all these which speak Galilaeans?', in which the original idea was that the Magus should be introduced.

For the Magus scene in Samaria Elgar had a number of musical ideas. The two associated with Simon himself are thoroughly chromatic as one would expect. This is the music that was doubtless intended to counter-balance the predominantly diatonic idiom of *The Kingdom* as completed. The first theme is marked for violin, and its reference is 28/III (ex.2).[36] Elgar returned

Ex.2

to this Simon idea at the end of his life, as also to the Magus's second theme, which occurs on the page referred to as 40/III (ex.3);[37] other suggestions for the scene are on 41/III.[38] The opening of Simon's speech is set, from Acts viii.10: 'To me they all gave heed, from the least to the greatest, saying: "This man is the power of God which is called Great"'. This is the crucial sentence linking him with Gnosticism and marking him as heresiarch. In addition are sketched his words, 'baptized in the Name of Jesus Christ', and the start of his quotation from the Samaritan woman, 'At Jacob's [well]'. The other passage concerns the entry of the chorus, 'With joy shall ye draw water out of the wells of salvation', the passage Elgar had scanned in the libretto notes and which is set to the *New Faith* motif from *The Kingdom*. The only libretto reference Elgar made to the sequence of musical ideas was the cryptic '40 Simon Magus (? & p 28 quick'), which proposed some link between pp.40 and 28 in sketchbook III (exx.3 and 2).[39]

The other musical references in the libretto notes concern the part of John in Samaria. They are three in number, two of which are crossed out, presumably because they were used in Scene IV of *The Kingdom*. 27/III refers to the start of the duet section between John and Peter at cue 143

Ex.3

[Acts viii.10]

to me they | all gave heed | from the least to the | great - [est] say - ing

(a)   (b)

This man | [is the power of God] | who is call - [ed] great

in *The Kingdom*; 58/III is the opening of John's aria, 'Unto you'. In 59/III it is less easy to understand Elgar's intention. He writes '3/4 slow? with John in Samaria', and the sketched music is a version of the *Kingdom's* 'Fellowship' theme in E minor. The music of John in Samaria ('Unto you') is of course in 3/4; but did Elgar propose a slow version of 'Fellowship' in 3/4 to introduce John and Peter in their confrontation with the Magus?[40]

These hints are meagre enough. In the libretto for the Simon scene are certain key words and phrases that would have allowed Elgar use of motifs he had already devised for the oratorios. We have seen the principle already at work. 'Christ is preached', 'the kingdom of God', 'may receive the Holy Ghost', 'Repent therefore' are phrases evocative enough in the Elgarian vocabulary, and one can hazard a guess at the sounds playing round Elgar's mind as the libretto took shape. The Judas links, which meant so much to Elgar and which are enshrined in Simon's words, 'I have sent thee silver and gold', coupled with Peter's harsh comment, 'I perceive thou art in the gall of bitterness, and in the bond of iniquity', would probably have conjured direct allusion to the Judas music of *The Apostles*.

What we have of Simon's music gives little hint that Elgar could have devised from it a musical character equivalent in weight to that of Judas. The account in Acts was bald and emphasised only the 'simony' in the Magus's make-up. Elgar's reading had revealed in Simon of Gitta a phenomenon of portentous importance in the early history of the Church. There was nothing in *Acts* of the formidable opponent Peter was supposed to have stalked throughout the Mediterranean world, nothing of the apocalyptic figure who could be equated with the 'second beast' in *Revelation*. A libretto to have encompassed such an antihero would have needed recourse to the most colourful and dramatic passages of the Bible, a painstaking gathering of epithets and phrases from here and there to produce a montage that should be lurid yet humanly convincing. Cardinal Newman tapped his own imagination to create the demons of *Gerontius*; and Elgar matched him with consummate skill. It is doubtless significant that Simon was to be introduced in that passage of *The Kingdom*, hissingly fugal, that most closely approximates to the demons' music. Perhaps with the demons and Judas, Elgar had written antiheroes out of his system. It is interesting that when, in *The Spirit of England*, Elgar came to set Laurence Binyon's wartime lines about opposing the perfidy of Germany, 'She fights the fraud that feeds on lies', his music knew no contortions save those of the *Gerontius* demons again. Elgar's apocalypse, if it is anywhere to be found, is perhaps most closely hinted at in the 'ghost' theme of the Second Symphony, which assumes in the Scherzo so menacing and overwhelming a presence.

Elgar's Simon Magus was finally set aside in February 1906, and *The Kingdom* ran its course with opposition to the apostles fragmented and generalised rather than concentrated in one formidable adversary. The three sketch pages, 28/III, 40/III and 41/III lay dormant for a quarter century. Speaking to Wulstan Atkins about his sketches, Elgar remarked: 'Mind you, I often use them in a totally different way to that which was in my mind when I jotted them down'.[41] So it was with Simon's sketches, which achieved further development only in Elgar's composition drafts for *The Spanish Lady*, the operatic project he embarked on in the last years of his life.[42]

Elgar's choice of Barry Jackson as librettist for the opera owed much to his friendship with Bernard Shaw. Jackson was a devoted Shavian, having given the first English performance of *Back to Methuselah* at Birmingham in October 1923. Shaw was convinced that Elgar's essential dramatic genius lay in distilling a *Falstaff* from Shakespeare's *Henry IV* plays and *Henry V*. What was opera compared with so splendid a symphonic study? But Jackson, who had recently had great success as founder-director of the 1929 Malvern festival, was interested that Elgar should hit on the idea of a Ben Jonson play as basis for an opera, and intrigued when told that his choice had fallen on *The Devil is an Ass*.[43] It was a curious choice in many ways. When he came to write the play for performance in 1616 Jonson went back on the view he had expressed ten years before in *Volpone* that plays with the devil on stage were antique relics of barbarism. The last line of the prologue to the play Elgar chose refers to a recent success of Dekker's, *If this be not a good play, the Devil is in it*. Marlowe's *Doctor Faustus*, with its faint echoes of Simon Magus, had demonstrated the popularity of devil plays more than 20 years before. Jonson was aware of their lingering appeal. So for the opening of his play he devised a hellish trio of Satan 'the great divell', Pug 'the lesse divell', and Iniquity 'the Vice'. But Jonson's main concern is still the moral comedy with which to lash the foibles of Jacobean society. Therefore Pug, though sent to earth to enlarge hell's confines with new recruits, finds himself consistently thwarted. He desires 'a little venery, / While I am in this body'. He gets none, and it is Jonson's delight to represent him as foolish and inept, so that in the end he the Devil has to be surreptitiously removed by the Vice (in the old plays it was always the Devil who triumphantly shouldered the Vice); otherwise he would disgrace the hellish powers by being clapped in prison. Jonson's point is that 'Hell is / A Grammar-schoole' compared with the corrupt society of 1616. He revels in stacking the odds against Pug, creating half a dozen characters who can readily outwit him.

But it was not Pug who was to inherit Simon Magus's music. Elgar was not interested in the devil play Jonson had intertwined with his social satire. Indeed, in the libretto drafted by Jackson and Elgar, the satire itself is much blunted in being accommodated to a less robust age. Yet there emerged a character worthy of the Magus's mantle. Meercraft is a Jonson creation of tremendous resource. He dismisses Pug with contempt: 'Why, if he were the Divel, we sha' not need him'. Meercraft is a masterful 'projector' with devices enough to make an easy gull of the greedy and ambitious Fitzdottrel, whom he incites to ever more fantastic flights of illusion and stupidity.

In a draft cast list Elgar has Meercraft 30 years old, 'A plausible rogue who will take anyone's money. Shrewdly cunning'. Thus he propounds his creed in the libretto:

> Money's a drudge, a bawd, a whore,
> Yet no man lives but must have more.
> Some cheat at cards and some at trade.
> And all to woo the queasy jade.
> I live by projects, skill'd and sound,
> Which by your leave I'll straight propound.

Jonson's Fitzdottrel, soon to be Duke of the Drown'd Lands reclaimed by Meercraft, outlines some of the schemes of this cunning plotter: 'He has his winged ploughes, that goe with sailes, / Will plough you forty acres, at once! And mills, / Will spout you water, ten miles off!' There seems no limit to his projects. The drainage scheme will produce 18 million; he will dress dogskin to the standard of finest leather; he'll produce wine from raisins, promote oral hygiene by means of toothpicks under his central control.

Elgar uses the Magus music of 40/III (p.40 of sketchbook III) in his projected Act 1 scene i of *The Spanish Lady*. Meercraft is addressing the crowd and bursting with fantastic plans:

> Money! You'll never want her!
> I'll coin her out of cobwebs, –
> Raise wool upon eggshells, –
> Grow grass out of marrowbones.

He is approached by Everill, whom Elgar describes as 24 years old, 'his cousin, debauched'. There then follows a dialogue that runs to 70 bars for the two baritones and piano, the longest stretch of connected vocal music that Elgar wrote for the opera. The exchange is ill-tempered because Everill is in financial straits (with pawned clothes) and Meercraft upbraids him for living beyond his means, wearing 'scarlet and gold – wedging in with lords'. The glissando bars of the Magus music are introduced for the first time at Everill's words, 'I come not for counsel'. They are referred to twice more, quietly, and at moments of doubt or cogitation. Everill touches his ear and Meercraft shrinks instinctively from the demand he knows will follow. It is at this point that Simon's chromatic semiquaver motif first appears in its new context, leading to Everill's 'I lack money!' (ex.4). It occurs twice more, when Everill scratches his ear again for money and when Meercraft unwillingly hands some over. Elgar worked hard at this scene interspersing new motifs with those of the Magus. Parts of it he copied many times, the whole more than once. The sketch of 28/III found place in an instrumental fragment for Act II of the opera.

The connecting thread between oratorio and opera is clear. It was on the Magus's misuse of money that Elgar concentrated for his proposed scene 'In Samaria'; it was with this in mind that he devised the shifty, chromatic motifs for Simon in his sketchbooks. Everill's importunate demands for money and Meercraft's eventual surrender signalled likewise an employment of coin to low purpose. In the oratorio Elgar planned to scale tragic heights, stirred by Peter's rebuke and the charge of 'simony' that was to echo down the ages. In the opera he prepared to plumb comic depths, pointing his finger at a commercialized society he felt had a stranglehold on all things including art, not least his own.

Ex.4

The Magus could pass through a mountain or through flames, he could make bread from stones, breathe flame and assume at will the form of an old man, child or youth. With such wonders he is said to have imposed on his followers and on Nero. Meercraft's projects worked a similar sorcery. 'This man defies the *Divell*, and all his works!' cries his dupe Fitzdottrel. Meercraft even gets him to feign possession by that same devil to escape bothersome commitments. Whether the sketches are more suited to Simon of Gitta or to the projector Meercraft must remain an open question. The demands of the Birmingham deadline for the first performance of *The Kingdom* and the BBC commission for the Third Symphony meant that neither character could come to full fruition in music. Elgar knew the value of a commission, undertook its responsibilities at whatever personal sacrifice, and appreciated its rewards; his art had often to pay the cost.

Notes

1. British Library Add.MS 63155, f.14*v*.
2. BL Add.MS 63155, ff.20*v*, 21.
3. p.108 of the vocal score.
4. So called in Jaeger, A J: *The Kingdom: Book of Words with Analytical and Descriptive Notes* (London, 1906); other thematic labels are from the same source.
5. See Moore, Jerrold Northrop: *Edward Elgar: a Creative Life* (Oxford, 1984), pp.361–506.
6. Moore: *op.cit.*, p.410.
7. BL Add.MS 47906, ff.3, 17.
8. Powell, D M: *Edward Elgar: Memories of a Variation* (London, 1937, rev. 3/1949), pp.52–3.
9. Moore: *op.cit.*, pp.386–7.
10. BL Add.MS 47905B, ff.221, 108.
11. BL Add.MS 47906, f.24.
12. From *Christus: a Mystery*, 'The Divine Tragedy: the Second Passover. xi'.
13. BL Add.MS 47906, f.20.
14. Hippolytus: *Philosophumena* vi.20.
15. *Acts of Peter (Actus Vercellenses)*
16. Moore J N: *Elgar and his Publishers* (Oxford, 1987), p.685.
17. Justin Martyr: *Apologies* i.26.56.
18. Grant, R M: *Gnosticism and Early Christianity* (New York, 1959, 2/1966), pp.70–96.
19. Irenaeus: *Adversus haereses* i.23–31.
20. Origen: *Contra Celsum* i.57.
21. Hereford and Worcester Record Office 705:445:2294.
22. BL Add.MS 47904B, f.21*v*.
23. Renan, E: *Les Apôtres* (Paris, 1866; Eng. trans., 1895); Elgar's copy, Birthplace Museum no.57; the English version wrongly places an acute accent on Renan's name, which Elgar copied correctly.

24. Vaughan, C J: *The Church of the First Days: Lectures on the Acts of the Apostles, I:* 'The Church of Jerusalem' (Cambridge, 2/1865); Elgar's copy, Birthplace Museum no.65.
25. Renan, E: *L'Antichrist* (Paris, 1876; Eng. trans., 1899); Elgar's copy, Birthplace Museum no.61.
26. Farrar, F E: *The Early Days of Christianity* (London, 1882); Elgar's copy, Birthplace Museum no.114.
27. Birthplace Museum no.115.
28. Birthplace Museum no.763; 1905 is almost certainly not the date of purchase, as Elgar has marked in the *Testament* passages for the Capernaum scene in *The Apostles*; I am grateful to Christopher Grogan for drawing this to my attention.
29. BL Add.MS 47905B, ff.193–6.
30. BL Add.MS 47906, ff.18–19.
31. BL Add.MS 47906, f.21.
32. Moore, J N: *Elgar and his Publishers*, pp.312–17.
33. BL Add.MS 63153–60.
34. BL Add.MS 47905B, f.202.
35. BL Add.MS 63154, ff.2v, 3.
36. BL Add.MS 63155, f.14v.
37. BL Add. MSS 47905B, ff.201, 213; 63155, f.20v.
38. BL Add.MSS 47905B, f.213; 63155, f.21.
39. BL Add.MS 47905B, f.213.
40. BL Add.MS 47905B, f.213.
41. Atkins, E Wulstan: *The Elgar-Atkins Friendship* (Newton Abbot, 1984), p.435.
42. MS material at present with P M Young, in preparation for the Elgar Complete Edition vol.41.
43. Jackson, B: 'Elgar's "Spanish Lady"', *Music and Letters*, xxiv (1943), p.1; repr. in Redwood, C, ed.: *An Elgar Companion* (Ashbourne, 1982), pp.209–29.

7 Elgar and Falstaff

Diana McVeagh

'... further, through and over the whole set another and larger theme "goes", but is not played.'

'... a larger canvas – & over it all runs – even in the tavern – the undercurrent of our failings & sorrows.'

The first of Elgar's two strikingly similar sayings has incited speculation for nearly a century. The second, made in a letter to Ernest Newman of 26 September 1913, a week before the first performance of Op.68, has attracted less attention. There is no mystery attached to it, for Elgar wrote out his 'failings & sorrows' theme:

Ex. 1

and its first occurs in *Falstaff* as the second half of a *cantabile e largamente* theme at 6 bars after figure 64.

It is characteristic of Elgar's creative process that it is not apparently one of the main themes, and he did not identify it among the 21 music examples in his own analysis[1] (nor did Tovey in the 33 examples in his[2]). It appears as a counter-melody in what Elgar described as 'a trio section of uproarious vitality'. But how much his comment reveals, made as it was about a work based on one of the great comic figures of European literature! In the same letter to Newman he wrote '*Falstaff* (as programme says) is the name but Shakespeare – the whole of human life – is the theme'.

Elgar's *Falstaff* has always challenged commentators and divided his admirers. He himself told Delius he considered it his best work and wrote to Gerald Cumberland that he had 'enjoyed writing it more than any other music I have ever composed ... I shall say "good-bye" to it with regret, for the hours I have spent on it have brought me a great deal of happiness'.

Yet in the year of its first performance it played to half-empty halls. The fact that Elgar published his own 'analytical essay' in *The Musical Times* the month before seems to have put some people off. Yet very detailed analyses of *The Dream of Gerontius* and the two oratorios were printed before their first performance, written by Jaeger. With Jaeger dead, who better than Elgar to write about his *Falstaff*? But the work has been faint-praised for being too learned, for smelling too much of the midnight oil and the study.

To an extent it is a problem common to all programme music. How can the composer best reconcile narrative and character study, descriptive and musical values? Incidental music usually needs short self-contained pieces, each setting a single atmosphere: Mendelssohn, Sullivan, and Finzi, in *A Midsummer Night's Dream, The Tempest*, and *Love's Labour's Lost*, did not have to shape the extended structural framework that Elgar (or Strauss) did. Opera has demands and opportunities of its own; but a symphonic work must make its own stage.

Elgar was of course aiming high. We like to think of Falstaff as English but before Elgar it was a German and an Italian who had portrayed him most notably in music. Shakespeare demands a double standard: how does a work measure up to its source and how fine is it in itself? The greater the composer, the more strongly he may bring out his own interpretation. The conjunction of Shakespeare and Elgar may not add up to the original Falstaff, but it makes an original work in its own right.

Three qualities should be present in any composer who sets Shakespeare: knowledge and love of the plays and genius in himself. In a symposium such as this the last quality may be taken for granted. Elgar's knowledge of Shakespeare went back to his boyhood, and (best of all) was not gained only from the printed page. Ned Spiers, his father's handyman and retired hack actor, would not have declaimed from a text in the back parts of the Worcester shop. Before *Falstaff*, Elgar had drawn from *Othello* (III iii) the brilliant title of his Marches:

> Farewell the tranquil mind; farewell content!
> Farewell the plumed troop and the big wars
> That make ambition virtue! O farewell!
> Farewell the neighing steed and the shrill trump
> The spirit-stirring drum, the ear-piercing fife,
> The royal banner, and all quality,
> Pride, pomp and circumstance of glorious war!

For his symphonic study Elgar needed, in effect, to edit the Falstaff plays, and subsume what he needed into music. In dismissing the 'caricature' in *The Merry Wives of Windsor* as an afterthought written at Queen Elizabeth's request, he was following scholarship of his time. As A C Bradley declared in 1902: Falstaff is 'to be found alive in the two parts of *Henry IV*, dead in *Henry V*, and nowhere else'. Even though Verdi's *Falstaff* is mainly based on the *Merry Wives*, it is curious that Elgar made no reference to it. Boito makes use of half-a-dozen passages from *Henry IV* and in design and characterization his libretto is far superior to *The Merry Wives*; Verdi's music, for all its merriment, brims over with tenderness for middle-aged folly and young love. It is just conceivable that Elgar had not seen the opera since, though it reached Covent Garden in 1894, the year after the Milan production, it was not revived there until 1914. There were, however, student performances at the RCM, Stanford having been at the premiere and written enthusiastically about it.

The earliest authority Elgar quotes in his Analysis is Maurice Morgann (1726–1802) whose famous *Essay on the Dramatic Character of Sir John Falstaff* was published in 1777 and reprinted in 1903 and – perhaps significantly – in 1912. Morgann was Under-Secretary of State with a special knowledge of American affairs, which accounts for such charming excursions as 'When the hand of time shall have brushed off [Shakespeare's] present Editors and Commentators ... the Apalachian mountains, the banks of Ohio, and the plains of Sciota shall resound with [his] accents'. The passage where he breaks away from Falstaff into general praise of Shakespeare's comprehension and poetry is superb, and the essay as a whole casts its gloss on Elgar's letter to Newman already quoted: 'Falstaff is the word only, Shakespeare is the theme'.

The famous paragraph from Morgann quoted by Elgar beginning Falstaff 'is a character made up ... wholly of incongruities' had also been quoted by Elgar's second authority, Edward Dowden, in his *Shakspere – A Critical Study of his Mind and Art* (1875). At once the paragraph raises two points. 'Incongruities': 'want of accordance or harmony' – how can such a state best be indicated in music? For composers of Elgar's period accordance still meant obedience to, or at least reference to, the diatonic system. A glance at his Falstaff themes shows how many of them are characterized by ambiguities or by direct chromatic contradictions. The very first, because it is unharmonized, does not properly establish its C minor key, but is full of implications, of Falstaffian shifts of attitude (Example 2 i). Each complete bar could be parsed to belong to a different key: bar 1 in E flat major, bar 2 in C minor, bar 3 in G minor. A less twisting, less evasive, but of course far less interesting version, could have run as example 2 ii:

Ex.2

Falstaff 'cajoling' (ex 3 in Elgar's analysis) and Falstaff 'boasting' (ex 4) are equally prone to accidentals. Most significant of all is the singing Falstaff at Eastcheap (Elgar's ex 8), the chordal passage on lower strings and wind, where the first bassoon part, for instance, runs:

Ex.3

F♯, F♮, F♯, F♮, G♯, G♮, E♮, F, G♯, G♮, G♯, G♮, A♯, A♮, F♯, G

A series of contradictions indeed! '... a man at once young and old, enterprising and fat, a dupe and a wit, harmless and wicked ...'

The second point that Morgann's paragraph raises is Elgar's treatment of the final sentence: '... a knight, a gentleman and a soldier, without either dignity, decency or honour'. Morgann's whole essay is a vindication of Falstaff's courage and was directed against the ignominious clowning he received on the eighteenth-century stage. He makes out a case that though Falstaff's actions appear cowardly, cowardice was not an essential part of his constitution. He draws a distinction between Impression and the Understanding, and declares that 'cowardice is not the impression which the whole character of Falstaff is calculated to make on the minds of an unprejudiced audience'. Elgar seems to accept this, and he repeats Morgann's 'knight, gentleman, soldier', but this time without the qualifying lack of dignity, decency, honour. Another example of Elgar's possibly unconscious suppression or misleading interpretation occurs in the final sentence of his Analytical Essay: 'Sir John Falstaff with his companions might well have said, as we may well say now, "We play fools with the time, and the spirits of the Wise sit in the clouds and mock us"'. But it was not Falstaff who spoke this, it was the Prince (II *Henry IV*, II,ii).

How then did Elgar see Falstaff? There was in Elgar a little part, as there was a large part in Falstaff, that kicked against convention. It comes out in Elgar's love of japes, in his punning letters to Jaeger and his occasional outrageous or cutting remarks. Not for nothing did he once contemplate a 'Rabelais' ballet. Rosa Burley noted how much more at ease he was abroad, away from the conventions of a society where he had to keep his place. 'Why', he had said one day, 'can't one live this free and happy life in England?' 'Why', she had asked herself, 'had the Genius been so much happier in Munich than in Malvern?' For *Falstaff*, Elgar quoted Dowden: 'From the coldness, the caution, the convention of his father's court ... Henry escapes to the teeming vitality of the London streets, and the Tavern where Falstaff is monarch'.

The parallel must not be pressed. Shakespeare's Falstaff was the heir to a long and mixed tradition. He has been seen as the Roman *miles gloriosus*, Plautus' bragging soldier. He also inherits his part from the morality plays where Vice, Vanity and Riot have their allowed place, with the functions and attributes of the Lord of Misrule and the Jester. The alluring old rascal provided an emotional and vicarious release for the disreputable side of everyone's nature; but his subversive effect was contained safely on the stage and his traditional end was under the Rule of Law.

This was the side of Falstaff that Morgann played down and romanticized and Elgar romanticized further. Tovey remarked that Elgar's Falstaff was composed 'entirely from Falstaff's own point of view'. It certainly is a partial point of view. 'The feeling of pleasantry which runs through the dialogue is almost courtly', writes Elgar of the opening scene between the Prince and Falstaff. 'Prince Henry apostrophises him as "Thou latter spring! All-Hallown summer!"'. Yes, but also as 'fat-witted with drinking of old sack'.

Elgar had of course to select from *Henry IV*, cutting here, expanding there. Absolute fidelity is not only impossible in moving from one medium to another but is no more automatically to be praised than is suppression of details or episodes. He used much the method he had in selecting from the Gospels to make his own *Apostles*. There he took a hint from the single sentence 'and continued all night in prayer to God' and expanded it into a nocturne. Here he takes a hint from Shallow's reminiscence 'Then was Jack Falstaff, now Sir John, a boy and page to Thomas Mowbray, Duke of Norfolk', and composed his delectable Dream Interlude. Similarly Boito gave 'Quand' ero paggio del Duca di Norfolk' to Verdi, who made it into one of the tiniest, freshest arias ever composed.

Holst in his opera *'At the Boar's Head'* (1924) covered almost the same ground as Elgar in the Eastcheap scenes. Since the one work uses words, the other not, comparisons must be made cautiously. But it is worth considering the means used by the two men to achieve Englishness. Elgar's music was wholly original ('I write the folktunes of this country!'). Holst, composing eleven years later, acknowledged nearly 40 old English melodies borrowed from the Playford, Chapell, Sharp and Gardiner collections. (Vaughan Williams, too, sought to make a peculiarly English opera combining his love of Elizabethan drama and of folksong, but *Sir John in Love* is based on *The Merry Wives* and so not strictly relevant. In any case, *Riders to the Sea* would make a musically more pertinent comparison with *At the Boar's Head*.)

Elgar gains sympathy for Falstaff by giving him tender, idyllic interludes. Holst on the other hand gains it for the Prince by setting the monologue which ends 'Redeeming time when men least think I will' and also by giving him two of Shakespeare's reflective 'time' sonnets. These lyrical passages are the most moving, the most poetic in Holst's score and tip the balance well towards the Prince. One point is apparently taken neither by Elgar nor by Holst, but is by Robert Nye in his extraordinary imagined autobiography, *Falstaff*[3]. Falstaff's famous 'Banish plump Jack, and banish all the world!' is answered by the Prince 'I do, I will!' In stage productions, as in Holst's opera, this is usually covered by Bardolph's precipitous entry. Robert Nye, on the other hand, sees it as foretelling the end: 'That eagle in his eyes was suddenly as cold as death, and I was the only person in the *Boar's* Head Tavern who heard him say, the future King of England, Henry the Fifth: *'I do, I will'*. In Nye's novel, it is *that* thunderbolt that knocked out Falstaff's wits, so that, worn out, he fell asleep behind the arras.

From then on, not one of Nye's readers would be unprepared for the eventual rejection of Falstaff by the Prince. Indeed, even that phrase, 'The Rejection of Falstaff', title of A C Bradley's essay, might seem as misleadingly pathetic as it would have seemed to Shakespeare's audience. For all that his learning has been praised (or caused a raised eyebrow) Elgar nowhere quotes Dr Johnson, whose estimate of Prince Henry was that 'the character is great, original and just'. Of Falstaff, Johnson concludes, 'No man is more dangerous than he that, with a will to corrupt, hath the power to please; and that neither wit nor honesty ought to think themselves safe with such a companion when they see Henry seduced by Falstaff'. For the essence of Falstaff as Lord of Misrule was that his reign must have an end, that when the reformed Prince became King he must side with Law, and the audience would accept the 'rejection' as both just and inevitable. In Elgar's *Falstaff* the person of the Prince has to carry the weight of the Lord Chief Justice, and 'we are shown', says Elgar, 'the inevitable degradation down to the squalid end'. But nothing in Elgar's music shows us, as Shakespeare does in Part II of *Henry IV*, that gradually, while Falstaff is over-reaching himself and becoming bumptious, the prince is growing into kingship and authority.

> I could have better spared a better man.
> O, I should have a heavy miss of thee,
> If I were much in love with vanity!

mourns Prince Henry earlier at Shrewsbury, thinking Falstaff dead. The first line is more often quoted than the following two, but they reveal the Prince's changing heart and mind.

In his Birmingham lectures Elgar had declared that the symphony without a programme was the highest development of art. This provoked Ernest Newman into asking why, if Elgar rated absolute above descriptive music, he himself had composed so much in a medium that his judgment condemned. At the time there was general, continuing controversy over such things and a belief that there was something inferior, even improper, about descriptive music. Towards *Falstaff*, then, Elgar's attitude was naturally mixed. He was careful not to call it a symphonic or tone poem, but a 'symphonic study' (the word study to be taken 'in its literary use or meaning'). He defensively pointed out 'it must not be imagined that my orchestral poem is programme music; that it provides a series of incidents with connecting links' such as in Strauss's *Ein Heldenleben* or *Domestic Symphony*. 'Nothing has been farther from my intention. All I have striven to do is to paint a musical portrait, or rather, a sketch portrait.'

Yet Tovey had written his analysis without reading Elgar's own and on only one significant point did they differ. Nearly all Elgar's 'corrections', which Tovey footnotes, are more precise, more specific than Tovey's guesses. In *Falstaff* things happen. Incidents of dramatic sequence are paralleled in musical sequence. The music lasts as long as a Mozart symphony and is full of changes and contrasts. So the study is *not* a portrait, not a timeless reflection of a man's qualities such as Nimrod's in the *Variations*, or Hans Sachs's in *Die Meistersinger* Act III prelude. Falstaff is not the same man at the end as he was at the beginning. Elgar's *Falstaff* is remarkable just because it combines portraiture and narrative in symphonically developing music which, in my opinion at any rate, deeply satisfies several opposing criteria at once.

The important point at which Tovey misread Elgar's intentions is not a matter of action but of sentiment. The theme referred to as example 3 was described by Tovey as 'blown up like a bladder with sighing and grief'. 'Not at all!', responded Elgar. 'A goodly, portly man, of a cheerful look, a pleasing eye and a most noble carriage.' Such a misunderstanding is fundamental. For all that Elgar was attracted to Falstaff the libertine, the liberator from convention, he himself could only go so far. He could choose to identify himself creatively with a character of gusto, liberality and lawlessness, but only by idealizing him. He was after all not writing a thesis on Shakespeare's Falstaff but composing an original work. If there is as much Elgar as Falstaff in it, it has total consistency; if it is subjective, it is emotionally authentic. It ranks with Verdi's *Otello* and *Falstaff* and Britten's *Dream*.

'... the undercurrent of our failings & sorrows.' Elgar gives a variant of that theme (example 1) as the dying Falstaff's final thought:

Ex.4

No longer a counterpoint, but at the last a prime, expressive melody, serenely accepted. So in his own way Elgar gives the old rascal a philosophical depth and craves our compassion.

Notes

1. Elgar, Edward, *Falstaff*. Analytical note. *Musical Times*, September 1913, p. 575.
2. Tovey, Donald F, *Falstaff*. Analytical note in *Essays in Musical Analysis*, Vol. IV (London, 1937).
3. Nye, Robert, *Falstaff* (London, 1976).

8 Elgar and the wonderful stranger: music for *The Starlight Express*

K E L Simmons

Take your seats for The Starlight Express!

Take your seats!
The Starlight Express is off to Fairyland.

Take your seats!
First stop the Milky Way.

Take your seats!
Or stay at home for ever.[1]

I

We all have our Fairylands, a state of mind we need to find, a goal we hope to achieve, an Ideal Place or Happy Otherworld where we long to go: the Land of Lost Content, Shangri-La, Where the Rainbow Ends, Deamland, Paradise . . . or the Neverland of Childhood and the nostalgia for the 'Before Times'. We are not willing 'to stay at home for ever'. Art comes to aid us at times, words and music especially, helped by our own imagination and sensitivity, our 'transport to the stars'.

For many, one or other of the great works of Elgar 'satisfies the longing soul' in such a special way but I know of none more potent, when the mood is right, than the music he wrote for *The Starlight Express*, a fantasy play by Algernon Blackwood and Violet A Pearn produced by Lena Ashwell at The Kingsway Theatre, London, during the post-Christmas period of 1915–16. Indeed, a distinct subspecies of Elgarian man has evolved in recent years over which this score has cast a particular and increasingly powerful spell.

142

We Starlighters hold a 'neglected child' kind of affection for the music having come to know it only in stages over many years. We want to know more about it and the play it was written to enhance.

The score, like those of the majority of Elgar's works for the stage, has never been published (only three songs with piano and a pianoforte suite of six movements[2]) and the full stature of the music was not revealed until a radio version of the play was broadcast in 1965 and 1968.[3] The original play was not published either and there have been no performances of it in the theatre since that first run at The Kingsway over seventy years ago. Nor does a definitive text appear to have survived.[4] So the full story-line remains obscure and exactly how the music fits into the structure of the play is still a closed book, to Elgarians as much as to others. As this last problem was not resolved when the first recording of the entire score appeared in 1976,[5] I set out on the track of *The Starlight Express* to try to discover its full history and answer some of the many questions that had remained obscure for so long.

The search for the story of *The Starlight Express*, both play and music, has been wide-ranging and my investigations have led me, by way of a large correspondence and literature and archive research,[6] in all sorts of unexpected and fascinating directions. Set against the background of The Great War – and of troop entertainment, women's suffrage, the peace movement, the theatre in London and the provinces (especially in the period 1913–18), the phenomenon of the matinée success through the medium of the fantasy play, and the early years of broadcasting – a web of complex inter-relationships has been revealed which touches on the lives, friendships, loves, sorrows, deaths, bereavements, work, disputes and collaborations of a host of people, not least amongst them those 'Prisoners in Childhood' Edward Elgar and Algernon Blackwood.

So absorbing was this story that, when my friend Raymond Monk asked me to write an account of it for his collection of *Elgar Studies*, I accepted with pleasure, cleared my desk and set to work. The subject then took me over again and stimulated further research so that, seven months and some 80,000 words later, I found I had drafted three-quarters of a book instead of the intended paper of modest proportions. As my own strong creative instinct was to expand the story still further, especially on the theatrical side, the time had obviously come for stock-taking.

The present essay, therefore, is limited mainly to the history of the composition of Elgar's music for *The Starlight Express* and the events leading to it, Elgar and Blackwood being the main protagonists. The bulk of the account is adapted from the chapter (here section III) called 'Elgar and The Wonderful Stranger: Preparations for The Kingsway Production' in the longer MS,[7] topped by an introduction (section I) and a linking digest (II) and tailed by a postscript (4). I am only too aware, however, that in restricting my scope thus I am doing less than justice to other key figures and topics of the full story but I hope to redress this imbalance elsewhere. In the Appendixes, however, I have given a descriptive analysis of the score and a summary of the action of the play with the music cues indicated; thus, those with a copy of the 1976 recording can, for the first time, follow the latter with a good idea of what is really happening when the music plays.

After their first meeting in November 1915, at the inception of The Kingsway Theatre production, Elgar and Blackwood became firm friends bound by the mutual attraction of personality, an enduring affinity of mind, and a number of common interests. 'Dreamers of Dreams', each had (quite independently and at about the same time) used O'Shaughnessy's *Ode* in one of his creations, Elgar setting the whole poem as *The Music Makers*, first performed in 1912 but started several years earlier, and Blackwood quoting its first verse in his powerful novel *The Centaur* of 1911. Elgar, in effect, became Blackwood's 'Music-maker' in the writer's first theatrical venture. So it is to Elgar as man of the theatre that we will turn first as a means of further introduction to the history of *The Starlight Express*.

The Stage, that world of make-believe and truth, was certainly one of Elgar's Fairylands. He had first entered it as a small boy in Worcester in the local theatre and music-hall and at home above the family music shop, encouraged by his father's handyman Ned Spiers who had once worked as a carpenter in a number of itinerant theatrical troupes. But it was for a magical allegorical play with music, devised with his brothers and sisters when he was twelve or so, that Elgar's own creative genius found its first tentative expression.

Set in another Fairyland, the Worcestershire countryside near his humble birthplace cottage at Broadheath where the Elgar children would go for visits and holidays, the play also had its own Fairyland of Youth: the 'hither side' of a woodland glade intersected by a brook where ordinary life could be forgotten and where those entering it were transfigured by 'that fairy feeling necessary for their well-being'. The misunderstood children tried thus to influence their parents (the despotic 'Old People'), first by luring them with The Little Bells across the bridge that separated the two worlds, then by sending The Fairy Pipers to charm them to sleep.[8]

Elgar never forgot his early music for this play and, in 1907 and 1908, arranged it (as his Opus 1) into two orchestral suites of seven and six movements, *The Wand of Youth*, the creation of childhood transfigured by the magic hand of its adult Music-maker. Subtitled 'Music to a Child's Play', this lovable work was dedicated to two West Country friends of youth (C Lee Williams and Hubert A Leicester).

Though the music of that unperformed play of youth survived, the words were gone for ever and not until he was an old man did Elgar return to a marriage of his own-selected words and music for the stage in an opera,

The Spanish Lady, adapted (with the help of Barry Jackson) from a comedy by Ben Jonson. He worked conscientiously but fitfully on his score but it was far from finished when illness and death finally intervened. So, like his childhood play, Elgar's opera never trod the boards.[9]

An opera by Elgar had been the dream of many music-lovers from at least the days of *The Dream of Gerontius* onwards but none of the many suggestions for operatic ventures he received came to fruition, due as much to his own dissatisfaction with the unsuitability of what he was offered as to the unfavourable musical climate of the time. After he had served most successfully in 1901 as Music-maker for the now largely forgotten play *Diarmuid and Grania* by those 'literary lunatics' George Moore and WB Yeats, he was pursued with great determination by Moore who was obsessed with the idea of a Wagnerian opera by Elgar and wanted to collaborate with him on it.[10]

Other playwrights and librettists also approached Elgar unsuccessfully with operatic ideas, including Laurence Binyon, Sir W H Gilbert, and the Duke of Argyll. There were further theatrical carrots dangled before him too, not least by Thomas Hardy[11], Sir Herbert Beerbohm Tree, and most persistently by Harley Granville-Barker (one of whose schemes involved the poet Laurence Housman and another that consummate dramatist Sir James Barrie). But all was to no avail and, until the advent of The Great War, Elgar accepted only one other commission for the stage, music for the masque *The Crown of India* put on at The Coliseum in 1912.

If none of Laurence Binyon's operatic schemes appealed to the composer, Elgar did eventually reward him handsomely by electing to set three of his celebrated wartime poems unforgettably in the last of the great Elgarian choral works with orchestra, *The Spirit of England* of 1915–17. Later, in 1923 during that creatively arid period after the death of his wife, Elgar also provided, against all the odds, music commissioned for Binyon's play *Arthur: a Tragedy*. Binyon had been Alice Elgar's friend too and that may well have tipped the balance. In those earlier unhappy years as a widower, Elgar increasingly sought solace in the theatre rather than the concert hall and made many friends among actors and others connected with the stage. So it is perhaps not surprising that he was also persuaded, in 1928, to be the Music-maker for one last play, Bertram P Matthews's *Beau Brummel*, though probably again largely out of a feeling of fellowship, this time for the actor-manager Gerald Lawrence.

Many years earlier, in 1914 a few months before the outbreak of The Great War, Elgar had refused a request from the writer and critic Robert Hichens to provide incidental music for a new production of the melodrama *The Garden of Allah* that Hichens had adapted from his novel of the same name in collaboration with Mary Anderson.[12] Yet, if we count the three works for reciter and orchestra *Carillon* (1914), *Une Voix dans le Désert* (1915) and

Le Drapeau Belge (1917), it was during the war that Elgar produced the majority of his stage works including, as well as the orchestral songs *The Fringes of the Fleet* (1917) and the ballet *The Sanguine Fan* (1917), the music for the play *The Starlight Express* (1915), his largest score for the theatre. This, as we have seen, was another work of friendship and it is to Algernon Henry Blackwood, the first link in the chain of its creation, that we must turn next.

II

Elgar and Blackwood could hardly have differed more in their family backgrounds. Born on 14 March 1869 at The Wood Lodge, Shooters' Hill, Kent (and so nearly twelve years Elgar's junior), Algernon was the second son of Stevenson Arthur Blackwood Esq (later Sir Arthur Blackwood KCB) and of Sidney the dowager Duchess of Manchester, the young widow of the sixth Duke. Then a civil servant at the Treasury, Blackwood senior rose to be the permanent Chief Secretary of the General Post Office and was knighted in the Jubilee Honours of 1887. The family was quite large, the Blackwoods producing three girls and two boys of their own in addition to the Duchess's son and daughter by her previous marriage.[1]

The boy Algernon was educated by tutors at home, at a series of private schools and at Wellington College. He also studied abroad in France and in Switzerland and later spent eighteen months at the Moravian Brotherhood School in the Black Forest before finishing up, after further tutoring, at Edinburgh University. His year's stay (when he was seventeen) in the Swiss Jura Mountains at Bôle near Neuchatel to perfect his French was to have a lasting effect on him.

Algernon spent his childhood (from the age of three) at the Manor House at Crayford, Kent, and his youth (from twelve to twenty-one) at Shortlands House near Beckenham. So his Victorian boyhood was one of relative affluence, large houses in their own grounds, servants, nannies, governesses, tutors, gardeners, home-schoolrooms and night-nurseries and also, no doubt, of visiting chimney sweeps and passing lamplighters, tramps and gipsies. In many ways, these were ideal years in ideal settings but there was one serious drawback which had a profound effect on such an imaginative, sensitive and introspective person as Algernon Blackwood.

His father, following his experiences as a volunteer officer in the Crimea campaign and the death (in 1856) of his beloved younger sister 'Ceci', had undergone a sudden and overwhelming religious conversion which utterly changed his life. Still only twenty-four, he was 'called to the Lord' in no uncertain way and spent the rest of his days in active and obsessive Evangelism, faithfully supported by his wife after their marriage in 1858.

The life of the Blackwood family revolved almost entirely round this crusade, which cut off its members 'from the amenities of the social life to which they were otherwise born'.[2] Algernon and his siblings, having been 'kept out of the "world" in every possible sense', entered that world eventually as true innocents abroad.

Instead of the novels of the day, Foxe's *Book of Martyrs* and the works of Lewis Carroll, which their father read aloud, were the children's 'imaginative fiction'. Algernon's own personal delight, however, was found in Hebrew poetry, the Psalms, the Book of Solomon and (especially) the Book of Job, all of which moved him 'in a different way and far more deeply'.

Then, just after he returned from his religious and educational retreat in the Black Forest, pure chance led him to read certain forbidden books on eastern philosophy and religion. These were to give him other, totally new perspectives. His reading broadened and, coloured by the poetry of Shelley (another great love), fed his growing sense of wonder. He examined the ideas of spiritualism, theosophy and all aspects of the occult. Though tempered eventually by the balance of scientific reading, many of the beliefs engendered by that escape from Evangelism (including 'the theories of Karma and reincarnation', and the belief in extension of consciousness) remained with him in maturity and justified themselves.

In 1887, Algernon was allowed to accompany his father on a short, semi-official trip to Canada and the United States. The visit to America was a turning point in young Algernon's life for it was in The New World, he decided, that his future lay. Three years later, after taking a short agricultural course at university, he left for Canada to seek his fortune. On 18 April 1890, barely a month after his twenty-first birthday, Sir Arthur saw his wayward son off from Euston; never were they to meet again for, by the time Algernon returned to England a decade later, his father had been dead for seven years. With an allowance, a small capital sum and 'a unique ignorance of life', young Blackwood arrived in Toronto, the following precious possessions in his baggage: a fiddle, the *Bhagavad-gita*, the poems of Shelley, Carlyle's *Sartor Resartus*, Berkeley's *Dialogues*, Patanjalli's *Yoga Aphorisms* and de Quincey's *Confessions*.

The years in America were Blackwood's real education in life. There he grew up and lost his innocence, together with his trust in the essential goodness of mankind. A rolling stone, he took a variety of jobs, pursued unsuccessful business ventures, was swindled out of his money, resorted to spells of teaching (the violin, French, German and shorthand), and underwent many character-forming adventures and humiliations.

Blackwood finished up eventually in New York where his fortunes fluctuated widely, mostly for the worse. Living hand-to-mouth and beset with poverty, he often faced near starvation, even posing as an artist's model and taking a one-line acting job, very briefly, in a third-rate touring company to earn a few dollars. The pawn-shop played a vital role in his economy. Eventually, after a prolonged and terrible stint as a crime-court reporter on an evening newspaper, a period of illness, and an interlude away in Ontario prospecting for gold, he landed a good job on *The New York Times* and finally a lucrative and satisfying post as personal secretary to the financier and philanthropist James Speyer, brother of Sir Edgar Speyer. He remained in Speyer's household until home-sickness finally drove him back to England in 1899 when he was on the brink of thirty.

There were three further early influences in Blackwood's life which his experiences in America strengthened: companionship, music and nature. The first of these, companionship, lies mostly outside the scope of the present account, though the importance of the part played by that procession of strange and wonderful, sometimes execrable, friends and acquaintances during his period of exile should never be underestimated. For one thing he was later to draw on their experiences using some of them as the basis of characters in his stories.

Even above companionship, however, Blackwood rated music, the importance of which as an influence on him has perhaps not yet been really appreciated by many Elgarians. When Blackwood left home in 1890, his beloved violin was the most important item packed and, during the difficult years which followed, that instrument (never pawned) was often his life-line to sanity and pleasure. In Toronto, with his friend Louis 'B' at the piano, he played Tchaikovsky, Chopin and Wagner, as well as Raff and the popular songs of the day. In New York he accompanied the tenor voice of his false-friend 'Boyde', who shared the squalid digs that Blackwood and his former partner John Kay occupied, and played old German songs to the morphine-addicted physician Otto Huebner, who had tended and befriended him. Huebner was also taken to chanting the hauntingly beautiful 'Invocation to Opium' passage from de Quincey's *Confessions* for which Blackwood invented 'a soft running accompaniment on the lower strings, using double stopping' with the mute on, adding a bass line with his own voice.

Though he attended concerts and organ recitals whenever he could, Blackwood found a greater and deeper delight in his own playing, preferably in the company of friends or alone out in the wilds, best of all under the stars and amongst the pine trees. Thus music and, at times, companionship were combined with the third, and even greater, of these seminal influences, 'Nature' with a capital 'n' – a pantheistic, intuitive, wholly unscientific love of which was, since the days of his Kentish childhood, the strongest sentiment in his life.

The return to England ended the education of Algernon Blackwood, the initial phase at any rate, because, for the curious and creative – and, above all, the self-taught – learning never really finishes. Like Elgar's, Blackwood's apprenticeship was long and difficult but there was a fundamental difference here between the two artists: whereas Elgar always knew what he wanted and was a musician from the start, Blackwood still (aged thirty) had no idea that he was destined to be a writer. In spite of his experiences as a reporter and feature writer in America, and an evidently intuitive and deeply entrenched ability as a story teller, he still had no literary ambitions at all and set about earning a new living, this time in the dried-milk business in London. However, fate would have it otherwise.

Back at his New York boarding house Blackwood had told strange stories for his friends; these imaginings, to his surprise, enthralled them. In London he continued with his tales but would write them down only for his own private amusement and delight – probably, he thought, to give expression to the accumulated horror of his harrowing experiences in New York, especially as a crime reporter. He also, in these years at the turn of the century, completed his first book, *Jimbo: a Fantasy*, expressly written for some children whom he had befriended at the time.[3] But still no thoughts of publication entered his mind until the intervention of an acquaintance he had made in New York – Angus Hamilton, a stepson of the dramatist Sir Arthur Pinero. Hamilton had been amongst the fascinated listeners to his stories there, and he now took it upon himself to show some of Blackwood's newly inscribed efforts to the publisher Eveleigh Nash.

Thus was the reluctant and self-doubting author launched. In 1906, the first collection of the tales of Algernon Blackwood appeared and by 1908 no less than three volumes were available to an increasingly appreciative readership. So it was by accident rather than design that Blackwood's reputation as a poetic teller of weird and macabre tales became established.

After the appearance of his third book, *John Silence: Physician Extraordinary*, Blackwood felt financially safe enough to abandon the dried-milk business for full-time writing. With a few possessions in a kit-bag he took himself, his typewriter and his precious new-found liberty off to The Jura Mountains – back indeed to Bôle itself, the village of his youth – where, he said, 'at frs. 4.50 a day, I lived in reasonable comfort and wrote more books'. Though he did not know it at the time, Blackwood had finally got on to the track of *The Starlight Express*.

In the eleven years or so that followed Blackwood, commuting between his Jura dreamland and London (where he lived in suburban lodgings but enjoyed the central amenities of The Savile Club), published three further collections of stories and seven novels. Three of the latter were of the now expected genre of the fantastic tale but the others all fall into a quite different category, that of the Blackwood 'novel-of-childhood'. One was *Jimbo*, published belatedly in 1909, but that lies rather outside the rest of the canon. The remaining three, which we may collectively call 'the Uncle-books', form its heart: *The Education of Uncle Paul* (1909), *A Prisoner in Fairyland* (1913) and *The Extra Day* (1915).[4]

Written about children they are not strictly speaking children's books at all but, rather, books for children of all ages. Coloured by his later adventures and experiences these all drew on Blackwood's memories and impressions of childhood. Each of the Uncle-books revolves about three children: an older girl ('Nixie'/'Jane Anne'/'Judy') and a younger boy ('Jonah' /'Jimbo'/'Tim') and a girl ('Toby'/'Monkey'/'Maria') and their parents. In all cases, however, the mother and father play a subsidiary role and, with one exception, lie partly or wholly outside the imaginative world of the children, the one perceptive, dream-focussing father having already died when the book, *Uncle Paul,* begins. So, to a certain extent, as in Elgar's cherished play of youth, there is a gulf of misunderstanding between the children and the figures of authority.

To some degree the children set about solving things in their own way but, in all three books, the vital role in unlocking the world of their fantasy is, paradoxically, played by a grown-up, always a man ('Uncle Paul'/'Cousin Henry'/'Uncle Felix'). Though a relative he is an outsider, a stranger to the children, a visitor. Having been taken prisoner by the youngsters this imaginative person (whose essential feature is that he retained or re-discovered many of his childhood characteristics, is still young-at-heart) gives a form or pattern to their dreams and fantasies. He is the real hero and it is his finding of himself, his fulfilment as he approaches middle age that is the core theme of the story.

In *Uncle Paul* (as in *Extra Day*) the visitor is a writer. Paul Rivers, a lumberman from Canada who had spent his boyhood in the gardens of Kent, returns to England and stays with his widowed sister and her children in their big old grey house that stands among pine-woods in the country. A lover of trees and wild places, he is a born story-teller but lacks confidence and an audience, finding both when the orphaned brood capture his sympathy and imagination, enrol him in their Secret Society and give him the task of writing down and reading out their 'aventures'. These take place in dreams, the first when they visit the sleeping winds in their nocturnal woodland resting place and meet 'The Little Winds' which depart last, dancing, when touched by the sun itself.

Paul and the children also explore 'The-Land-Between-Yesterday-and-To-morrow', entering initially through 'The Crack' between the two as they rush apart when To-day begins at midnight (everybody being thin somewhere, as Jonah says). This is a 'live-happily-ever-after' place, an enchanted garden where the harried spirit can take refuge, where lost things are found when you remember them, where ideals that have gone astray come to fruition, where hopes are renewed. This mystical haven, or state of mind, comes to mean more and more to Uncle Paul, especially after the death of the older girl, the wonderfully imaginative, endearing, and sprite-like Nixie who, Paul comes to realise, had carried within her the essence of the ideal woman whom he will now never meet. Eventually he finds fulfilment in philanthropy working for the good of child waifs and strays in London, and in writing a book *Adventures of a Prisoner in Fairyland* for 'those myriad, faint, unhappy voices' of the world's neglected children. It becomes a success and 'may now be found upon the table of every house in England where there dwells a true child seven or seventy'.

If in *Uncle Paul* our hero remained a bachelor, in *Prisoner* he finds his long-awaited soul-mate in the end – the whole book, in fact, being one big karmic love story, though The Countess (its amber-eyed heroine) does not appear in person until the very last few of its five-hundred pages. This time the visitor, Henry Rogers, is a London businessman who has retired early in order to put his money to good philanthrophic use in some scheme or other. The details, however, are far from clear in his mind because, like most of the other adults in the story, he is (in this one respect at any rate) 'wumbled' – Blackwood's coined word for a state of muddle, uncertainty, and frustration.

While hatching his schemes, Henry is reminded (quite by chance and for the first time in many years, as the spring sunshine in all its morning splendour pours through the window of his flat) of his boyhood. Then in the newspaper the name of the Kentish village in which he had lived in childhood and youth,'Crayfield,' happens to catch his eye. On the spur of the moment he decides to go there. Inexorably he is being drawn into some fateful process lying beyond his own control.

Alighting at the railway station, Henry leaves the village behind at the churchyard and walks towards The Manor House. At the old square grey house, on the lawns where he had once chased butterflies, he sees the night-nursery window from which he had once netted stars. His reveries are interrupted by his old tutor, the local Vicar, through whom, then and later, further childhood memories are stirred. Alone again as dusk falls, Henry explores the house and, finally, the garden. As he steps out on to the lawn,

> he knew suddenly that he was not alone, but that shadowy figures hid everywhere, watching, waiting, wondering like himself. They trooped after him, invisible and silent, as he went about the old familiar garden, finding nothing changed . . . *'He has come back!'*[5]

As he passes down the dark tunnel of lime-trees in The Long Walk more figures slip out of the house and join the others.

> Then suddenly, looming against the field that held the Gravel-Pit and the sleeping rabbits, he saw the outline of the Third Class Railway Carriage his father bought as a Christmas present, still standing on the stone supports

that were borrowed from a haystack ... That Railway Carriage had filled whole years with joy and wonder. They had called it the Starlight Express ... It looked mysterious, old, and enormous as ever ... The memory of the thrilling journeys he had made in this Starlight Express completed his recapture, for he knew now who the troop of Presences all about him really were ...

They are The Sprites, his sprites, the everyday figures of a Victorian childhood transformed by imagination into fantastic creatures of the night, the passengers of The Starlight Express now waiting his return. He steps out of the trees, doffing his hat like a signal flag, and utters the long-awaited invitation which brings them back into full consciousness:-

Take your seats ... for the Starlight Express. Take your seats! No luggage allowed! Animals free! Passengers with special tickets may drive the engine in their turn! First stop the Milky Way for hot refreshments! Take your seats, or stay at home for ever!

A hoard of travellers, animals and people rush for the train, all showing their tickets to The Blue-eyed Guard, her glance being the passport.

Of course, he remembered now – both guard and engine-driver were obliged to have blue eyes. Blue eyes furnished the motor-power and scenery and everything. It was the spell that managed the whole business – the Spell of the Big Blue eyes – blue, the colour of youth and distance, of sky and summer flowers, of childhood.

Among those getting into the train Henry recognises The Tramp, The Lamplighter, The Sweep, The Gypsy, The Woman-of-the-Haystack, The Laugher, The Head Gardener and The Dustman. Seeing them he remembers The Star Cave where they stored lost starlight at night for later use in 'un-wumbling'. He himself had never actually found it though, for The Interfering Sun had always risen too early and spoilt things as The Morning Spiders flew over the fields at dawn on their threads of gossamer and fairy cotton.

As Henry jumps into the train too, it starts off on its journey, rising quickly to a tremendous height. Prompted by The Blue-eyed Guard he directs its course to The Star Cave. Asked for a precise locality the name of Bourcelles a little village in The Jura flashes into his mind, probably because of its associations (mountains, caves, and children) and because, only that morning, he had received a letter from his cousin John Campden with whom he had spent a year learning French there many years ago. Campden and his family now live at Bourcelles where he writes books. Waking from his day-dream Henry decides to visit the children at Bourcelles.

Without realizing it, he has started a process which, with the children's co-operation and that of The Sprites, will bring fulfilment to their parents and others, not least to himself. The rest of the book, set mostly at Bourcelles, deals with this transformation. In helping others

Henry unwittingly helps himself, meeting his soul-mate in the end, a mysterious and anonymous noblewoman. But, it transpires, it is she, The Countess, who has been the instigator of all the wonders from the time of their childhood, she who set up The Net of Stars and 'thought-alive' The Sprites. She, in her spirit, had been seeking him for all those years, trying to establish contact, haunting him with a vision of her amber eyes. Thus it is that Orion finally catches his lost Pleiad.

The 'Bourcelles' of *Prisoner* is, of course, Bôle itself (which Blackwood, like Henry Rogers, first visited to learn French) and some of the people he met at Bôle found their way into the novel. The shadowy figure of The Countess, however, is based on the woman who was its dedicatee and inspiration: the mysterious 'M.S.-K.', his real soul-mate and dear friend, who had broken his heart by marrying someone else, a baron.[6] Thus, The Baroness of true life, who called herself 'Maya', was Blackwood's own lost Pleiad ('Maia', of course, being the eldest and fairest of the Pleiades, daughter of Atlas and the mother of Hermes). It is in *Prisoner*, too, that The Starlight Express makes its appearance and who can doubt but that an old third-class railway carriage was among the objects of interest that Sir Arthur Blackwood was known to have installed in his garden at Crayford ('Crayfield') for the pleasure of his children?[7]

Nothing further would have been heard of that magical train if Blackwood had been left to his own devices but now fate intervened again when, shortly after the appearance of *Prisoner* in 1913, someone wrote to him out of the blue and asked for permission to use the novel as the basis of a play.[8] It is to this person, the second link in the chain of creation leading to *The Starlight Express*, that we turn now. So, enter Miss Violet Alice Pearn, dramatist.[9]

Born in 1880 in Portsmouth, Violet Pearn was eleven years Blackwood's junior. With her lifelong companion Gertrude Pratt and a gang of huge dogs she lived at St Michael's Cottage in Guildford, Surrey, on The Mount, a hill out of the town. As well as dogs the two ladies adored children and Violet put on plays for them to take part in locally. In 1913, when she wrote to Blackwood, Violet was on the threshold of a career in the theatre as a playwright. That year (when she was thirty-three and thus, like Blackwood and Elgar, rather a late-starter) Violet had won a competition for amateurs in *The Era*. She had already written two successful books before trying her hand at plays, her very first effort *Mountain Lights* being set in Wales. Then came her prize-winner, *The Minotaur*, and recently she had completed yet another play, *Wild Birds*, set in her native county of Devon and spoken in a modified version of the local dialect, which she hoped would be put on by a leading London manager.

In 1913, Violet was now also busy with her new Algernon Blackwood play 'By Starlight Express to Fairyland', as she then called it. Quite bowled over by his *Prisoner* novel, she worked quickly and soon had a synopsis ready to send him. As the book was too big and complex to use all its themes and events, dreadful decisions had to be made on what should go in and what should be left out. It was soon settled that the story would be set entirely in Bourcelles and concentrate on the Campden family and the visit that Cousin Henry makes to them. The love story was to be jettisoned, so no countess. But all The Sprites were in: The Dustman, The Sweep, The Head Gardener, The Lamplighter, The Tramp and The Gypsy, The Laugher, and The Woman-of-the-Haystack — with The Little Winds (imported from *Uncle Paul*) to blow her along.

There was also to be another mystical figure: accompanied by a troop of London street-urchins who dance to his music, this is The Organ-Grinder, a character not found in any of the Uncle-books. A kind of super-sprite, yet perhaps not a sprite at all, he is in some way a replacement for The Countess as the puppet-master of events. This concept, however, was slow to develop and never quite matured; lying increasingly outside the action, The Organ-Grinder eventually became the musical interlocutor of the play, introducing each act with his song.

The focus of interest, now that Cousin Henry was no longer really the hero, shifted to the people in Bourcelles. These included the English family living in 'The Den': the two younger children ('Monkey' and 'Jimbo', who believe they get 'OUT' of their bodies at night and go travelling amongst the stars), their elder sister (Jane Anne or 'Jinny', who gets 'OUT' but does not know it), and their 'wumbled' parents — Daddy (an author who cannot find his inspiration) and Mother (a housewife who is overwhelmed by drudgery and worry). And there were to be 'wumbled' neighbours too, all of whom live at the 'Pension Wistaria': the proprietoress, Madame Jequier (an amusing Swiss widow who is desperately worried about her establishment which now faces bankruptcy); Miss Waghorn (an old lady who has lost her memory and is always looking for her long-dead brother and friends); and The Three Retired Governesses (who have come home to die). The solving of the 'wumbled' adults' problems, particularly Daddy's, through the induction of sympathy (symbolised by 'Star-dust' which gets them 'OUT'), became the main theme of the play, the 'un-wumblers' being the children, Henry, The Sprites, and The Organ-Grinder. And, in keeping with her strong Christian beliefs, Violet introduced a quasi-religious ending in the finale linking everything with The Star of Bethlehem.

With Blackwood's advice and encouragement, Violet's work on the play progressed rapidly during 1913. Blackwood, who always maintained that he had no dramatic sense, was happy to leave things to her at first but they later decided that it would be a joint effort and they both worked on it, separately and together, exchanging many letters. Blackwood soon became a familiar visitor at the little terrace house in Guildford. He gave Violet the nickname

'Gingerbread' and signed his letters to her 'Uncle Paul' (the name by which he was known to his special friends).

Together they laboured away. The original four acts of Violet's draft were reduced to three. The first, which caused them much trouble (both then and later), was set in two scenes (both in The Den), the one during the morning as the family awaits the coming of Cousin Henry, the other later that afternoon when he arrives. They added another character 'Grannie' (Mrs Campden's mother), an embittered old lady who lives with Madame Jequier at the *pension* where she engages in a running feud with Miss Waghorn: and much light-hearted 'business' centred on the arrival of a large packing case (called 'The Magic Box' by the children) of old clothes and the distribution of these cast-offs amongst the family and their friends. The rest of the play followed Violet's outline closely: Act Two contained the night scenes set in the pine-forest and those of 'un-wumbling' back in the village; and Act Three the last scene in The Den and the dénouement back in the forest, where Daddy now finally finds his true inspiration.

More and more now, Blackwood was assuming the dominant role in the partnership and came to think of the play as primarily his.[10] But it was on Violet's contacts in the theatre, late in 1913, that they now drew in an attempt to have the play performed on the stage. What was needed was someone who would interest a theatre management in the idea and get backing for it; and a producer (director), a designer, a cast and a composer. Although Blackwood later maintained that music 'only emerged as quite an afterthought',[11] it was implicit in the whole conception from the start and an important ingredient, as Violet's draft instructions made clear:

> It is essential that the words of the songs should be heard,

she stressed; and for the finale,

> The music, which has now reached the carol 'Nowell, Nowell', proclaims whose Star has arisen again for the sake of the wumbled world.

For the required help Violet turned to an old friend, the actress Muriel Pratt, niece of her companion Gertrude, and she was not unforthcoming. Muriel, then at The Gaiety Theatre, Manchester, with the repertory company run by the legendary Annie Horniman, had recently decided to establish her own company and, in co-operation with her actor-director husband William Bridges-Adams, try her hand as a manager in repertory. Making plans for her new venture, she certainly had hopes of mounting her friend Violet's new Blackwood play as well as appearing in it (as Jane Anne).

As director, Muriel wanted Basil Dean, then an assistant producer with Sir Hubert Beerbohm Tree at His Majesty's Theatre, London, after a spell as the first director of The Repertory Theatre in Liverpool (where he had mounted, with great success, the fairy frolic *Fifinella* in December 1912). A former City clerk turned actor, he had been among the young men in the company at The Gaiety when Muriel was first there and was later destined to rise to great eminence in the theatre and films as a producer-manager-director, as well as in the field of troop entertainment in both world wars.[12]

Dean's duties were ill-defined but he soon landed a major chore as Tree's reader of new plays. It may well have been in this capacity that he saw the script of *The Starlight Express* in one of its earlier versions, perhaps then (late in 1913) being touted round The West End managements. With ambitions of his own as an independent producer of plays (if possible at his own art theatre in London where poetic drama would be given its head), Dean may have earmarked *Starlight* as his own (just as he had done with Flecker's *Hassan*, which had come under his hand in the autumn of 1913 and which he was trying to revise, as it was then far too long). More likely, however, it had been sent or given to him directly by his former Horniman colleague Muriel Pratt on behalf of her friend Violet Pearn.

Be all this as it may, Dean's interests and Muriel's coincided and they joined forces. Towards the end of 1913 Blackwood was able to write to his publishers (Macmillan) that the play he had recently written had 'been accepted next autumn by a London Theatre'.[13] Whether, in fact, matters were really so definitive, plans were far enough advanced early in 1914 for Dean to find a backer (Algernon Greig), arrange for a draft lease to be drawn up for a London theatre (The Savoy, no less), and think of commissioning music for *Starlight*. For this he turned to his friend Clive Carey, composer, singer, opera producer, and actor, who was later to have a distinguished musical and theatrical career at home and abroad (not least with the formidable Lilian Baylis at Sadler's Wells and as a vocal teacher with Elsie Morrison, Joan Sutherland, and David Ward among his pupils). Carey, then in his early thirties and already experienced both in the theatre and in writing music for it, accepted Basil Dean's invitation.[14]

Born in 1883, F C S Carey studied music at Cambridge University and, under Sir Hubert Parry, at The Royal College of Music in London. He had first gone to Cambridge as a boy-chorister returning in 1900 as an organ scholar at Clare College; then only seventeen, he divided his initial studies between London and Cambridge and already had 'something of a reputation as a singer, composer, pianist and conductor'.[15] In 1902, he first met and came under the strong influence of E J Dent (eventually Professor of Music there) who then held a fellowship at King's, the two becoming close and life-long friends. Edward Dent thought highly of Carey's gifts as a composer of song and music for the theatre and gave him critical advice and every encouragement.

In the years immediately following, though still a student, Carey was active in various musical ways at Cambridge and, in the autumn of 1906, he started post-graduate studies there. Although he also studied abroad (Germany, France, Italy) and was organist at Guy's Hospital, Cambridge became the centre of Carey's life and not inconsiderable achievements in the years up to The Great War, the single most important event being his historic production in 1911 of Mozart's *The Magic Flute* in Dent's new translation, with Carey singing the role of Papagano and Cyril Rootham conducting. These performances put the work back in the repertory and launched Edward Dent on his career, ably assisted by Carey, as the champion of opera in English.

Basil Dean first met Carey, and his pal C R C ('Bobby') Maltby, at Cambridge in 1910 when on tour there with Miss Horniman's Company and the three of them became firm friends. Maltby, the son of an archdeacon in Southwell (Nottinghamshire), and an Oxford man, later shared lodgings with Dean in London, being then obsessed in pursuing a career as a dancer, having been quite bowled over, like so many others, by the season of Russian ballet at Covent Garden in 1913. It was Carey and Maltby, Dean acknowledged, who helped him to appreciate the importance of music and rhythm in the theatre and in 1912 he had invited them both up to Liverpool to take part in *Fifinella*. This venture was particularly dear to his heart and his 'first real opportunity "to have a go"'[16] in the capacity which was to prove to be his real forte in the years to come.

Dean produced *Fifinella* again at Christmas 1913, not at Liverpool but back in Manchester (at the Gaiety), having managed to interest a young newcomer to his old Liverpool company to finance the revival. This was Algernon Grieg straight up from Oxford where (like Bobby Maltby earlier) he had belonged to the university dramatic society. Already he was keen to try his hand at theatrical management. Among the cast again were Clive Carey and Bobby Maltby. Edward Dent, journeying up to see his two friends, enjoyed himself immensely in Manchester 'in spite of the cold and the general horribleness of that city'.[17] Thus, in Manchester that December and January were the plans for a production of *Starlight* likely to have been settled. Like Clive Carey, Basil Dean was an obvious choice for the venture.

After the Manchester run, Carey and Maltby (using his stage name 'Robert Crighton') both threw in their lot with their friend Muriel Pratt and her infant repertory company which was due at The Theatre Royal, Bristol, for a short experimental season in May 1914. The visit met with such approval locally that the company was asked back again in September, with hopes of establishing itself permanently there.[18]

One of the highlights of the first Pratt season in Bristol was the *première* of Violet Pearn's four-act play *Wild Birds* − now transferred from London where Granville Barker was to have done it at The Kingsway Theatre (which he still had on lease from its proprietor Lena Ashwell). This, Violet's first big success, opened on the evening of Tuesday 19 May with Muriel as the ill-fated Janivred Gurney, a role especially written for her, and Clive Carey as the vagabond Zachary with whom Janivred falls in love: the two of them, both children of nature, being the 'wild birds' of the title.

Meanwhile back in London, Basil Dean, with plans for *Starlight* ticking over, was exceptionally busy. In April, he also found time to get married interrupting his continental honeymoon to pursue Flecker over the theatre rights of *Hassan*.[19] In June, after his return there was the first production of his play *The Love Cheats* to be faced. Later he and his new wife threw a flat-warming party for their friends, including Bobby Maltby. Wider forces, however, were already at work leading inexorably to The Great War and to changes in everybody's hopes and plans.

Soon after hostilities were declared in August, Dean (like Elgar) joined the special constabulary. Plans for *Starlight* were still alive, however, in New York as well as at home, for a copy of the play had been sent to The American Play Company. On 2 September 1914, Dean wrote to inquire after this and received disappointing news from Helen Tyler, the General Manager, who declared the play 'not practical'.[20] Whether, dispirited, Dean then decided to drop the idea is uncertain, but in October 1914 he cut himself off entirely from the world of the conventional theatre and enlisted in the army, thus effectively disappearing from our story.

The outbreak of war cast a temporary shadow over Muriel Pratt's plans for another season at The Theatre Royal in Bristol but it was soon decided locally that it should go ahead. All seemed set for a successful visit but Muriel, with no capital of her own and working on a week-by-week basis, was walking a financial tightrope. In spite of all their efforts attendances were not high enough and the money ran out, the season ending well before Christmas. Whether or not Muriel had had plans to put *The Starlight Express* on in Bristol at Christmas 1914 we shall probably never know (and it may always have been intended for London anyway) but, though hopes for a production remained into October, Dean's departure finally put an end to the project. What the Dean/Pratt production of *Starlight* would have been like with music by Carey, sets and costumes by George W Harris (Dean's genius of a designer), and the roles of Jane Anne, The Organ-Grinder and the Lamplighter taken by Muriel, Carey and Maltby respectively, we can only now guess.

No one, after Dean's departure, thought to tell Carey that *The Starlight Express* project had been abandoned and his music was no longer needed. In November 1914 Carey himself (though like Maltby at heart a pacifist) volunteered for the army, joining the RAMC. He had continued with his music for *The Starlight Express* since March, concentrating on the songs of which three survive (as his Opus 18): The Organ-Grinder's Song ('Oh! Children'), the Dustman's Song ('The busy Dustman'), and The Gardener's

Song ('Stars are seeding in the air').[21] Edward Dent had written to encourage him in August just after war was declared:-

> I hope you are going on with *The Starlight Express*. The song you showed me was really delightful. Don't chuck composition: I am sure you have real originality of your own in a certain genre.

And again in September:-

> I am glad that *The Starlight Express* is still running. I suppose the song about *Fraulein* will have to be altered to *Mademoiselle* now . . ..[22]

Meanwhile, Muriel Pratt had not given up her hopes of making her way in the theatre as a manager and producing her friend's *Starlight* play. In April 1915 she returned to Bristol and tried again to establish her company in permanent repertory there. Luck, however, was against her and by the end of May the company had disbanded for ever. Muriel retreated to her mother's home at Ewhurst in Surrey and by September was back on the London stage in a revival of *Hindle Wakes* at The Duke of York's, where its short run ended on 2 October.

By then, however, she had landed her next job and on 16 October opened at The Kingsway Theatre in the small part of Muriel Hudson in John Hasting Turner's play *Iris Intervenes*. With Muriel came her husband Bridges-Adams. He both acted in and directed the play while she also took on the job of stage manager for the production. The invitation had come from Lena Ashwell, the proprietor of The Kingsway who herself played the title role of Iris. She had visited Bristol in 1914 at the end of Muriel's first spell there with her company, when determined efforts were being made locally to find support for its return, and had addressed a public meeting on Muriel's behalf. It may have been then that she first heard of the plans for *The Starlight Express*, but in any case, would have learned that they had floundered when she and Muriel were working together in October 1915. It must have been during the run of *Iris Intervenes*, which continued until 20 November 1915, that Lena Ashwell decided to put on *Starlight* herself at her own theatre that Christmas.

In Lena Ashwell we find one of the great personalities of the English theatre. Born in 1872, she first decided on a singing career, studying for a while at The Royal Academy of Music in London, but gave this up for acting in 1891. By 1901 she was one of the most sought-after actresses on the London stage but in 1907 she changed course and became a theatrical manager, taking a 99-year lease on W S Penley's theatre in Great Queensway (off the High Holborn end of Kingsway). After refurbishing it and doing everything that could make it 'original, attractive, and full of well thought out individuality',[23] she renamed it 'The Kingsway Theatre' and launched out in repertory there in October. Music was to be a distinctive feature at her theatre. She recalled the result of this policy many years later:-

> The music was really beautiful. How could it be otherwise when such artists as Albert Sammons, Lionel Tertis, Eric Coates played for us, and Sir Thomas Beecham would be sitting in the orchestra? Everything was done by artists who loved their work.[24]

The venture at The Kingsway was not a lasting success, however, and the lease became a burden to her – even after her second marriage, to the distinguished surgeon Dr (later Sir) Henry Simson in 1908, had given her security – and she was forced at times, in those years of hard work and anxiety, to take acting engagements elsewhere and to let out her theatre to other managements in order to pay the rates and taxes. The final pinch came with The Great War when her normal theatre activities started to clash with the war-work on which her heart was set from the outset: organising cultural entertainment for the troops abroad. By late 1914, in spite of many obstacles, she managed to establish (under the auspices of The Women's Auxiliary Committee of the YMCA) her now famous 'Concerts at The Front' organisation consisting of actors, singers, dancers and musicians.

The first party had gone out in February 1915 and she herself, after a fund-raising matinée at The Coliseum, followed for a tour in March and again in June. Most of her time at home now, however, was spent in recruiting artists, organising the parties and raising funds. She was also making use of her theatre at times where 'business as usual' helped to boost public morale as well as bringing in some income to pay the bills. Also, as we have seen, plans were afoot by October or early November to put on *The Starlight Express* there ('as a piece of Red Cross work for the mind', she said, 'during the first agony of the war').[25]

Just what factor had attracted Lena Ashwell to this particular play is far from clear but a sympathetic feeling for Algernon Blackwood and his ideas must have played a part. Like Blackwood (and Elgar) she was certainly a 'dreamer of dreams', later quoting part of the O'Shaughnessy *Ode* in one of her books.[26] But in the closing months of 1915 dreams needed to be turned into reality and she had to assemble a cast of actors, dancers and singers. Though she may have been aware of Muriel Pratt's and even Basil Dean's preferences here, the choices were probably largely her own at this stage.[27] For some reason Muriel herself (Violet Pearn's approved 'Jane Anne') was excluded from the venture, a cause of lasting bitterness on her part.

To design the costumes and scenery Lena Ashwell obtained the services of the artist Henry Wilson who had recently taken over the presidency of The Arts and Crafts Society.[28] He appears to have had no previous experience of designing for the London stage but his assistant Stanley North had and to him fell the task of actually painting the sets. North was also responsible for the now well-known comet design that appeared as a symbol of *The*

Starlight Express itself on hand-bills, posters and other advertisements for the production, as well as later on the programme cover. The stage manager was R Wynne (assisted by Jane Wells, who also took the part of The Dustman) and the lighting electrician W E Siday; as business manager, Lena Ashwell brought back the former proprietor of the theatre Arthur Penley.

The choice of singers and dancers must have come at rather a later stage for the extent of the music for the production had still to be decided and seems to have been left, relatively speaking, almost to the last moment. As we have seen, music was important to Lena Ashwell and had been a speciality at The Kingsway since she took charge of that theatre. Now, in wartime, it assumed an even greater importance as became increasingly clear to her as her experience in troop entertainment grew. The laughter, the interest and the music were more than mere 'amusement', she said,

> to those armies of men ... out there − where life and death were stark realities, where life was swept bare of all artificialities and death was abroad, visible and undisguised − there, music, the straightest road to the unseen world of spiritual beauty, fulfilled more than its tangible function of cheering up the men, although that is 'a work of great military value' ...; it was more than food for their spirits, hungry for loveliness after the abnormal hideous experience of weariness or pain and tension. Music ministers with magical results to minds distressed, destroying the seeds of despondent thoughts, the black moods that dullness, pain, or loneliness sow in the most gallant hearts, for 'where music is, there can no ill thing be'.[29]

It must have been in this spirit that she sought a composer for *The Starlight Express* in war-torn London during the closing months of 1915. She consulted Algernon Blackwood who in turn sent her to his close friend and fellow member of The Savile Club, Robin H Legge, the music critic for *The Daily Telegraph* and a strong champion of the music of his friend Sir Edward Elgar.

Lena Ashwell knew the Elgars well but, even though she was using his *Chanson de Matin* (played by the Anzac Quartet along with pieces by Gounod, Rubinstein, Sullivan, Irving Berlin, and others) during the run of *Iris Intervenes*, it seems doubtful that she was aiming so high in her present search. However, with the approval of the backer, a Mr Phillipson, an approach to Elgar was agreed and Legge attempted to contact him by telephone at Severn House early on Wednesday, 9 November, barely seven weeks before the opening matinée, following it up with a letter from his home in Chelsea which reached Elgar later the same day after his return from a short visit to Leeds.

> My dear Elgar, I rang you this morning about an important matter with Lena Ashwell, who came down here to ask me to suggest a composer of incidental music with some chorus work for a play she wants to produce at Xmas. I of course 'went for' you tooth & nail. As you were not at home Miss Ashwell is going to write to you. The play is founded upon a story by her friend & mine,

Algernon Blackwood, & is one that I am sure will attract you. Most sincerely I hope you can see your way to undertaking the music. PLEASE do take it up if you like the play. We want something more from you now, & this is so beautiful a thing. Nobody else can do it as you can.[30]

The letter from Lena Ashwell, also written on 9 November, from her house in Grosvenor Street must have arrived close behind Legge's.

Very dear Sir Edward. Robin Legge has encouraged me to ask you if you would consider writing music for a play I hope to do at Christmas by Algernon Blackwood. The play is half reality and half fairyland & it is your help in fairyland I want so much. There is a great mystic quality in the play which I am sure will help people to bear the sorrows of the war, & the end is really wonderful in its beauty. Would you ring me up tonight & say if I may come to see you about it.

The rest of the initial story can be pieced together from the entries in Lady Elgar's diary.[31] Lena Ashwell called at Severn House the next day and showed Elgar the texts of the play and the songs ('very nice and interesting'), Elgar driving back into town with her at the end of her visit. On the 11th he and Alice attended the Thursday afternoon matinée of *Iris Intervenes*; taking tea with their hostess afterwards, her acting as well as one of the themes of the play (a husband's fidelity) meeting with Alice's approval. By this time Elgar was evidently warming to the possibility of taking on the task, spending much of Friday reading the script and lyrics and planning out how he might do the music. The next day his mind was made up and when Lena Ashwell called to learn his decision he agreed to provide the music for *The Starlight Express*. This might, he suggested, be specially composed for it or, in view of the rather short notice, be adapted from his *The Wand of Youth* suites. As a possible example he played her some of this music on the piano, moving her to tears.[32]

Thus did Algernon Blackwood find his Music-maker. Elgar told him later that he had been waiting a generation for just such a story to set.[33]

III

But on one man's soul it has broken,
A light that doth not depart;
And his look, or a word he has spoken,
Wrought flames in another man's heart.[1]

1915 had not been a happy year for Elgar. The war was going badly and the end of it was not in sight. Everything had not been over by Christmas 1914 as most people expected; indeed, events were proliferating with landings at Salonika and Galipoli and the campaign in Mesopotamia begun. There were huge losses on both The Western and Eastern Fronts and the Germans used poison-gas and flame-throwers for the first time. At sea the enemy

U-boats increased their deadly activity and sank *The Lusitania*. On The Home Front, with the increasing shortages and deprivations and the first Zeppelin raids on London, morale was low. Determined to be seen to be 'doing his bit', Elgar resigned as a special constable in February and joined the local Hampstead unit of The Volunteer Reserve, but his spirit, ever subject to periods of depression, was not really in this mock soldiering and he worked away on the war-music that was expected of him, mostly with a heavy heart.

The first months of the year had been spent, frustratingly, over the initial composition of *The Spirit of England*, a self-initiated project dear to Elgar which he had to leave unfinished out of consideration for Cyril Rootham who, he discovered, had already set Binyon's concluding poem of the cycle (*For the Fallen*). Elgar then started work on his Polish commission, *Polonia*, which he finished on the first day of July just six days before its first performance. He then turned his attention to a second work for speaker and orchestra, *Une Voix dans le Desért*, again (as in their successful collaboration of 1914 with *Carillon*) setting lines by the Belgian writer Emile Cammaerts, completing the new work two weeks later. In August and October he conducted further runs of *Carillon* at The Coliseum, the second of these with his close friend Lalla Vandervelde as reciter. The wife of the exiled Belgian politician Emile Vandervelde, she was the daughter of Edward Speyer, another of Elgar's friends and a kind patron. On 24 August Cammaerts himself called in at Severn House to discuss *Une Voix dans le Désert*, Elgar's playing of it through moving them both profoundly. Elgar then returned for a while to *The Spirit of England*, again however laying it aside uncompleted.

In October too, he visited his sister Pollie at Stoke Prior in Worcestershire as he had done a number of times that year. Indeed, whenever he could in 1915 he got away on holiday to the country fleeing the worries of London and the war. On one such trip in August he had made friends with a dog 'Ship'[2], this and the nostalgic visits to Worcestershire evidently reminding him of his youth and better times when he himself had owned a dog ('Scap'), thus further increasing his mood of dissatisfaction.

A key event that October was Elgar's trip to Bournemouth where, on the 23rd, he was to conduct a concert. Uprooted from Stoke Prior against his will, he felt decidedly out of sorts in spirits and confided this to Alice, who wrote in her diary: 'E. not liking music at all & saying it was all dead &c'. But the music was from *The Wand of Youth* and this revived his spirits. Indeed when *The Starlight Express* project came up a couple of weeks later the tunes for the old play of youth may well have still been going through his head and helped to clinch the matter.

There may have been another contributory factor too. On 3 November Elgar went down to stay with his friend Frank Schuster at 'The Hut', the latter's home near Maidenhead. Two days later his host entertained a group of wounded soldiers with whom Elgar engaged in 'much interesting talk'. This, undoubtedly, heightened his awareness of the horrible reality of war and perhaps made him all the more responsive to Lena Ashwell's plea for musical balm when it came. It is likely, too, that another of Elgar's close women friends, Alice Stuart-Wortley, put in a good word for the project when she came for tea at Severn House on 12 November to take a look at the script of the play for, like Lena Ashwell, Mrs Stuart-Wortley was active in fund raising for 'Concerts at The Front'.

On Sunday 14 November, the day after he had agreed to provide the music for *The Starlight Express*, Elgar was 'unwell' and still felt so on the 15th, a bitterly cold day. His spirits were revived, however, by a visit from two friends, Lena Ashwell and Claude Phillips (the art critic). They brought with them a stranger – Algernon Blackwood.

They all talked about the play and to give his guests an idea of the possibilities Elgar played through some of the music from *The Wand of Youth*, moving them to tears. When they left, Elgar felt well enough to return to town with them. There he visited Novello's his publishers and settled that he could indeed use the *The Wand of Youth* scores as a basis for the incidental music and songs for The Kingsway production.

It had been the 'very pleasant and interesting' Mr Blackwood's first meeting with the Elgars and he charmed them both immediately. The conversation was 'delightful' Alice reported in her diary. When it turned to turf racing, Blackwood 'told E. about rearing a horse to run in the Derby on dried milk'. The horse had been 'Azote', owned jointly with his business partner during the years in London after his time in Canada.[3]

Other commitments, however, prevented Elgar from settling down to work seriously on the score for the play until 19 November when, feeling much better, he started to look through his sketch-book for ideas, discussing matters with Lena Ashwell the next morning when she called. One question which would have had to be settled early was the size of the pit band needed to play the music. For obvious reasons the full orchestra required for *The Wand of Youth* was out of the question, but neither could Elgar be expected to make do with just the handful of strings which usually played at The Kingsway. So for his benefit it was agreed to increase the basic forces to a complement of at least twenty-five players: some ten to eighteen strings; two flutes (one doubling piccolo), two clarinets, oboe, bassoon; two horns, two trumpets, two trombones; harp; timpani and the usual percussion. To this list, however, there were to be later additions as Elgar faced the demands of his inspiration.

In these early days too, the need to have a professional in charge of the musical side of the production at The Kingsway would already have been realised. The eventual choice as music director was the 30-year old

Worcestershire-born conductor and composer Julius Harrison. A student of Bantock at Birmingham University he had been present when Elgar delivered his lectures as Peyton Professor there a decade earlier and had long admired him. In the closing months of 1915 Harrison had come into the employ of Thomas Beecham whose newly founded opera company was then based at The Shaftesbury Theatre where Harrison conducted *Pagliacci* and *Carmen* in November and December, fitting in his *Starlight* duties with the help of an assistant, Anthony Bernard, who deputised for him as necessary.[4]

By the 23rd Elgar was busy with the music, taking time off on the 24th to visit the dialogue rehearsals, now in full swing at The Kingsway. Pleased with what he saw Elgar arranged for Blackwood to call early next day to go through the script with him in the morning. By this time, it seems certain, he was already having ideas for some new music for the play, probably to fit the words of the songs, an early priority for the singers still had to be chosen.

While Elgar and Blackwood were at work on the 25th, a Mr Green called to audition for the singing role of The Organ-Grinder: 'fairly good – not ideal' was the verdict, Alice noted. Then in the afternoon, when Schuster and Alice Stuart-Wortley dropped in for tea, Elgar played them the 'new tunes' he had sketched. Blackwood came back for dinner that day; sitting round the fire he and the Elgars engaged in 'nice out-of-the-world talk' together late into the evening.

Next day, Alice noted, Elgar was 'very hard at work' on the music and busily telephoning round to various publishers, 'Elkin, Enoch, Novello, &c &c &c' and to Lena Ashwell. He had got the bit between his teeth. Already then the Blackwood magic was having its effect and, even by this stage, any remaining idea of merely adapting *The Wand of Youth* score for the job had clearly been abandoned. Elgar was now determined to provide his new-found friend with as much new-composed music as possible while still retaining the nostalgic link with his own music of childhood.

The tall, humorous Blackwood – an endearing, balding, sprite-like boy-man, full of fun and fantasy – had made a most striking impression on both Edward and Alice Elgar, evidently being 'one of us' (unlike the dreadfully affected and 'very phantasmagoric' Thomas Beecham who had called on the 21st). With Alice Elgar, herself once a writer, Blackwood had of course much in common including a similar privileged background and upbringing, their fathers both having been knights of the realm. For Alice as much as Elgar himself, however, the attraction of opposites must also have been at play for it is unlikely that either of them had ever before encountered quite such a strange and fascinating character as Algernon Blackwood.

When Blackwood came into their Hampstead home that November day he also entered the Elgars' hearts in a special way, and their feelings of friendship and love for him increased over the weeks and months that followed, long after staging of *The Starlight Express* had come and gone. Perhaps in some way they had even been waiting for him. Certainly he filled an empty niche in their lives.

He himself identified the phenomenon in *Extra Day*, published that very same year. For Algernon Blackwood was their 'Wonderful Stranger'.

> A wonderful stranger was ... on the way. Children possess this sense of anticipation all the world over ... the feeling that some day or other a Wonderful Stranger will come up the pathway, knock at the door, and enter their lives, making life worth living, full of wonder, beauty, and delight, because he will make all things new ... grown-ups have it too in the form of an unquenchable but fading hope.

Through Blackwood and the music he wrote for him, Elgar found another route back to his own childhood. Just as Blackwood delighted in him, Elgar delighted in Blackwood and the two of them became bosom chums. Elgar soon expressed the nature of his feelings for his new-found friend to the mutual friend who had brought them together. Legge wrote back:-

> My dear Elgar, More than words can say I rejoice in your letter & its meaning. Why on earth it never dawned on me to bring you & Alg Blackwood together [before] I cannot think. He is wonderful to me, & you must be wonderful to him (as you are to me). When can I hear the music? Robin H Legge'.[5]

Violinists both, Elgar and Blackwood had many other traits in common including a boyish love of jokes and games. In relaxation, especially when the run of the play was over, they spent hours at Elgar's billiard table in hilarious sessions of plate-pool, much to Alice's amusement, like two overgrown schoolboys – her boys (for she was just old enough to have been Blackwood's mother, and had long been one to her husband).

But there was a serious side to the friendship too, and we can now only guess what topics of life and death those two deep-thinking men might also have talked about. In Blackwood's expanded philosophy of life and religion for instance Elgar, the lapsed Roman Catholic, may have found comfort from the threat of eternal damnation as well as support for his own growing humanistic agnosticism.[6] Whether he knew any of Blackwood's writings before Lena Ashwell brought him the text of *Starlight* is uncertain but he soon started to read *Prisoner*, finding immediately that it inhabited a similar world of sleep and dreams as did many of his own compositions.[7] As for Blackwood it would seem that he knew next to nothing of Elgar's music at the time of their first meeting[8] except, presumably, by repute.

At some time or other, however, their conversation must have turned to Elgar's own play of childhood as well as to the music he wrote for it. Then, perhaps, they may have identified a symbol they had in common, that of the threshold, gateway, or entrance to a special place, which in Blackwood's writings amounts almost to an obsession.

In Elgar's play the gateway had been a bridge across a stream leading from the everyday world of the Old Folk into the Fairyland-of-Youth. In Blackwood's novels and stories it took many forms even within the same work. In *Prisoner* for example, it was the pair of big iron gates that barred the drive up to Henry Rogers' old home at Crayfield, separating the world of fields and copses outside from the childhood memories waiting to be freed within; later, at Bourcelles, it was (among others) a lone sentinel poplar tree that lay between the village and the pine forests in the mountains where The Star Cave and other marvels were located. But, if the most striking of Blackwood's gateways, the portal into the old Garden of the World-Soul, occurs in *The Centaur*, perhaps the most significant of them in those days of war and loss is to be found in *Extra Day*.

> Most wonderful of all ... was the door in the old grey fence; for it was a Gateway, and a Gateway, according to Uncle Felix, was a solemn thing. None knew where it led to, it was a threshold into an unknown world. Ordinary doors ... were not Gateways ...; but out-of-door doors opened straight into the sky, and in virtue of it were extraordinary. They were Gateways. At the End of the World [the neglected part of the garden which the children made their head-quarters] stood a stupendous, towering door that was a Gateway. Another, even more majestic, rose at the end of life.

There was such a threshold after death, of course, set to unforgettably exciting and onward-impelling music in Elgar's *The Dream of Gerontius* as The Soul approaches Its God.

The two men, and Alice Elgar, may well also have touched upon the day/night theme of *Prisoner* and the *Starlight* play derived from it, for the same life/death imagery had long haunted the Elgars too, as it had so many other creative artists, not least Wagner who gave supreme expression to it in *Tristan*, a work particularly beloved by Elgar himself. In his own compositions such a theme is found of course in *Gerontius* and *The Light of Life* as well as in the song *Pleading*, *Scenes from the Saga of King Olaf*, *Caractacus*, and a number of other works including *The Apostles* in which Judas sings:-

> If I say, Peradventure the darkness shall cover me, then shall my night be turned to day — yea, the darkness is no darkness with Thee, but the night is as clear as the day. [Psalm 139, v. 12]

The Apostles certainly entered their conversation in those early days as we shall see. The Elgars could well have told Blackwood that words similar to those of that psalm were known to them many years earlier when they were courting for, after Alice's mother (Lady Julia Maria Roberts) was interred with her late husband (Major-General Sir Henry Gee Roberts) in the churchyard at Redmarley d'Abitot in 1887, the inscription 'Night and Day are both the same to Thee' was added after her name on the tombstone. Possibly Elgar, even then collecting words for *The Apostles*, suggested these words to Alice though (as in her novel of 1882, *Marchcroft Manor*, she had said of her suffering hero, Roger Osbourne, that it was 'as if day and night were all the same to him') her own literary interests may already have been set on a similar path.

Perhaps it was during those early days of growing friendship at Severn House that Blackwood introduced the Elgars to his friend The Baroness who then entered Alice Elgar's social circle when she came up to town from her home in the country. Then too the Elgars and Blackwood may have discovered their common link with the Speyers: for Edward Speyer, Lalla Vandervelde's father, was a cousin of another mutual acquaintance Sir Edgar Speyer (Chairman of The Queen's Hall Orchestra), and Blackwood had met him when working for his brother and partner James Speyer in New York all those years before. Edgar Speyer's wife, Leonora von Stosch, a violinist like Blackwood and Elgar, had helped Elgar when he was composing his concerto.

Most of their conversation, however, must have concentrated chiefly on the *Starlight* play and Elgar's setting of Blackwood's lyrics for it. By this time the script had been thoroughly revised, especially Act One, now cast in a single long span set in The Den at Bourcelles at evening, during which the evening sunlight is replaced by starlight after the arrival of Cousin Henry. And perhaps in an attempt to overcome Helen Tyler's criticism that the play lacked some kind of exposition at the beginning, but eschewing the obvious solution of setting it in the garden at Crayfield, there was to be a kind of prologue, a prelude sung by The Organ-Grinder to a group of small urchins (The Street Arabs).

Blackwood had wanted this scene to be set in a London Street with Cockney children and an old-fashioned, Italianate organ-grinder, thus preserving the original link, but he was overruled and had to settle for the neutral backcloth of the stage curtain. His disappointment was further increased when it was also decided that the implied location was not to be London after all but Switzerland with The Organ-Grinder clad in continental garb and his attendant children as Swiss peasants.

But even more disturbing changes were being made. As an expediency, perhaps to save money, the role of The Organ-Grinder was to be combined with that of The Tramp, the new character becoming a sort of organ-grinder-tramp. That meant cutting out not only all the stage 'business' of the original tramp but his constant companion The Gypsy too. So two of the most endearing and potentially comic of The Sprites were lost at a stroke, and at the cost of some confusion to the composer, as much as anyone, for the consequences of the decision had not always been thought through.

The opening song 'To the Children' ('O Children open your arms to me') was set to existing verses from *Prisoner*. That it had always been the author's intention to use these lines somewhere in the play is certain, for Clive Carey had already set them for the abandoned Dean production. Now, however, there were to be songs in front of the curtain before the other acts also. The second of these, 'The Blue-Eyed Fairy' ('There's a Fairy that hides in the beautiful eyes'), also came from verses in the novel but the lyrics for the third, 'My Old Tunes' ('My old tunes are rather broken'), was specially written by Blackwood for the play.

The music Elgar provided for all three of The Organ-Grinder's songs was largely 'new' in the sense that he had not used the various themes in them before, with the single exception of some from 'The Little Bells' movement of the second *The Wand of Youth* suite which he incorporated into the first and third song. Standing for sleep, dreams, expectancy, mystery, night, wonder and the like, this 'Star Music' came to play an important role in the whole composition along with some from the 'Fairy Pipers' movement of the second suite.

Otherwise, if we remember the original intent, *The Wand of Youth* contributed surprisingly little to *The Starlight Express* apart from the use of a shortened and simplified form of *Moths and Butterflies* (Suite 2) as an interlude and, probably as a last-minute expediency, the complete *Sun Dance* (Suite 1) as background music to end one scene. Elgar seems not to have had time even to adapt the last piece to meet the requirements of his reduced theatre orchestra and it had to be played from the existing parts of the published Novello score.

The first of The Organ-Grinder's songs, into which Elgar incorporated a brief overture, also introduces a number of tunes that re-occur elsewhere in the score including the simple 'Children' motif and The Organ-Grinder's barrel-organ theme which is almost like a happy version of its fateful predecessor in the last song of Schubert's *Die Winterreise* cycle. The main music of the second song, a waltz, had been written long ago Elgar told Algernon Blackwood, and he had been waiting for many years to find suitable words for it.[9] Now Blackwood's fitted perfectly and the delighted composer made much use of his old-new tune elsewhere in the score, including turning it into an extended interlude in Act Three.

At some stage also it was decided to convert one of The Sprites' chants into another song for The Organ-Grinder, and this became 'The Curfew Song' ('The sun *has* gone') in the first scene of Act Two, using both new music and old (based again on 'The Little Bells' and 'Fairy Pipers'). Much later, after the run had started, a fifth song *The Song to The Little Winds*, ('Wake up, you little night winds!'), was added to the same scene. Other changes made during the initial rehearsal period gave even more verses intended for The Sprites to The Organ-Grinder to sing, all in the last scene: 'They're all soft-shiny now' and, during The Finale itself, 'Hearts must be soft-shiny dressed', in which he leads the soprano in the closing duet.

Thus the singing role of The Organ-Grinder increased in importance as the music grew. To a large extent this reflected Elgar's desire to give musical life to as many of his new friend's verses as possible but the voice and personality of the singer that Elgar had, from the start, wanted for the part also inspired him to provide tunes for him too. For the chosen Organ-Grinder was to be another friend, the operatic baritone Charles Mott, whose place in the *Starlight* company was probably confirmed some time between 26 November and 2 December, during the days when the blank pages in Alice's diary indicated feverish activity at Severn House as the work for the play got seriously underway.

Mott's vocal training had been unconventional. Of a highly musical temperament, he had started singing as a boy at St James's Church in Muswell Hill, London. Then as a young man he took whatever amateur engagements he could find. At the age of twenty-two, when participating in a club concert at Alexandra Palace, he attracted the attention of the vocal teacher Henry Stanley and became his pupil for a period of four years. He was then noticed favourably by the authorities at Covent Garden who sent him to study in Berlin where he was coached in a number of operatic roles by the famous bass Paul Knupfer for about one year. After this Mott's fortunes improved dramatically when he was appointed as principal baritone at The Hof-Oper in Dessau where he remained for two years and was a great success. He was now ready to return to England where, in about 1909, he immediately took up concert and operatic work in London and elsewhere.[10]

Now probably in his mid- or late thirties[11], Charles Mott had only begun to make a real name for himself during the 1913–14 seasons at Covent Garden singing Wagnerian and other roles: Melot, Kurwenal, Kothner, Nachtigall, Frederick, Donner, Gunther, Escamillo, etc., under Artur Rodzinsky, Albert Coates, Artur Nikisch, Hamilton Harty and other conductors, among them Julius Harrison (who, with Adrian Boult, then worked on the musical staff there under Percy Pitt). Elgar had heard Mott in *Die Meistersinger* in February 1914 and, much impressed, had invited him to Hampstead to sing for him. Keen to hear Mott in *Gerontius*, Elgar wrote in March to Ivor Atkins recommending him as a suitable new voice for the parts of The Priest and The Angel of the Agony at The Three Choirs Festival which was being held in Worcester that year.[12]

Elgar heard Mott in further Wagnerian roles in April and May then wrote and invited him and his wife to a gathering at Severn House in June. Mott, busy with an engagement 'singing two concerts daily' in Torquay before returning for a last performance (in *Manon Lescaut*) that season at Covent Garden, telegraphed his acceptance, then wrote on 7 June from 'Nepaul' the private hotel where he was staying with his wife and daughter.

> Dear Sir Edward Elgar. I am just following up my telegram with a few lines to thank you for your very kind letter ... My wife and I will be delighted to come along & of course I shall be happy to sing a song or two. I have two other engagements on the same afternoon (!!) but I am determined to "work" them all & in any case I shall "save myself up" for your "at home". I am delighted about Worcester & am quite aware that it is entirely through you that I am engaged ...

He had obviously been trying through some of Elgar's songs and continued:-

> By the way, I would love to sing one or more of your beautiful songs when I come to you next week ... I am having great success now wherever I go & I feel that it is now just a matter of opportunity to give me a good standing among British artists. With my best regards to Lady Elgar & yourself, and renewed thanks for your kind letter, I remain Yours sincerely, Charles Mott.[13]

Atkins had auditioned and subsequently engaged Mott to sing in *Gerontius* that September but, after the outbreak of war in August, the Worcester meeting was cancelled. So Elgar, who managed only to rehearse the choral sections, never heard Mott as soloist in *Gerontius* in his beloved cathedral, being unable even to attend the memorial service to Field Marshall Lord Roberts there later that year when Mott sang the angel's *Proficiscere* for the first time.

Now, in December 1915, Elgar was anxious to hear Mott sing again but from 3–5 December much of the composer's time was occupied with rehearsals and performances of *Carillon* at The Albert Hall and The Coliseum. On the 3rd, while waiting for the reciter Tita Brand to arrive, he had taken up a violin and played in the orchestra much to the players' delight. Perhaps it was because the violin was very much on his mind in those December days that Elgar decided to incorporate a number of important violin solos into the *Starlight* score.

The weekend over Elgar settled back to his work. His two visitors that Monday morning (6 December with just 23 days left until curtain-up) were a Mr Bradley, probably his copyist, and, at last, Charles Mott whose singing was 'very good & nice' reported Alice. The relatively muted tone of her praise suggests, however, that it was not at this stage any of her husband's new tunes that the singer had sung.

Lunchtime was given over to financial discussions with another friend, the musician Landon Ronald, head of The Guildhall School of Music and now (like Harrison) conducting for the Beecham opera. Long a champion of Elgar's music, and the dedicatee of *Falstaff*, he had 'like an angel' taken charge of all business matters connected with the new score, including performance royalties thus taking the worry off the busy composer's mind. Within the week, as Novello's was not interested, 'kind Landon' had found another publisher, Messrs Elkin & Co., the small firm which had already issued *Carillon* the previous year.

In the afternoon that hectic December day came the choreographer and ballet mistress, Flo Martell, for it was now evident that dancing would be an important feature of the production. As well as the eight children (all little girls) who were to accompany The Organ-Grinder on all his appearances, some of them doubling up as The Little Winds, seven older girls were needed as The Pleiades, later described thus by Blackwood and Pearn in the programme book:-

> These seven sisters, virgin companions of Artemis, were pursued by Orion, the giant-hunter, for their beauty. Their prayer to be rescued was heard by the gods, who changed them into pleiades (doves) and placed them among the stars. Orion still hunts them from east to west across the skies, for they have the softest light of all the Constellations and the finest Star-dust!

The chosen maidens came from young dancers and actresses known to Flo Martell. Only one of them, the twenty-three-year-old Lynn Fontanne, had appeared on the London stage before and she alone was later to make her name in the theatre though, in December 1915, that great actress to be was still obscure enough for the programme to spell her name incorrectly.[14] Although mentioned (and even heard) earlier, The Pleiades make an appearance in the play only in The Finale when their descent from the heavens to earth provided a challenge to the producer and her staff that, in the event, was hardly met.

The other main *Starlight* singer was to be the operatic soprano Clytie Hine in the role of that peculiar sprite The Laugher. She arrived later the same day, her '*very* delightful singing' also being approved. She may have been the choice of Lena Ashwell for, like several other women in the cast, she belonged to 'The Concerts at The Front' organization. Like Mott however, she had sung in Wagner at Covent Garden and was also known to both Harrison and Beecham, having performed under the latter (in Mozart, as First Lady in *Die Zauberflöte*) in 1914. She was to appear again under both Beecham and Harrison in 1916, when she also appeared in the second run of Stanford's opera *The Critic* under Eugene Goossens at The Aldwych, to which the Beecham company had moved from The Shaftesbury Theatre in April.

Just as a great deal of music had accrued to The Organ-Grinder, as much as possible was now re-allocated to The Laugher for obvious practical reasons. To her existing music in Act Two, 'I'm everywhere' and 'They'll listen to my song' was added 'Oh, stars shine brightly' (previously given to all The Sprites) and, as the curtain falls, 'We shall meet the Morning

Spiders', previously indicated, not for Jane Anne, as sometimes stated but for Henry, Jimbo, and Monkey ('The Dawn Song'). In the last scene of Act Three, where her only lines before had been 'Laugh a little every day/At yourself—that is to say', The Laugher now took over the part previously given, during an extended ensemble for Daddy and others, to a mysterious 'Voice from the Pleiades' (in the novel actually The Countess), starting with the line 'Oh, think beauty'. As well as joining in the closing duet with The Organ-Grinder she was also to sing the opening verses of The Finale 'Dustman, Laugher, Tramp and busy Sweep' originally given optionally to The Pleiades or to The Voice.

With a cast chiefly of actors, and the main singing roles given to the only two professional singers, the original idea of having choral sections was now dropped. All the remaining verses, mainly for The Sprites, were to be chanted though, in some cases, individual sprites (The Dustman and The Gardener especially) came to half-sing their lines to other tunes in the play. Indeed, had there been time, Elgar might have got round to providing music for them too, as Clive Carey had done.

There was, however, to be a special Sprite-call. Elgar wrote to Julius Harrison about it on 6 December:-

Dear Mr. Harrison: I have made the 3 Acts as clear (& *clean*) as I can – there only remains the short section in Act III which the copyist has not yet returned. Will you see if anybody everybody can make the sprite call – it is wanted behind the sc: several times, roughly it is thus

in any key, falsetto by the men – it comes in the orch. as you will have noticed. It does not in the least matter about its being out of *tune* or anywhere near it – only get the quick drop . . ., and then the longer note either [diminuendo] or [crescendo/diminuendo]/ Kind regards/Yours sincerely/Edward Elgar'.[15]

The letter also indicated what surprising progress Elgar had already made with his score, though, as rehearsals continued and new problems arose, there was still quite a long way in fact to go.

On 7 December Elgar, helped by Mr Bradley, stayed in all day 'absorbed in his "Starlight". Relief came in the evening when Blackwood arrived to dine. Reversing roles Elgar 'told him many stories'; he also played through some of the music, entrancing him. When the talk touched on Orion and The Pleiades, they all went outside and found those very stars in the evening sky:

'Glorious', Alice observed. This experience may well have decided author and composer to make more, musically, of Cousin Henry's speech to the children about them in Act Two. So these words, like Daddy's about Star-dust in Act One, came to be set as a formal melodrama with each phrase precisely notated in the score for the actor to follow.

For the next three days Elgar continued to be deeply absorbed in his 'most fascinating & lovely' new music. The choreographer called again on the 8th but much of the 9th was taken up by a strange quest:

> E. to try & find an Organ – went to all sorts of wonderful places in London – no success.

If not a barrel-organ for The Organ-grinder, this must have been the portable harmonium that Elgar had decided was needed to supplement his *Starlight* orchestra at The Kingsway for the extended music for the end of Act Three, Scene 2, including The Finale with its Christmas theme and hymn.

But was this not a great deal to ask of the limited financial resources at that little theatre? Already the basic forces of the orchestra had started to swell alarmingly and were, relatively speaking, assuming huge proportions. The percussion section now included side-drum, bass-drum, cymbals, jingles, wood-blocks, tambourine, triangle, tubular bells, cow-bells and a glockenspiel and a wind-machine! An organ as well seems excessive, especially as Elgar was quite capable of providing an alternative instrumentation for it, as indeed he eventually did. The clue may lie in the choice of two other extra instruments as well as organ: cow-bells and wind-machine. Though neither of them had been used before by Elgar, nor were ever again, the script did clearly ask for cow-bells while the wind-machine was just about justified as an accompaniment for The Little Winds. But an organ?

Could it be that Elgar was keeping faith with his friend and early champion, the German composer Richard Strauss, officially now an enemy? The latter's *Alpine Symphony* had finally appeared that year and reports of its first performance must have reached England in spite of the hostilities. Elgar could have read these or have been told about them by Thomas Beecham who had promoted the music of Strauss in this country before the war. In any case, Elgar may well have known all about the symphony from his correspondence with Strauss in happier times for that gigantic composition had been in progress since 1911. In it there were cow-bells, and a wind-machine and an organ (even sprite-like calls in the section with the cow-bells). Was Elgar deliberately using the same exotic instruments in his Jura score, perhaps as an eventual musical signal to Strauss that he had been thinking of him in that dreadful year of 1915?

That evening Lena Ashwell called to dine and go over points of the play. Next day (Friday, the 10th) Elgar, busy with his score, interrupted work to visit the theatre and lunch there. He also took time to dash off a delayed reply to a letter from Clare Stuart Wortley (written the day after she and her parents had come to tea with the Elgars on Sunday, 28 November) in which she had enclosed a copy of Walter Pater's famous description of da Vinci's *La Gioconda* in his book *The Renaissance* (a work that both she and Elgar loved).

> Dear Clare: I have been so *sumptuously* busy over the play – slow copyists – inferior & rejected singers – etc., etc. – that all the nicest things in the world – & you the very best of all – have had to be neglected, but not forgotten. Thank you very much for the quotation – a real riot of language. I have the essay somewhere and you lead me to look at it again. Bless you, Your affectionate friend, Edward Elgar.[16]

If not due to pure chance, one wonders what could have prompted Elgar's interest in this particular passage at such a busy time. It may possibly have arisen out of conversation with Algernon Blackwood, however, for Pater's words touched on a major theme of his which Elgar may have mentioned to his other friends afterwards:-

> She is older than the rocks among which she sits; like a vampire, she has been dead many times, and learned the secrets of the grave; and has been a diver in deep seas, and keeps her fallen day about her; and trafficked for strange webs with Eastern merchants ... The fancy of a perpetual life, sweeping together ten thousand experiences, is an old one; and modern philosophy has conceived the idea of humanity as wrought upon by, and summing up in itself, all modes of thought and life.

Elgar spent the weekend at home going through the numbers written so far. Charles Mott arrived early on Saturday '& sang through some of the music & so delighted with it'. With Bradley at work also, Elgar had another visitor, W W A Elkin, there to discuss the publication of the *Starlight* score by his firm. On Sunday, with snow about, Julius Harrison came and played through the music with the composer, staying to lunch. Everything now seemed clear for a final onslaught on the music with seventeen days to go to the first performance.

On Monday Alice's diary reported: 'Breathless time with 'Starlight Express', then fell tantalizingly silent for nearly a fortnight as the back of the task was broken, the activity at Severn House, the comings and goings, the rehearsals there (and at The Kingsway) and the rest all unrecorded. An undated letter from Blackwood sent at about this time was encouraging (he had heard from Violet Pearn that Elgar was anxious for him to hear Mott sing.)

Dear Sir Edward, . . . I suppose you realise that your music is the most divine, unearthly thing ever written. I don't believe you do. I never can tell you what I think of it (even if I did forget that you wrote The Apostles!). It makes me happy all day long, and I want to cry and sing. It will go all over the world I know. I shall simply burst when I hear Mott sing it . . . Please let me know any time you want me. I shall love to come. Yours sincerely, A.B.[17]

Blackwood was, however, under rather a cloud with Lena Ashwell who seems to have found his presence at rehearsals somewhat disruptive.

I shall be in town again early Monday morning but not at the theatre. I am staying away . . . for a week at Miss Ashwell's request. It's a good idea. I shall come back fresh and be able to judge the progress.

Clearly there were many problems with the script still to sort out and overcome but the main trouble lay elsewhere! Blackwood himself gave a clue to the likely cause later to a newspaper interviewer, who found him on stage at The Kingsway half-concealed behind the trees of a mountain forest romping with the children.

We have some awfully happy children . . . and what I enjoy most at rehearsals is to have a game of hide and seek with them before Miss Ashwell arrives. The note of high spirits that is thus struck goes right through the play.[18]

But there were much more serious clouds on the horizon as Blackwood reported to Elgar in the same letter:-

I hear that Mr Wilson, the artist, has designed the Sprites in the spirit of Greek fantasy – Lamplighter a quasi-Mercury, Gardener as Priapus, or someone else, and Sweep possibly as Pluto. It is a false and ghastly idea. There is nothing pagan in our little Childhood Play. It is an alien symbolism altogether. It robs our dear Sprites of all their significance as homely childhood Figures. Don't you think so too? If our Play means anything at all, it means God – not the gods. But Mr Wilson is obsessed with Greece, dear thing. I have written to Miss Ashwell as urgently as I know how. I only tell you this in a whisper, please, a whisper that even the presiding Gollywog could hardly hear!

To the delight of both Blackwood and Elgar this particular aberration of Henry Wilson, Lena Ashwell's designer, was soon thwarted, but there was to be still more trouble with him before they were finished. Obviously all was not going well at the theatre during those hectic days. Hints at the nature of the tribulations there were given many years later in his autobiography by O B Clarence, the actor who played the role of 'Daddy':-

During rehearsals there was constant bickerings and difficulties which were very regrettable and unpleasant . . . There were disagreements about the symbolism of the decor, which was all rather highbrow and obscured the beauty of the story. There were even dissensions among the orchestra . . . There was so much allure in the conception of this fantasy that one felt that it only wanted harmony among the interpreters to secure success . . .

I don't know what Elgar thought of it all; it was altogether very sad. He made no remonstrance to my knowledge. He was geniality itself and entertained the cast one day to lunch at the Connaught Rooms opposite . . .[19]

So the play whose theme was 'sympathy' and understanding was floundering during rehearsal for the lack of those very qualities. There were grumbles too about Lena Ashwell's direction, Violet Pearn for one being most unhappy about what was emerging. Blackwood, however, remained loyal and put a brave public face on things:-

It is a very happy play, which will, I hope, cheer everyone up. The extraordinary intuitive grasp which Miss Ashwell has shown has been a very keen delight to me. Her enthusiasm and her zeal are beyond anything I could have expected.[20]

Whatever he might have said publicly, Blackwood was far from happy as he pointed out to Elgar in a letter from The Savile Club on Christmas Day cataloguing his grievances after the dress rehearsal on the day before (24th), at which they had both been present and had seen the costumes and sets for the first time:-

. . . I have written to Miss Ashwell to say the light in Act 1 must be healthy sunlight, instead of gloom that conceals the expression on every face. I wrote it 'evening sunset light' in the Play. I have also tried to show her how Mott's songs lose half their effect by being set against an ugly gauze, and entirely out of the picture. In the Play I wrote 'a street scene', of course. Mott was most depressed about it himself.[21]

And Henry Wilson was the cause of yet more worry. For one thing having dropped the idea of Greek gods, he had still got the costume for The Organ-Grinder wrong.

I further objected to his Piedmontese brigand appearance with those ghastly tight breeches. No English child will recognize the familiar organ-grinder of the country lanes in that untrue and silly costume. The vulgarity of the Dustman [*sic*][22] I did not refer to. It is most painful to me, though.

But there was worse still, as Clarence's words have indicated, for Blackwood's Christmas letter had started thus:-

My dear Sir Edward, I know what you're feeling. Probably you guess what I'm feeling. Can we do anything? I have, of course, the right of veto. That means getting a new artist, postponement of opening [scheduled for the 29th], heavy loss of money to Miss Ashwell, and so forth. You know better than I do what a sweeping veto would involve. That our really big chance should be ruined by her strange belief in a mediocre artist is cruel.

The letter continued . . .

This murder of my simple little Play (qua words) I can stand, for the fate of my books has accustomed me to it; but this suburban, Arts & Crafts pretentious rubbish stitched on to your music is really too painful for me to bear. If you feel inclined to help me with advice (privately and quite between ourselves) I shall be grateful. But, after a horrid night of thinking it all over, I can see no course but to veto it all and face postponement, change of artist etc etc – or to insist upon what compromise is possible at this late hour. We can talk on Monday [27th] if you like. I am ready to do anything. If I have to be firm and nasty, I can be so. Only I feel so inexperienced. And the free and friendly discussion of things has never been possible somehow. I only had hints that something was going on. I felt exceedingly uneasy. Then this awful crime was sprung upon me when the money had been spent, and the lateness of the hour made sweeping changes so horribly difficult for me to insist upon. I stopped the Sprites being Greek Gods, but the rest . . .!

. . . and closed:-

I found it quite useless to say anything last night, as the atmosphere was electric rather . . . In fact, a new artist seems our only hope. And someone to be called in (Harry Grattan, say) who understands something, at least, about proper lighting. I believe, however, it will all be much better by Wednesday. I shall be at Best Beech Hotel over Sunday . . . but shall come up to [the] theatre on Monday – by an effort of will. Yrs A.B..

The main disappointment, of course, was the scenery, now revealed in all its awfulness for the first time. Its designer, Henry Wilson, as it later transpired, may well not have been Lena Ashwell's first choice as designer for both she and Elgar seem to have wanted Charles Raikes (a relative of Alice Elgar[23]) who was greatly proficient in the imaginative design and construction of stage scenery and in the art of stage lighting. Charles Raikes' son takes up the tale:-

. . . my father knew about 'The Starlight Express'. He saw the show at the Kingsway Theatre, and indeed disliked the settings and costumes almost as much as Elgar did. My father was much involved with the professional theatre in pre-1914-war days, and was something of a scenic artist: he had, I believe, been approached by Elgar and Lena Ashwell to do the 'sets' but it was wartime and he was already in the army.[24]

Elgar's overwhelming antipathy was expressed in a letter to his friend the Malvern architect Troyte Griffith on 28 December. Wilson, he said, had entirely ruined any chance the play had of success.

. . . he's an ignorant silly crank with no knowledge of the stage at all & has overloaded the place with a lot of unsuitable rubbish & has apparently never read the play. He ought to be put in a Home![25]

The day before, Monday of opening week, Alice's diary had finally broken its silence. Those blank pages hid a family tragedy under the impending shadow of which most of the music for *The Starlight Express* had been written. On 21 December, the previous Tuesday, Elgar's nephew and godson William Henry Elgar, the elder son of his brother Frank, had died at 10 High Street, Worcester, aged only 25.[26] Named after his grandfather, and like him a piano-tuner, he had been ill with pulmonary tuberculosis for the past year, the condition suddenly worsening so that his end (though not entirely unexpected) came as a sad shock. Because Christmas was imminent the burial was arranged for the 23rd, the day before the dress rehearsal at The Kingsway, so it is doubtful if Elgar was able to be present, which must further have increased his grief and perhaps induced a measure of guilt at his absence.

That Monday, then, Elgar was still busy with his music. Blackwood came in the afternoon as did Anthony Bernard 'who helped'. Whatever Blackwood's intentions had been, his talk with Elgar evidently dissuaded him from postponing the *première* which went ahead mainly as scheduled on Wednesday afternoon (29 December) in spite of all their misgivings. Not that all the disagreements had been resolved, however. A letter from Lena Ashwell sent at this time to the now fractious composer gives us an indication of the kind of problems they still faced and the stress they were under.

> Dear Sir Edward, I have been dreaming about the difficulties & I see them very clearly. How would it be if the music started with the descent of the Pleiades. Then the crescendo would be sharper [?] & I can easily make the people speak right with the music. I've been doing it for years in a small way. I *can't* do the play without you, & it is really life or extinction for me to get the play right & it can't be right without you. Yours always.[27]

Dismayed by all these complications, both practical and temperamental, Lena Ashwell may well have regretted her impulse to produce this particular play at such a troubled time: whoever was to receive balm from this work of sympathy, it would not be her! But perhaps it would all work well enough after all? Increasingly, she must have pinned her hopes on her 'Great Un-wumbler' and his music to supply the required magic and pull everything together.

In an interview given at the dress rehearsal and published in *The Referee* that Sunday (26 December) she put on a brave face and said:-

> I think I would rather produce a play like this ... than do anything else on the stage. Although producing a play in War time has its minor difficulties in the way of procuring materials and getting them delivered, the serious difficulties have solved themselves. The first serious difficulty might have been the music – the play needed music – but when I took the script to Sir Edward Elgar and he promised to write it, I knew that that difficulty was overcome before it had arisen. And now it is so wonderfully a part of the play that it has grown to be much more than incidental music. It is as much a part of the play as the Sprites and the children and the setting.

And, stubbornly, she stood by her designer:-

> Another difficulty that 'might have arisen' is the scenery and dresses. Because when anything hasn't been dramatised before (Mr Blackwood's Sprites, for instance) it is a matter not only of giving 'airy nothing a local habitation and

a name', but clothes as well – a much more complicated proposition. But Mr Wilson, the president of the Arts and Crafts Society, knew exactly what Mr Blackwood's Sprites looked like and did. In fact, he seemed to know just as much about it as the authors, Mr Blackwood and Miss Pearn. So that difficulty did not arise!

In fact, after the traumas of the dress rehearsal, one would have believed that all had gone marvellously well:-

> The children in the cast seem to be looking upon the rehearsal as a game of their own, and if the play had been got up specifically to amuse them they couldn't have been in wilder spirits. I really think they'd like to go on rehearsing all night as well as every morning and afternoon.

Meanwhile, another problem had arisen, one from which Elgar was probably shielded by his friends. Clive Carey (by now a lieutenant in the Ordnance Corps) had finally learned that Elgar had been asked to write the music for the Ashwell production. Bitterly disappointed he wrote to Blackwood to find out why he had been dropped. The reply (dated 26 December 1915) came from Violet Pearn.

> Dear Mr Carey, Mr Blackwood has sent me a copy of your letter to him. I am so sorry you feel aggrieved with regard to 'The Starlight Express'. I understood your arrangement with regard to the music was made with Mr Basil Dean & therefore when – to our mutual misfortune – his production of the play fell through, your connection with the play lapsed at the same time as his did. When the question of the production at The Kingsway arose I much regretted that you had enlisted – to be exact I regretted it as soon as I heard of it – but it did not occur to me there was any chance of your doing the music while you were in the Army: I wish to heaven you were not!

She continued:-

> But in any case I could have done nothing about it. Sir Edward Elgar was the choice of the financier and Miss Ashwell. Mr Blackwood delights in him … With every possible good wish, and many regrets that you should feel yourself to have been discourteously treated. Very sincerely yours Violet Pearn.[28]

Carey had heard of the new project from his friends. All of them thought he had been shabbily treated including Edward Dent who, throughout the war, wrote innumerable letters of cheer to his young friends in the forces, keeping them abreast with musical activities at home (and suffering personal distress when some of them lost their lives).

It is most unlikely that Elgar even knew that Carey had been involved in the previous *Starlight* project or that Carey held Elgar to blame in any way for what had happened. It was an ironic situation for, unlike his mentor Dent, Carey had always admired Elgar's music, even *The Dream of Gerontius*, dismissed by Dent as 'Gerry's Nightmare'! (The last laugh here was on Dent, for, as he left no instructions, The Angel's Chorus from *Gerontius* was played by the organist at his cremation in 1957. A bogeyman to many

Elgarians because of his publicly stated dislike of Elgar's music, Dent would have himself probably enjoyed the joke too.)[29]

And what of Violet Pearn all these hectic weeks? It is clear that she too was far from happy with the whole business. In her letter to Clive Carey, she indicated her misgivings:-

> The Starlight is advertised to go on on Wednesday. Judging by the dress rehearsal on Friday it probably won't go on at all!! It was ghastly.

Unlike Blackwood and Lena Ashwell she was wholly unimpressed by Elgar's music and the letter also contained this comment about the composer:

> He's done the songs before the curtain quite well. The rest of the music – and there is masses of it – bores me to tears.

And referring many years later (in letters to Val Gielgud) to Lena Ashwell's 'pompous and dreadful production', she told him:-

> It was a terrible production – Muriel Pratt would love to tell you about it. It was financed by a man in loving memory of his wife and there were bits put in because the dear departed would have liked them.[30]

Violet had communicated some of her spirit of discontent to her friend at the time when, excluded by Lena Ashwell from *Starlight*, Muriel was languishing unhappily in Ewhurst. On 24 November, Edward Dent had written to Clive Carey and told him of a visit he had recently paid Muriel with Bobby Maltby with whom, since their Bristol days, she was on more than friendly terms, much to the disapproval of her mother and husband. (Then on leave from the front in Flanders, Maltby and his men in the 12th Rifle Brigade had experienced a terrible time in the trenches which had re-inforced his views on the urgent need to find peace. He was to die of wounds received in The Battle of The Somme on 27 August 1916.)

> Bob took me to call on Muriel Pratt and we heard a lot about *The Starlight Express*. It is so disgusting that it is not to have your music. But from M.P.'s description I think you are well out of it. Lena Ashwell seems to have treated her very badly. They have got Elgar to do the music to it and apparently Lena Ashwell and Algernon Blackwood go about saying in perfect seriousness that the play is being produced by God.

Dent repeated the story to Carey a week or so later, adding

> ... so you are well out of it, as I imagine God would be as tiresome to collaborate with as Stanford.

On 22 December Maltby wrote to Carey to wish him a merry Xmas, finishing with this comment:

> Of course the 'Starlight' won't be worth 2d, quite absurd & hopeless – Why write it at all?

And again on the 28th:-

> Oh Damn – and the 'Starlight Express' is to be produced this week by Lena Ashwell with music by Elgar and a loathsome looking female playing the mother. I should think the scenery will be by Harker and wigs by Clarkson, costumes by Natham – it will in any case be perfectly bloody and an entire failure. With which happy thought I leave you – God bless us all.[31]

Elgar, meanwhile, who was to have directed the music from the pit, did not even attend the opening of the play, as Alice recorded in her diary on 29 December:-

> First performance of the Starlight Express. E. wd not conduct as the mise en scène was so repulsive – & was not even present – music wonderful.

The official reason given for his absence was quite different, however, for on that Monday there had been a serious distraction: Alice, involved in an accident with a taxi-cab, was brought home dazed from Chelsea; remembering nothing about it (but told 'she spoke most politely & behaved with much dignity'), she took to her bed for about ten days. There as the year closed she wrote in her diary:-

> End of year of anxieties D.G. Much success in many ways to England. Sad losses & awful atrocities by the Germans who have become more diabolical than ever. May victory for the Allies & peace come in the New Year.

Thus did *The Starlight Express* start out at last on its theatrical journey but neither of the Elgars was there to wish it *bon voyage*.

IV

Altogether (with later additions during the run) Elgar had, in a great burst of creation unequalled since the final composition of the second symphony in 1910–11, produced a huge score of some fifty musical numbers. As well as the songs there are passages of notated melodrama, dances, entr'actes and interludes; also much incidental music (used as the background to dialogue or to accompany stage 'business', and so on). Most of the numbers are discrete and clear-cut but some are linked in complex sequences, most notably in the closing scene where the music is almost continuous.[1]

There is, alas, room only briefly to summarize the rest of the history of *The Starlight Express* here. The opening matinée on Wednesday 29 December 1915, though starting late, went surprisingly well with a full house and an enthusiastic audience. The reviews of the play itself, however, were mixed and, much to Blackwood's disappointment, often critical to a greater or lesser extent, a few being almost hostile, though some of the critics and most of the public loved it. But the acting, singing and even the production received almost universal praise. So did Elgar's music, with an enthusiasm that sometimes bordered on the rapturous; though there were a few dissenting voices it was widely held that it was the saving of the piece (a visit to which, in those troubled times, developed almost into a cult).[2] Elgar, of course, soon put aside his chagrin and started to pay frequent and increasingly enthusiastic visits to the proceedings at The Kingsway though Alice Elgar, confined to her bed, saw little of them.

Thus *The Starlight Express* continued on its run until falling houses, probably only temporary, caused Lena Ashwell to announce its closure a week or two before its scheduled time, much to the disappointment of everybody involved. So after forty performances, the play came to a halt on 29 January 1916. It had by no means been the abject failure claimed by some later writers and there were plans to revive it in the following December though for various reasons these came to nothing. Neither did Elgar prepare any of the concerts suites that were widely expected of him, though he did record thirty minutes of music from the score in February 1916 with Blackwood in attendance and Charles Mott singing The Organ-Grinder's songs.[3] After that, and two performances by Mott of the three prelude songs in April with The Hereford Orchestral Society under Dr G R Sinclair, the theatre parts were returned to The Kingsway (where they were later destroyed by fire) and the MS score to Elkin's (where it languished for the rest of Elgar's lifetime and long after).

It was fitting that an old friend, indeed 'one pictured within'[4], should have been the first to programme some of Elgar's *Starlight* music and the composer was heart-broken when, early the next year, Dr Sinclair died at the age of only fifty-four. But there was an even more untimely loss to bear for Elgar's Organ-grinder, Charles Mott, succumbed from wounds received on 13 May 1918 during The Second Battle of The Marne. One of his last letters (perhaps *the* last) was written to Elgar; in it Mott quoted The Little Bells theme from *The Wand of Youth* and *The Starlight Express*.[5]

Elgar had heard Mott sing in *Gerontius* after all when he conducted it in May 1916, during the series of performances organised by Clara Butt in aid of The Red Cross, and in November the same year at Manchester. For a time too, until his military duties intervened, Mott had sung in another Elgar work for the theatre, *The Fringes of The Fleet*, written for Mott and a chorus of three other baritones and orchestra to words by Rudyard Kipling, and they were able to record these songs in July 1917.[6]

Blackwood and the Elgars remained firm friends and (between expeditions abroad on behalf of The Red Cross and secretly for the British intelligence service)[7] he continued to visit them at Severn House and later also at Brinkwells, the cottage in Sussex that the Elgars took in 1917 to get away from London. If anything their fondness for him increased and they came to call him 'Starlight'. At Brinkwells, the two men, both of them lovers of trees and all Nature, were in their element. The friendship lasted throughout The Great War and long beyond though they appear to have seen less of each other after the death of Alice Elgar in April 1920, soon after which Blackwood, then travelling in Europe, wrote the following grief-stricken letter.

> My dear dear E. Is it really true? I can't believe it. I've seen no papers, but a man here said it was true, & I find your letter saying the illness was serious. It's an awful shock. What it is for you & Carice is beyond anything I can say, and I simply cannot realize it. Your life companion & comrade, and oh how dear & sweet she was to me always. My dear friend, I do feel & pray for you & Carice, & Severn House without her is unthinkable, & little Brinkwells.[8]

The letter closed:-

> *I really can't write.* I long to see you. I shall be home soon. I have to meet my sister-in-law in Switzerland first.[9] It all makes me ache so for you – & the impossibility of helping or comforting is terrible. My love to you. A.B.

Blackwood and Elgar did not work together again, even on the theatre piece that Blackwood hoped one day they would.[10] Elgar seems to have lost interest in his *Starlight* music during most of the remaining years of his life. Blackwood however, both before and after Elgar's death, made repeated attempts to get the play performed again, both in the theatre and on the wireless: it mattered not to him whether this was in an improved edition of the version done with Violet Pearn or in a completely new version, so long as Elgar's music was featured again in its entirety.

Violet however, was not interested in preserving the music, only in getting the play performed again; for this in 1944–45 she obtained the help once more of her faithful friend Muriel Pratt, then with the BBC. On Muriel's untimely death in 1945, that attempt (like all the others) came to nothing and both Violet and Blackwood died (in 1947 and 1951 respectively) without seeing their first venture together ever performed again. They had collaborated on three further plays and had had a modest success with the second of these, *Through the Crack* (a performance of which Elgar attended some time in the 1920s). Sad to say by the time of her death Violet and Blackwood were scarcely on speaking terms, perhaps on account of this very matter of *The Starlight Express*.

However, some of the other *Starlight* music, in its full orchestral garb, was performed on the wireless during the lifetime of all three of them. The conductor Joseph Lewis, in charge of light music at the BBC under Boult, received both Elgar's and Elkin's permission to broadcast a selection of the score and this he did from time to time between 1933 and 1940 (when the BBC parts were destroyed in The Blitz). The first programme of the music went out on 22 December 1933 when Elgar was still alive but whether the then mortally ill composer heard it is not known, though it would be nice to think so and it is likely that he did.

The Blackwood/Pearn version of *The Starlight Express* has yet to come into its own as a play but, in recent years, the Elgar score has been recognised for the masterpiece it is. Indeed, the 1970s proved to be the decade in which *The Starlight Express* finally steamed into people's hearts. George Hurst recorded a suite of the music in 1974,[11] then came the complete EMI recording of the full score in 1976 under Vernon Handley. In 1978 there was a new stage version of the play by Thérèsa Kitchin and The Acorn Children's Theatre; like Raymond Raikes's radio version of the 1960s it went back to *Prisoner* for its story and used the Elgar music (but in a reduced orchestration).[12] That same year, *The Starlight Express* reached Elgar's Worcester when a substantial suite was conducted in the cathedral by Donald Hunt during Three Choirs Festival week,[13] and it went on to Elgar's Malvern in 1980, when Simon Rattle programmed a short suite at the festival there.[14] In 1979, however, substantially the full score had been given in the concert hall for the first time, *en suite*, at Uppingham under the direction of Barry Collett, a brave pioneering venture that has yet to be repeated by other conductors.[15]

How best to perform the music for *The Starlight Express* outside the theatre still remains a problem. We need the devoted hand of a gifted and sympathetic musician to construct, on the basis of a thorough knowledge of the original play as well as the music, one or more substantial orchestral suites from Elgar's score, perhaps through an 'Elgar Commission'.[16] And if the full score is to be performed *en suite* in the concert hall and on radio at all frequently there is urgent need also for the preparation of a linking narration to accompany it. Perhaps too, as the 1980s draw on, we can hope that the original play and the music will come together again in a recreation of that collaboration between The Wonderful Stranger and his Music-maker over sixty years ago.[17]

Acknowledgements

My research was done in part at the following establishments and I am most grateful to those in charge, and their staffs, for help and facilities: The Elgar Birthplace Museum, Broadheath (Mr James Bennett, Curator and earlier Mr J G S McKenzie); The Hereford and Worcester Record Office (HWRO), St Helen's, Worcester (Mrs E A Howard, Assistant County Archivist and earlier Miss M Henderson); and The Library, University of Leicester. An equally fruitful source of information has also come from my correspondence with the following individuals, to whom I am especially indebted: Mrs Lavender M Jones (Literary Executor for the late Violet A Pearn), the late Mr H F C Carey (nephew of Clive Carey), Mr Raymond Raikes (former BBC producer), Mrs Thérèsa Kitchin (Acorn Children's Theatre) and Mr Mike

Ashley (biographer of Algernon Blackwood). I would also like to thank my wife Marion Simmons (University of Leicester Library) for her continued support and help, not least in the archives at Worcester and Broadheath and for her critical reading of the penultimate draft of this article.

Valuable information and material was also obtained by post from: The John Ryland's Library, University of Manchester (Miss Glenise A Matheson, Keeper of Manuscripts); The Rowe Music Library, King's College, Cambridge (Mrs M V Cranmer, Librarian); The BBC Written Archives Centre, Caversham Park, Reading (Mr Neil Somerville, Senior Assistant); The Central Library, Torquay (Mr P J Bottrill, Area Librarian); and in particular, through the good offices of Dr Robert Anderson (Co-ordinating Editor of *The Elgar Complete Edition*), from Novello & Company, London (Mr Robert Langley, Publisher). I am also indebted to Dr Anderson for most kindly checking Appendix 1 for me against the hire-score of the music for *The Starlight Express*.

For permission to quote from the writings of Algernon Blackwood, Violet A Pearn, and E J Dent, I am grateful respectively to: A P Watt Ltd on behalf of Mrs Sheila Reeves, Mrs Lavender M Jones, and Mr Nicholas Wooler (Dent/Trend estate). I also extend my thanks to any other copyright-holders not traced by me and express the hope that they will contact me so that acknowledgement may be made when the complete study is published. I would also like to extend my thanks here to the following for help with that wider study: Mr E Wulstan Atkins, the late Sir Adrian Boult, Mr Alan Childs, Mr Barry Collett, Mrs Pauline Collett, Mr Neil Crutchley, Dr Winton Dean, Mr Denys Grahame, Mr Mike Grundy, Dr Donald Hunt, Mr Ian Lace, Mrs Vivienne McKenzie, Mr Raymond Monk, Dr Jerrold Northrop Moore, Mr Robin Prytherch, Mr Ronald Taylor and Dr Percy M Young. To my friend Raymond Monk I owe a special debt for without his encouragement and persistence this chapter would not have been written at this particular time.

Finally I have to say that, like all those writing on Elgar today, I do so in the security of knowledge given us from his major biographers, Percy M Young, Michael Kennedy and J Northrop Moore, to whom all Elgarians should be ever grateful.

Notes

I

1. Adapted from *A Prisoner in Fairyland* by Algernon Blackwood.
2. Arranged by Julius Harrison and Alfred W. Ketelbey respectively.

3. Adapted and produced by Raymond Raikes; music played by The BBC Welsh Orchestra, conducted by Lionel Salter (who also edited the music from Elgar's original MS).
4. An edited 'full-text' version has now been prepared by the writer, based on a variety of sources (including Violet Pearn's and Elgar's own copies of the script).
5. EMI Records: London Philharmonic Orchestra, conducted by Vernon Handley, with Derek Hammond-Stroud and Valerie Masterson; album notes by J. Northrop Moore.
6. See Acknowledgements.
7. Provisional title: *Elgar and Company in Theatreland: The Story of 'The Starlight Express'*.
8. See Moore (1974, 1984) for further details.
9. See Jackson (1943).
10. See Kennedy, E (1968) for a full account and transcriptions of George Moore's letters to Elgar. (Note the correct spelling of 'Diarmuid'.)
11. See Mitchell (1984).
12. Mary Anderson is better known to Elgarians as Mary de Navarro, a friend of the Elgars, especially of Alice Elgar, who called her 'Maime'. The music for the 1921 production of *The Garden of Allah* was provided by another friend, Landon Ronald.

II

1. Information on the Blackwood family (here and later) has been gleaned from various sources, including Anon. (1897) and Blackwood's own account of his earlier years (1923, 1934).
2. This and following quotations from Blackwood (1923).
3. See Hudson (1961). Blackwood himself said they were 'cousins' but Mr Mike Ashley, his biographer, tells me he used this term very loosely.
4. Hereafter shortened to *Uncle Paul, Prisoner*, and *Extra Day*, following the practice of Blackwood himself and of his biographer.
5. This and following quotations from *A Prisoner in Fairyland*.
6. I am indebted to Mr Mike Ashley for identifying 'M.S.-K.' for me and for other information about her. I have now established that she later became a friend or acquaintance of Alice Elgar — but that is another story!
7. See Anon. (1897).
8. See Keeton (1945). Blackwood told Miss Keeton that this was in 1915 but that was clearly a *lapsus* on his part.
9. I have received much information on the early career of Violet Pearn from Mrs Lavender M Jones (see Acknowledgements). Unfortunately, for reasons of space, much of the material on Violet Pearn (and on theatrical aspects of *The Starlight Express* story in general) has had to be omitted from the present account.
10. See (e.g.) *The Observer* for 26 December 1915.
11. See Keeton (1945) — though the account that Blackwood gave to her of the history of *The Starlight Express* there is something of a confabulation!
12. See Dean (1956, 1970, 1973) for details; in none of his writings, however, did Dean mention anything about *The Starlight Express*.
13. Information per Mr Mike Ashley.

14. The fact that Clive Carey was commissioned to write music for *The Starlight Express* came to light only fairly recently (Carey 1979). See also Taylor (1979b) and Kennedy (1982), but the implication that Elgar was only second choice as composer for The Kingsway production is not, of course, correct.

15. See Carey (1979), a source of much interesting and relevant information on which I have drawn here.

16. See Dean (1970).

17. Letter to Clive Carey, 2 January 1914. This, and other letters from Dent to Carey cited later, per the late H F C Carey; the letters themselves are now in Rowe Music Library (see Acknowledgements).

18. See Barker (1974).

19. See Redwood (1978).

20. Letter in the Basil Dean collection (now in The John Ryland's Library – see the Acknowledgements).

21. Together with a fourth song ('Do you remember?' from *Guenevere*), they survived, apparently unpublished, as *For Songs from Plays* (per the late H F C Carey).

22. 'Fraulein' was changed, but not exactly as Dent suggested.

23. Ashwell (1936).

24. Ashwell (1936).

25. Ashwell (1929).

26. Ashwell (1929).

27. The full cast-list, omitted here for reasons of space, is given in Simmons (1982).

28. Wilson's name was definitely Henry, not 'Harry' as usually given.

29. Ashwell (1922).

30. This and the following letter are from the Novello archives (see Acknowledgements).

31. Consulted over the years in the HWRO (Hereford and Worcester Record Office) St. Helen's, Worcester; see the Acknowledgements.

32. Said, by Alice Elgar in her diary, to be the 'Fountain Dance' from the second suite though, in the event, it did not find a place in the score of *The Starlight Express*.

33. *The Daily Telegraph*: 30 December 1915.

III

1. From *Ode* by A W E O'Shaughnessy.

2. See Moore (1984).

3. See Blackwood (1934).

4. Anthony Bernard's full role in the proceedings still has to be fully established (see Simmons 1982). He clearly was, or became, a friend of the Elgars (who both thought highly of him) and may well have helped Elgar with practical musical matters.

5. Letter dated 29 November (Elgar archives, HWRO).

6. This question will, I hope, be explored in more detail elsewhere by Mr Ian Lace.

7. Elgar's copy of Blackwood's novel survives at The Elgar Birthplace Museum, Broadheath, with the numbers of all the pages that contain verses noted on the flyleaf.

8. See Keeton (1945).
9. See *The Daily Telegraph*: 30 December 1915.
10. Based largely on a cutting from *The Clubman*, June 1918, in the Elgars' scrapbook for 1909–19 (The Elgar Birthplace).
11. Little is known about Charles Mott, even the place and year of his birth – suggested as about 1875 by Moore (1974).
12. See Atkins (1984).
13. Elgar archives, HWRO.
14. See Simmons (1982).
15. Quoted from Young (1956).
16. Elgar archives, HWRO (with additional punctuation)
17. Novello archives.
18. *The Observer*: Sunday, 26 December 1915.
19. Clarence (1941).
20. *The Observer* (idem).
21. Novello archives.
22. Evidently a *lapsus* for The Sweep (played by Leonard Calvert). Blackwood, in fact, thought highly of Jane Wells as The Dustman as shown by his inscription of her copy of *Prisoner* (now in the possession of Mr Mike Ashley).
23. Charles Stanley Montgomery Raikes (1879–1945), son of William Alves Raikes (Alice Elgar's cousin) and Vera Maria [James] Raikes.
24. Letter from Mr Raymond Raikes to the writer (22 January 1980).
25. Quoted in Young (1955).
26. See Simmons and Simmons (1984, 1985–86) for further details of the history of the Elgar family in Worcester.
27. Novello archives.
28. Per the late H F C Carey.
29. See Carey (1976). As his diary shows, Dent attended a performance of *The Starlight Express* at The Kingsway; what he, and other of Clive Carey's friends, thought of it all is another story!
30. Letters in BBC Written Archives, per Mr Raymond Raikes and Mr Mike Ashley.
31. Per the late H F C Carey. (Joseph Harker, William Clarkson, and the firm of L & H Natham were all well-known in the theatrical world of the time for their work in pantomime.)

IV

1. For further details, see Appendix 1. The full score will, of course, be published eventually in *The Elgar Complete Edition*. At present, the orchestral score and parts are available from Novello's on hire only, in a version edited by Lionel Salter.
2. A full, analytical account of over thirty reviews has been prepared for the longer version of this study.
3. See Moore (1963, 1974) for details.
4. In the *Enigma Variations* of course.
5. Elgar archives, HWRO (part of this letter is quoted by Moore 1984).
6. See Moore (1963, 1974) for details.
7. The full story of Blackwood's wartime activities as an undercover agent in Europe (see Ashley 1983) remains to be told.

8. Elgar archives, WRO.

9. This was Kate, the widow of his older brother 'Stevie' (Stevenson Arthur Blackwood, 1867–1917) – information from Mr Mike Ashley. Kate and Stevie had visited the Elgars at Severn House with Algernon and their young son on 13 July 1916 (Lady Elgar's diary).

10. Blackwood wrote to Elgar about this early in 1916; their mutual friend Percy Anderson was suggested as designer.

11. Originally issued by Polydor, later re-issued on Chandos. The orchestra was The Bournemouth Sinfonietta, the soloists John Lawrenson and Cynthia Glover.

12. First produced at The Rhoda McGaw Theatre, Woking, on 27 October 1978, the music arranged and conducted by Nigel Carver. See Taylor (1979a) for review.

13. 30 August 1978: the orchestra was The City of Birmingham and the soloists those on the George Hurst recording (see above).

14. 24 May 1980: the orchestra was The Philharmonia, the soloists Thomas Hemsley and Nan Christie.

15. 30 September 1979: the orchestra was The Rutland Sinfonia and the soloists Peter Weight and Rita Jones. See Simmons (1980) for review.

16. The Elgar Commission is a fund administered by The Elgar Foundation primarily to finance a new composition every three years for performance at Worcester during the week of The Three Choirs Festival.

17. A planned stage performance – under the sponsorship of The Starlight Express Project, in a performing version edited by the writer, and with the full Elgar score in strict original sequence – was announced for the 1988 meeting of The Three Choirs Festival but had to be postponed.

References

Anon. (1897). *Some Records of the Life of Stevenson Arthur Blackwood K.C.B.,* Hodder and Stoughton: London.

Ashley, M. (1983). 'A touch of Pan'. *Introduction to Tales of the Supernatural* by Algernon Blackwood. The Boydell Press: Woodbridge.

Ashwell, L. (1922). *Modern Troubadours: A Record of the Concerts at the Front.* Gyldendal: London.

Ashwell, L. (1929). *The Stage.* Geoffrey Bles: London.

Ashwell, L. (1936). *Myself a Player.* Michael Joseph Ltd: London.

Atkins, E W. (1984). *The Elgar-Atkins Friendship.* David & Charles: Newton Abbot.

Barker, K. (1974). *The Theatre Royal, Bristol, 1766–1966: Two Centuries of Stage History.* The Society of Theatre Research: London.

Blackwood, A. (1923). *Episodes Before Thirty.* Cassell & Co.: London.

Blackwood, A. (1934). *Adventures Before Thirty.* Jonathan Cape (The Travellers' Library): London.

Carey, Hugh (1979). *Duet for Two Voices: An Informal Biography of Edward Dent compiled from his Letters to Clive Carey.* Cambridge University Press: Cambridge.

Clarence, O B. (1941). *No Complaints.* Jonathan Cape: London.

Dean, B. (1956). *The Theatre at War*. Harrap: London.

Dean, B. (1970). *Seven Ages: An Autobiography 1888–1927*. Hutchinson: London.

Dean, B. (1973). *Mind's Eye: An Autobiography 1927–1972*. Hutchinson: London.

Hudson, D. (1961). 'A study of Algernon Blackwood'. *Essays and Studies* 14: 102–14.

Jackson, B. (1943). 'Elgar's "Spanish Lady"'. *Music and Letters* 24: 1–15.

Keeton, A E. (1945). 'Elgar's music for "The Starlight Express"'. *Music and Letters* 26: 43–46.

Kennedy, E. (1968). 'George Moore to Edward Elgar: eighteen letters on *Diarmuid and Grania* and operatic dreams'. *English Literature in Transition* 21: 168–187.

Kennedy, M. (1968, 1982). *Portrait of Elgar*. Oxford University Press. London.

Mitchell, K D. (1984). 'Elgar and Hardy: the projected opera'. *The Elgar Society Journal* 3(6): 13–15.

Moore, J N. (1963). *An Elgar Discography*. British Institute of Recorded Sound: London.

Moore, J N. (1974). *Elgar on Record*. Oxford University Press: London.

Moore, J N. (1984). *Edward Elgar: A Creative Life*. Oxford University Press: London.

Redwood, D. (1978). *Flecker and Delius – the Making of 'Hassan'*. Thames Publishing: London.

Simmons, K E L. (1980). 'THE STARLIGHT EXPRESS at Uppingham'. *The Elgar Society Journal* 1(5): 7-8.

Simmons, K E L. (1982). 'A message, an oath, and a bag of stardust'. *The Elgar Society Journal* 2(5): 16–20.

Simmons, K E L. and Simmons, M. (1984). *The Elgars of Worcester*. Elgar Society: London.

Simmons, K E L. and Simmons, M. (1985–86). 'A walk round the Elgars' Worcester'. *The Elgar Society Journal* 4(2): 7–13; 4(3): 18–26; 4(4): 8–20.

Taylor, R T. (1979a). 'THE STARLIGHT EXPRESS'. *The Elgar Society Journal* 1(1): 9–10.

Taylor, R T. (1979b). In *The Elgar Society Journal* 1(3): 4.

Young, P M. (1955). *Elgar O.M.: A Study of a Musician*. Collins: London.

Young, P M. (1956). *Letters of Edward Elgar and Other Writings*. Geoffrey Bles: London.

Appendix 1   Elgar's music for *The Starlight Express*

The 50 musical numbers in Elgar's *Starlight* score are listed below in straight sequence, with the numbers used on the Lionel Salter version of the Novello hire full-score given in brackets. After consulting my 'full-script' edition of the play, I have allocated provisional titles to the individual numbers so as to characterise them more memorably; in addition, certain sections have been classified as 'Sprite Music' or 'Star Music', for obvious reasons. I would stress that this is my own personal classification (that of a musical non-musician) and not an official one (which must await the publication of the music in *The Elgar Complete Edition*).

First Prelude
(before the curtain, Act One)

1. (1)   Overture and The Organ-Grinder's Song 1 ('To the Children')

     (a) Overture: *Allegro non troppo – Moderato con moto*)(bar 1–36)

     (b) First Prelude Song: 'O children, open your arms to me': — (bar 37–131)

     (c) Conclusion: *Moderato* – ending with cow-bells faintly on stage (bar 132–145)

Act One
(Bourcelles: The Den at La Citadelle)

2. (2)   Incidental Music 1
     The Earth has forgotten it's a star – The Lamplighter Passes (Sprite Music 1): *Allegretto* (10 bars; strings)

3. (2a)   Incidental Music 2
     Light and hope (Star Music 1): *Lento* (2 bars; strings)

4. (3)   Incidental Music 3
     The Organ-Grinder is heard (Sprite Music 2):—
     (14 bars; clarinet and violas – barrel-organ off)

5. (4)   Incidental Music 4
             The Star Society (Star Music 2): *Allegretto* (8 bars [4
             bars repeated]; strings)

6. (5)   Melodrama 1
             Daddy's star story (Star Music 3): *Moderato – Allegro*
             (20 bars)

7. (6)   Incidental Music 5
             The Star Cave (Star Music 4): *Lento* (11 bars [5 bars
             repeated, plus one bar]; strings)

8. (7)   Incidental Music 6
             The Gardener comes (Sprite Music 3): *Allegretto* (14
             bars; strings)

9. (8)   Incidental Music 7
             A great Un-wumbler's coming (Sprite Music 4): *Allegro*
             (35 bars [14 bars repeated, plus 7 bars]; strings and
             clarinet – barrel-organ off)

10. (8a)   Incidental Music 8
             Jinny tries on the veil (violin solo): — 5 bars [2 bars
             repeated, plus one bar].

11. (9)   Incidental Music 9
             The Organ-Grinder and The Sprites bring Henry's
             luggage (Sprite Music 5): *Allegro molto* (44 bars
             [including a 4-bar repeat] – with opening horn solo)

12. (10)   Incidental Music 10
             What jolly stars! (Star Music 5): *Lento* (6 bars; strings)

13. (11)   Incidental Music 11
             The Children's secret – The swearing-in of Cousin 'enry
             (Star Music 6): — (35 bars [including 6-bar and 4-bar
             repeats and a 6-bar da capo]; strings, harp and
             percussion)

14. (12)   Finale, Act One: Incidental Music 12
             Good night – I'll come to you when you're dreaming
             (Star Music 7): *Andantino* (30 bars [including a four-bar
             repeat])

Second Prelude
(before the curtain, Act Two)

15.   (13)   The Organ-Grinder's Song 2 (The Blue-eyes Fairy)
                   (a)   Introduction: *Allegro* (bar 1–42)
                   (b)   Second Prelude Song: 'There's a Fairy that hides in
                          the beautiful eyes': — (bar 43–166)
                   (c)   Conclusion: — (bar 167–199)

Act Two: Scene 1, First part
(Outside Bourcelles: The Pine Forest at Dusk)

16.   (14)   Entr'acte 1 and Incidental Music 13
                   In The Pine Forest at Dusk (Star Music 8): *Allegro non*
                   troppo (38 bars)

17.   (15)   Melodrama 2
                   Orion and The Pleiades (Star Music 9): *Moderato* (19
                   bars; strings and harp, *seque* ...)

18.   (15a)   Incidental Music 14 ('Melody') and The Organ-Grinder's
                   Song 3 (The Curfew Song)
                   (a)   The Scaffolding-of-The Night (Star Music 10):
                          Allegretto (bar 1–44 [including a 10-bar repeat])
                   (b)   The Sprites at work – The busy Dustman (Sprite
                          Music 6): — (bar 45–97 [including one 5-bar and
                          three 4-bar repeats])
                   (c)   Song: 'The sun *has* gone': — (bar 98–121)
                   (d)   Conclusion (with curfew-bell): — (bar 122–129,
                          leading to ...)

19.   (16)   Interlude 1
                   Home to sleep – The Children get 'OUT' (Star Music
                   11): *Andantino* (80 bars, including flute solo near end
                   [and an 8-bar repeat])

Act Two: Scene 1, Conclusion
(Outside Bourcelles: The Pine Forest at Night)

20.   (17)   Incidental Music 15
                   Outside The Star Cave (Star Music 12): *Lento* (12 bars;
                   strings and harp – with concluding violin solo)

21. (18)   Incidental Music 16 and Baritone's Melisma
                  The Wumbled People call out for star-dust (Star Music
                  13): *Lento* (4 bars; strings – and off-stage voice)

22. (19)   Incidental Music 17
                  Arrival of The Starlight Express (Sprite Music 7):
                  Allegro (14 bars [including two 2-bar repeats])

23. (20)   Incidental Music 18
                  Entry of The Sweep (Sprite Music 8): *Allegro molto*
                  (9 bars, *seque* ...)

24. (21)   Incidental Music 19
                  Entry of The Organ-Grinder (Sprite Music 9): — (9 bars,
                  seque ...)

25. (22)   Incidental Music 20
                  Entry of The Gardener (Sprite Music 10): — (9 bars)

26. (23)   Incidental Music 21 and The Laugher's Song 1
                  (a) Entry of The Laugher (Sprite Music 11): *Presto*
                       (bar 1–18)
                  (b) Song: 'I'm everywhere' (bar 19–64)
                  (c) Conclusion: — (bar 65–75)

27. (24)   Incidental Music 22
                  Entry of The Lamplighter (Sprite Music 12): *Allegro*
                  (9 bars)

28. (25)   Incidental Music 23
                  Let's ask The Organ-Grinder (Sprite Music 13): — (15
                  bars, including organ/barrel-organ [and a 5-bar repeat])

29. (26)   The Organ-Grinder's Song 4
                  'Wake up you Little Night Winds': *Allegro non troppo*
                  (44 bars, including wind-machine [and a 4-bar repeat])

30. (27)   Ballet 1
                  The Dance of The Little Winds: *Moderato – Lento* (116
                  bars, including wind-machine [and one 16-bar and
                  three 8-bar repeats])

31.   (28)   Incidental Music 24
        The kind old Dustman (Sprite Music 14): *Moderato* (21
        bars [including a 7-bar repeat])

32.   (29)   Incidental Music 25 and Soprano's Melisma
        Into The Star Cave (Star Music 14): *Lento* (7 bars;
        strings, with solo soprano and solo violin)

33.   (—)   Incidental Music 26 (not in the hire-score)
        Loading up with Star-Dust: *Presto* (52 bars) to the music
        of the 'Sun Dance' from *The Wand of Youth* (First Suite)

34.   (30)   Interlude 2
        The Wistaria Pension at night (Star Music 15): *Adagio*
        (12 bars; ending with short cadenza for harp and solo
        violin)

Act Two: Scene 2
(Bourcelles: The Wistaria Pension)

35.   (31)   Incidental Music 27
        The Lamplighter at work: the death of Miss Waghorn
        (Sprite Music 15): *Andante* (15 bars; strings)

36.   (32)   Incidental Music 28 and Interlude 3
        Off again: *Allegretto* (41 bars [including a 17-bar repeat]
        seque ...) to a version of 'Moths and Butterflies' from
        The Wand of Youth (Second Suite)

Act Two: Scene 3
(Bourcelles: The Den at La Citadelle)

37.   (33)   Entr'acte 2
        The Den at night (Star Music 16): *Più lento* (7 bars;
        strings – ending with solo 'cello cadenza)

38.   (34)   Incidental Music 29 and The Laugher's Songs 2 and 3
        (a) Un–wumbling Daddy 1 (Star Music 17): *Allegro*
              molto moderato (bar 1–43 [including four 4-bar
              repeats])

38. (cont.)   (b) Song: 'Oh stars shine brightly': — (bar 44–76
                          [including a 16-bar repeat])
                     (c) Un-wumbling Daddy 2 (Sprite Music 16): — (bar
                          76–101)
                     (d) Song: 'They'll listen to my song': — (bar 102–115)

39.   (34a)   Incidental Music 30
                     The Lamplighter at work again (Sprite Music 17):
                     Adagio (7 bars, ending in viola solo with harp)

40.   (35)   Incidental Music 31
                     Departure of The Sprites (Sprite Music 18): *Allegro*
                     (9 bars)

41.   (36)   Finale, Act 2
                     The Dawn Song (soprano): 'We shall meet The Morning
                     Spiders': — (30 bars [including a 4-bar repeat])

Third Prelude
(before the curtain, Act Three)

42.   (37)   The Organ-Grinder's Song 5 (My Old Tunes)
                     (a) Introduction: *Allegro* (bar 1–10)
                     (b) Third Prelude Song: 'My old tunes are rather
                          broken' (bar 11–79)
                     (c) Conclusion: — (bar 80–86)

Act Three: Scene 1
(Bourcelles: The Den at La Citadelle)

43.   (37a)   Jane Anne's Song (soprano)
                     (a) Cow-bells on stage
                     (b) Song: 'Dandelions, daffodils': — (5 bars,
                          unaccompanied)

44.   (38)   Incidental Music 32
                     Miss Waghorn – 'OUT' for ever (Star Music 18): — (12
                     bars; strings)

45.   (39)   Melodrama 3
The source of life – Daddy's inspiration: *Lento* (19 bars, ending with a flourish by The Lamplighter)

46.   (40)   Interlude 4
The Waltz of The Blue-eyes Fairy: *Tempo di Valse* (176 bars [including six 4-bar and two 8-bar repeats])

Act Three: Scene 2
(Outside Bourcelles: The Pine Forest at Night)

47.   (41)   Entr'acte 3 and Opening Sequence
(a)   Entr'acte
Outside The Star Cave again – Chant of The Lamplighter 1 (Star Music 19/Sprite Music 19): *Lento* (bar 1–14)
(b)   Incidental Music 33
This is a special night (Star Music 20): *Allegro* (bar 15–30)
Jinny's little stars – Arrival of Madame, etc. – Sweep, Sweep (Star Music 21/Sprite Music 20): *Moderato e grazioso* (bar 39–66 [including one 8-bar and two 2-bar repeats])
(c)   The Laugher's Song 4: 'Laugh a little every day': — (2 bars)
(d)   Incidental Music 33 (continued)
Chant of The Lamplighter 2: — (2 bars)
Here comes Mother (Star music 22): — (bar 71–84 [including two 1-bar and two 2-bar repeats])
Mother and The-Woman-of-the-Haystack (Sprite Music 21): *Moderato* (bar 85–92)
Chant of The Lamplighter 3 – Gathering Star-dust (Star Music 23): — (bar 93–99 [including two 1-bar repeats])
(e)   The Organ-Grinder's Song 6: 'They're all "soft-shiny" now': *Moderato* (bar 100–107)
(f)   Incidental Music 33 (concluded)
Arrival of Grannie (Star Music 24): *Allegretto* (bar 108–124)

48. (42)   Incidental Music 34
      (a) The Spirit of Miss Waghorn (Star Music 25):
          Andante – Lento (bar 1–9)
      (b) Daddy's tender light (Star Music 26): *Allegretto* (bar
          10–15)
      (c) Daddy enters and prepares for his speech (Star
          Music 27): — (bar 16–21)

49. (43)   Incidental Music 35
      (a) Our Fairyland (Star Music 28): *Moderato*
      (b) Ensemble
          Chant: 'Fling you starry Pattern wide ...' (The
          Sprites, etc.)
          Song (soprano): 'Oh, think beauty ...' (A Voice/The
          Laugher): — (bar 15, etc.)
          Chant: 'In the cave, you work for others ...'
          (Mother, etc.)
          Song (soprano): 'Every loving, gentle thought ...'
          (A Voice/The Laugher): — (bar 21, etc.)
          Chant: 'Every wish that you surrender ...' (Jane
          Anne, etc.)
          Song (soprano): 'While the busy Pleiades ...' (A
          Voice/The Laugher): — (bar 25, etc.)
          Chant: 'Light desire/With their fire ...' (Cousin
          Henry): — (bar 29–30, *attacca* ...)

50. (44)   Finale, Act Three
      (a) Ballet 2
          The Dance of The Pleiades (Star Music 29):
          Moderato (bar 1–9)
      (b) Song (soprano): 'Dustman, Laugher, Tramp, and
          busy Sweep' (A Voice/The Laugher): — (bar 10–24)
      (c) Song (baritone): 'Hearts must be soft-shiny dressed'
          (One of The Sprites/All The Sprites/The Organ-
          Grinder) – leading into duet with soprano: — (bar
          24–45)
      (d) Incidental Music 36
          The rising of The Star (Star Music 30): *Grandioso*
          (bar 46–71 – with bells near close)

Appendix 2   The story of *The Starlight Express*

This is a summary of the version of the Blackwood/Pearn play which
finally emerged after those hectic, difficult, and often acrimonious weeks
of rehearsal at The Kingsway Theatre in November and December 1915.
There were later changes during the run but these are not described
here except when they affect the music.[1] The numbers inserted in
square brackets in the text refer to the relevant music in Elgar's score
(see Appendix 1).

Prologue (First Prelude)

The Starlight Express begins with the curtain still drawn. As the overture
gets well under way [Music 1a], The Organ-Grinder enters accompanied
by his special theme and a troop of children who listen to his song [1b]
and dance about him from time to time, their steps echoed in the music.
The song introduces some of the themes of both play and music: of the
innocence and imagination of childhood; of night, sleep and dreams; and
(set to 'The Interfering Sun' motif) of adults as wearisome and troublesome
folk who do not understand children, or the childlike, and scorn their
fantasies. As the music moves to its conclusion [1c] the Organ-Grinder
and the children leave and, to 'The Morning Spiders' theme, the curtain
rises on Act One.

Act One

To the sound of distant cow-bells from the mountains behind, The Den,
a comfortable but muddled and untidy room in the building known as 'La
Citadelle', is revealed. This is the home of the Campden family – Mother,
Daddy, Jane Anne ('Jinny') and the two children Jimbo and Monkey – in
the Jura village of Bourcelles where they live while Daddy tries to scrape
a living by writing. ('It's cheap and nourishing', Jane Anne says, 'and the air
is a sal . . ., a salutation'.)

The grown-up Campdens are charming people but, loveable as they
are, they are troubled. Things never go well with them or with their
friends: Madame Jequier (the amusing Swiss widow who keeps the 'Pension
Wistaria' where they go for their meals), old Miss Waghorn (who has lost her
memory and is always looking for her brother and friends who have died),
and The Three Retired Governesses (who, with Miss Waghorn, live at the
pension). They are, in the expression used by Daddy, 'WUMBLED', living out
of sympathy and out of touch in such a way as to produce ineffectiveness,
muddle, discontent and unhappiness.

Daddy's a wumbled author, and Mother's a wumbled housekeeper. And Jinny's wumbled in her mind when she doesn't get her words right … And this is a wumbled room where everything gets lost.

This opening act, consisting of a single long scene, is concerned mainly with introducing the main human characters and their problems. It is Jinny's sixteenth birthday and, as a treat, she is to be allowed to unpack a large box of used clothes that richer relatives have sent, just as soon as Grannie (Mrs Campden's mother) arrives and the ladies from the pension. Daddy's cousin, Henry Rogers, is also expected from England on a visit.

At first, only Daddy, 'a spare, gentle-looking man' of about forty,[2] can be seen. He is at work on his new book, writing and muttering away, crossing things out, obviously in a thoroughly muddled (or 'wumbled') mood. Jane Anne, his elder daughter, enters. Dusting, she sings a fragment of the song of 'The Morning Spiders'. Her movements are 'gentle and deliberate', her face 'charming in its quaintly polite and attentive expression'. An earnest, sympathetic, and endearing *ingenue* who hardly seems awake in the glare of the day, she tends to use big words which she makes a special effort to learn from the newspaper, but in a 'wumbled' way.

Encouraged by the girl, Daddy pours out his troubles: he cannot get his great new shining ideas on life 'out' into a proper form. They have come to him from he knows not where but, primed, he is desperate enough to seize on any clue or remark as a further source of inspiration. One such, 'The Earth has forgotten it's a star' (a key theme of the play), now comes from Jane Anne and, as Daddy makes a note of it, she sees a lamplighter pass by outside [Music 2].

Was he *The* Lamplighter, one of Henry Roger's sprites? Reminded of Cousin Henry who, Daddy tells her, will arrive tonight from London, they talk about him and his childhood sprites. Were they real? Well, Henry thought so hard about them that they had 'come alive' for 'Thinking is being' you know. As well as The Lamplighter 'who lights us up and makes us glow', giving hope [Music 3], there were others: The Tramp (who 'does things by instinct'), The Laugher ('who laughs until trouble turns into fun'), The Head Gardener ('who makes things grow'), The Sweep (who 'sweeps the blacks and blues out of us'), The Dustman (who 'brings the dream-dust from the stars, the dust of love and sympathy and beauty') and the Woman-of-the-Haystack ('the mother of 'em all') blown along by The Little Winds.

Eagerly anticipating Henry's arrival, Jane Anne hopes he will come before bed-time so she can take him out and show him the village as it lies under the stars. This is too much for Monkey, who, having overheard (and misunderstood) the words 'OUT' and 'stars', comes tumbling in, protesting, for these are words associated with The Secret Star Society to which only she and Jimbo belong. A 'merry sprite of a girl of twelve, full of laughter and impudence', her 'quick and darting movements' contrast with those of her much more sedate sister. While they talk, the long-forgotten sound of The Organ-Grinder comes to them from outside — but far away, as if they were hearing it once again all the way from England [Music 4].

Jimbo comes in next: a 'jolly, manly little boy of ten' with 'a good carriage of the head', he has 'a gentle, courteous manner'. Jane Anne, hushing, tells him that Daddy is working but, again innocently dropping the words 'OUT' and 'stars', she receives her young brother's protestations too.

Jimbo and Monkey wait impatiently for the unpacking of the box of clothes, 'The Magic Box', as they call it, from which Jinny says 'Everybody gets exactly what they want'. They discuss the ladies from the *pension* whose absence is holding up the ceremony: Madame (who loves her garden), The Three Governesses (with only twenty pounds each a year to live on) and poor old Miss Waghorn (who lives in the past). Their sharp-tongued Grannie is coming too and her visit, as usual, is not anticipated with any pleasure. As Jane Anne helps Daddy get into an even greater muddle with his papers, the two children draw aside and discuss their Secret Society [Music 5]. Has Jinny found out about it? Probably not, they decide, for she is 'too slow' and 'couldn't "get OUT" in her sleep if she tried'.

Their conversation turns to starlight: 'It's what we get', Monkey says, 'when we're "OUT" at night'. Then, of course, only the body is asleep but they are far from certain about it all and go and ask Daddy: 'What ... are ... stars and starlight ... exacurately?' He gathers them round him and tells them what he knows, but in an uncertain, 'wumbled' fashion speaking slowly, half-chanting to the music, partly to himself and partly to the children [Music 6]:-

> '*Star*light
> Runs along into my mind
> And rolls into a ball of golden silk —
> A little skein
> Of tangled glory;
> And — when I want to get it out again
> — to weave the pattern of a verse or story —
> It must un-wind.
>
> It then gets knotted, looped, and all up-jumbled,
> And long before I get it out again, 'UN-WUMBLED',
> To make my verse or story,
> The Interfering Sun has risen
> And burst with passion through my silken prison
> To melt it down in dew,
> Like so much spider-gossamer, or fairy-cotton.
> Don't *you* ...?
> *I* call it — rotten!'

Jinny nods in a knowing way but Jimbo and Monkey, disappointed (especially with the ending), press him further. Daddy tells the three of them more about starlight:-

> It's the softest light in the whole world. When it touches our Earth ... it disappears. Goes out like a candle in the wind. Yet it's never really lost.

Speaking to the children thus, he finds, is helping him sort out the hidden ideas for his book, which must be coming to him from them in some way.

Asked where the starlight goes, he is suddenly struck by a delightful idea [Music 7]: into 'Star Caves', he says, where unused starlight gathers. And there is such a cave just near them, 'on the slopes of Boudry where the forests dip towards the precipices of the Areuse'; if one walks through the starlight 'you get all clothed and covered with it and come out all "soft-shiny"' for

> it sticks to you, and so you "stick" to other people. That's sympathy – insight.

Monkey says that she wants to get into The Star Cave; Cousin 'enry will know the way. This reminds Daddy, who had forgotten until now, to pass on this message to the children from Henry:-

> Please give my wildest love to the wicked children in advance, and tell them (*in a whisper mind*) that I'm coming with all my sprites in "The Starlight Express" and may arrive at any moment. Be sure (*this is most important please*) to tell them to look out; whatever they do, they must LOOK OUT.

Fending off an excited torrent of questions Daddy tells them to wait for the answers from Henry himself later.

To his temporary relief, they are interrupted by the arrival of Mother, an 'ample, motherly woman with a certain large grace about her' and 'a touch of Irish brogue and also of Irish charm'. A kind person she is, however, quite overwhelmed by the worries of her humdrum existence of endless sewing and mending. The ensuing conversation reveals what a muddled life theirs is. As usual, they eventually get round to discussing Daddy's 'new thing', so big and yet so strangely simple it will 'light up the world'. He is choking with it and will burst unless he can find expression for his ideas, but all Mother can wonder is: will it pay, like the love-stories he used to write? Finally, she unwittingly manages to kill his growing enthusiasm, for the moment at least, with her talk of the unpaid bills and Daddy retires to his desk to look them over.

Just at this moment Grannie enters, ill-tempered as ever. A 'little old lady, white-haired, wrinkled and wizand', she is 'like a Fairy Godmother pretending to be a witch' and carries a gold-headed ebony stick. She, too, is Irish with a touch of the brogue and has 'a very quick sharp manner' about her. As she grumbles Daddy can be seen tearing up the bills.

The ladies from the *pension* now straggle in at last. First of all comes Madame, 'an eager anxious-looking, brown-faced, dark-eyed woman, very thin' with 'stray whisps of grey hair breaking out everywhere'. Desperately anxious about her establishment which now faces bankruptcy, she is shrill of voice, 'quick and darting in her movements' and 'wildly dressed', still in her gardening clothes. The Governesses arrive next: the first 'aristocratic and an exclusive snob', the second 'mean and grasping', the third 'a sentimental, plaintive little woman whose air and costume suggest a struggle to retain her vanished youth'. Finally comes Miss Waghorn, 'an old lady, past seventy, thin and erect, with restless eyes and old hands knotted with rheumatism'; 'fustily and untidily dressed, she is extraordinarily vague and disconnected in her manner', recognises none of those present (except Jinny), and has to be introduced formally to most of them all yet again, to Monkey's heartless amusement.

But the time for the opening of The Magic Box is now at hand and an amusing sequence begins. Jinny is allowed to unpack and Daddy must try on everything first, which he does, to ludicrous effect. All those present receive gifts from the box but, to Mother's great sorrow, few if any of them are satisfied with what they get except Miss Waghorn, who finds a key in the old cloak she is handed and believes it is the lost one her long-dead brother entrusted to her that will unlock his papers (and, the others hope, her memory too). When Madame, examining the tea-gown she has been given, complains that it is unsuitable for gardening, The Gardener is heard and glimpsed through the window [Music 8][3]. Jane Anne rushes after him and he too receives a gift from the box.

The ensuing conversation leads Monkey and Jimbo, outrageously kitted out with items from the box, to conclude that everybody (except themselves of course) is 'wumbled'. But help is at hand for Jane Anne is convinced that 'a great Un-wumbler's coming'. As she speaks, the sound of The Organ-Grinder is heard again [Music 9]. Finally, before The Magic Box is put away, Jinny at last picks out something for herself, a piece of gauze veiling, blue spangled with gold; she flings it over her head and dances about [Music 10] for it reminds her of the story of her favourite stars, The Pleiades.

The Governesses leave but the other visitors linger on. There is a loud knock on the door: it is The Organ-Grinder[4] come with Cousin Henry's luggage and to tell them Henry will soon be here. Behind him, in the gathering dusk, other mysterious figures can be seen [Music 11].

Not long after, Cousin Henry himself steps into the room. Dressed in tweeds with 'square-toed boots and a soft felt travelling hat', he is a 'tall and brown-faced man about forty' with 'very blue eyes that twinkle'. He is introduced to the three visitors in turn and, after they have departed, to Jane Anne and the two children with whom he makes instant friends.

Jimbo, it is quickly decided, will be Henry's 'seketary' while he is with them in Bourcelles and will help him with his schemes to do good with his money now that he has retired. Henry looks through the window and admires the perfect network of stars he can see, including Orion and The Pleiades [Music 12 begins]. The latter, Jane Anne confides to him, are her 'special consolation' and he admits to her that his constellation is Orion. They are 'star-cousins' therefore, Jinny tells him delightedly.

When Henry is left alone with Jimbo and Monkey, he starts to tell them of his scheme for helping 'disabled – er – thingumajigs' but they think, correctly, that it is a 'wumbled' idea. They let him into their secret: they have a Star Society for 'un-wumbling ... the whole world'! [Music 13 begins]. Jinny does not know for she would never understand. They pause as she comes and goes, looking for the table-cloth, then enrol Henry as their third member, all of them choosing their special stars [13 continues].

The children tell him that they get 'OUT' of their bodies at night and go shooting up into the stars and believe he does too. When they ask him what The Starlight Express is 'exacurately' and The Sprites, he says that such things can only be spoken about under the stars, so a regular meeting of The Star Society is called for tomorrow night, 'up in the mountains ... by the precipices of the Areuse'.

When the others return the children receive a 'bed-sentence' from Mother and say goodnight. Jinny kisses her star-cousin goodnight [Music 14 begins]. She then tells her father that she will help him with his work for she can pull like anything and will get him 'OUT' and 'un-wumble' him tonight. 'I'll come to you while you're dreaming', she says, as the curtain falls.

Second Prelude

Before the curtain rises for Act Two, The Organ-Grinder, accompanied by his troop of dancing urchins, again sings another prelude song, this time casting the spell of The Blue-eyes Fairy over all that follows [Music 15].

Act Two: Scene 1 (first part)

As The Organ-Grinder leaves, an entr'acte begins [Music 16] and before long the curtain opens to reveal the first scene. It is set at the edge of The Pine Forest at dusk with all the stars (including The Pleiades) already faintly visible in the sky through a great space in the trees. The location of The Star Cave can be seen among rocks on one side as Henry tends a smoking fire. Monkey and Jimbo stand on each side of him. The children know of the cave but it is too narrow even for them to enter. Henry tells them 'There's a way into everything – everyone's thin somewhere'. Monkey calls the meeting of The Star Society to order.

They talk of starlight, of sympathy, of lost starlight and of The Star Cave; that idea, Henry suggests, came to Daddy from him via the stars which catch your thoughts and pass them on. How, the children wonder, can you get into The Star Cave? In a train, is the answer, 'a train of light' and of thought, The Starlight Express. Its passengers are those 'practised "un-wumblers"', The Sprites who carry the Starlight-of-sympathy – Star-dust – all over the world. The children ask Henry where Star-dust comes from. From 'one big star', he says, 'that the world only sees now and then' when the other stars, which help by sending it earthward, need a new supply. Orion knows this and The Pleiades. He tells them the story of Orion and The Pleiades [Music 17].

> The Pleiades were maidens once on earth.
> Orion, the giant, chased them for their beauty,
> and the Gods tossed them up amongst the stars
> – so that everybody should see their loveliness – always.
> But Orion never gave up.
> He hunts them still – always half-an-hour behind them.
> You can see his splendid head and shoulders tilting above the horizon –
> his gleaming sword, his shining belt – never tired – never resting –
> and his hungry arms stretched out across the sky . . .
> Only *really*, you know, he *has* caught 'em up,
> because their beauty *is in his heart*.
> His arms are in their hair;
> and they toss their golden rain over him with their song,
> their tears, their laughter.

As the dusk deepens and the stars become clearer they begin to feel drowsy, as if The Dustman had already been at work on their eyes. Can they hear The Starlight Express coming, the children wonder? No, it is the night, The-Scaffolding-of-the-Night has started [Music 18a]. They fall asleep . . .

Sprite-calls sound off-stage, faint and mysterious at first [Music 18b]. Then The Organ-Grinder tiptoes in, followed by all but one of The Sprites one by one, looking 'as if the blue shadows of The Pine Forest had taken form and shape'. Glimpsed in the daytime, The Sprites 'have only a slight air of strangeness and mystery to distinguish them from their types of every day' but now at night 'they are super-tramp, super-sweep', and so on, 'mysterious swift, singing creatures, with their strange musical call not unlike birds . . . blue-shadowy, or faintly luminous' suggesting 'something big and vague at the edges', though each of them always retains his distinctive appearance and character.

Moving with fantastic dancing movements round the sleepers they utter the chant about 'The busy Dustman':

> He's off to gather star-dust for our dreams . . .
> He dusts the Constellations for his sack,
> Finding it thickest on the Zodiac,
> But sweetest in the careless meteor's track . . .

Soon The Dustman himself enters. The Bringer-of-Dreams, he completes the verse while sowing his golden Star-dust of sleep:-

> *That* I keep only
> For the old and lonely . . .
>
> The rest, –
> The common stuff, –
> Is good enough
> For Daddy, or for Grannie, or for Mother,
> Or any other . . .'.[5]

Then The Organ-Grinder sings his Curfew Song [Music 18c], but he and The Sprites hide when the curfew bell sounds [Music 18d] and Henry, Monkey and Jimbo awake.[6] Henry decides they had better go home where the two children will sleep more tightly; then they can get 'OUT' quickly, return and get to work. He promises, 'by The Pleiades and all the other stars', to come back too in The Starlight Express 'as soon as the moon is high enough to cast a shadow'. As they leave, the curtain falls to mark the passage of time.

Interlude [Music 19] leading to the second part of Scene 1

The curtain rises as the music ends. The scene remains the same but it is now night: the fire is out, the pines are lit by starlight, and from the hidden mouth of The Star Cave streams a broad shaft of golden brilliance. Monkey and Jimbo, their clothes faintly radiant, stand hand-in-hand at the edge of the trees looking a little startled and wondering where on earth they can be [Music 20 starts]. They become even more surprised on seeing what appears to be a shooting star and discover that it is their sister Jane Anne [violin solo] shining in a new-found beauty with a soft light much brighter than theirs. Already busy collecting Star-dust, she enters The Star Cave without seeing them and they realise that she too is a Star Person after all.

When Jinny comes out of the cave, crammed with Star-dust [end of Music 20], she tells the others that she is collecting for Daddy and Mother, that all three of them are 'OUT', and that this is Daddy's cave. Then, after they hear the voices of all the 'wumbled' people in the world calling out for Star-dust [Music 21], Jinny shoots off, calling back to the two children that The Sprites will soon arrive in The Starlight Express and show them the way into The Star Cave.

Monkey and Jimbo hear a deep rumbling sound, then The Starlight Express sweeps like a comet across the sky and drops behind the trees [Music 22]. Sprite-calls can be heard and the voice of The Blue-eyed Guard. The children hide and watch. One by one The Sprites enter and, uttering their chants, go into the cave.

First, in quick succession come: The Sweep, 'a dear old dirty chimney sweep with circular brushes, etc.' [Music 23]; The Organ-Grinder[7] [24]; and The Head Gardener, 'a big burly man, very sunburnt, with a deep earthy voice and earth-stained garments' [25]. Next, singing, The Laugher flashes by, 'a vague swift figure, seen for only moments at a time,' moving with 'a flitting dancing gait, her face almost hidden' [Music 26]. The children catch her mood and almost give themselves away with their giggling. The Lamplighter follows, 'extraordinarily swift in his movements' [Music 27].

Monkey wonders where The Woman-of-the-Haystack has got to, so she and Jimbo call to The Organ-Grinder to fetch her. He comes out of the cave [Music 28] and sings to The Little Winds [Music 29] to blow her in.[8] But all their attempts [Music 30] to get The Haystack Woman, 'an enormous spreading person, with hair like hay, dressed in a tarpaulin, etc,' into the cave fail and she collapses exhausted on the ground. The Little Winds then call on The Dustman to give her his dust before her moans wake up the Interfering Sun ahead of its time. The Dustman enters [start of Music 31]. 'A hurrying, shadowy thing with dreaming eyes, long hair like waving grass, and hands that spread as though sowing something in the air', he puts her to sleep then, as The Little Winds thank him and dance off, himself goes into the cave, chanting.

The Organ-Grinder re-enters the cave.[9] He makes the children think of Cousin Henry. Where can be be? At that moment in comes Henry, all soft-shiny like the children; too excited to get to sleep, he tells them, he was delayed till now. As Jane Anne flashes by again, Monkey and Jimbo ask him, 'you Great "Un-wumbler"', to take them into The Star Cave.

The three of them move along the stream of starlight and slip in for, he reminds them, 'Everybody's thin somewhere' [Music 32]. The sound of sweet, wordless singing is heard from far away [end of Music 32] and The Pleiades can be seen dancing in the dome of the sky, sending starlight earthwards [start of Music 33].

The Sweep then The Gardener come out of the cave, chanting, and go on their way loaded with Star-dust. Henry and the children follow them out. They too have all that they can carry and, as they watch The Pleiades, the rest of The Sprites stream from the cave. Last of all emerges Jane Anne. As she leaves, she urges them to hurry and help with Daddy before The Interfering Sun catches them. The other three depart too but decide to call at The Wistaria Pension for some 'un-wumbling' practice first [end of Music 33]. As the interlude begins, only The Haystack Woman remains, still sleeping near the entrance of The Star Cave. The curtain falls.

Interlude [Music 34] leading to Scene 2

When the curtain rises, just before the interlude music ends, the scene has changed to a room in The Wistaria Pension where Madame Jequier and Miss Waghorn lie asleep in their beds.

Henry, Jimbo and Monkey enter by the window. Watched by The Organ-Grinder from without, they start to work first on Madame, who has nodded off with her bills and account books around her, then call on her special sprite, The Gardener, for help. He enters and, as the others touch her things with Star-dust, gets to work. When he has finished, he sings his song ('Dandelion, daffodils . . .') then shoots out. Henry bends over the sleeping figure and tells her to call in at the bank tomorrow.

Now for Miss Waghorn. They call The Lamplighter and in he hops. He starts to give of his light but soon realises that she no longer needs it [Music 35] and will soon be 'OUT' for ever, for she has remembered at last and has found her brother. He leaves and The Dustman now enters to sow his special dust for the old and lonely about her [start of Music 36]. He too departs and, as his voice dies away, Henry and the children follow and the curtain falls.

Interlude [Music 36 continued]
and Entr'acte [Music 37] leading
to Scene 3

When the curtain lifts this time we are back in The Den where Mother and Daddy are asleep in two made-up beds [Music 37 ends]. Jane Anne is already there and 'un-wumbling', with The Sweep to help her.

Henry, Jimbo and Monkey soon enter and Jinny tells them that she comes every night and has already nearly got Mother 'OUT'. Watched again by The Organ-Grinder from without, they all gather round Mother (whose needlework has fallen from her tired hands) but decide to finish her off tomorrow with the help of her special sprite, The Haystack Woman.

So they concentrate now on Daddy. They rush in a body around him and get to work with considerable difficulty. It is his head that sticks! They pull and pull to no avail; he is like elastic [Music 38a begins] and they cannot disentangle him. They call on The Sprites and Sprite-calls echo all about the house. Then the voice of The Laugher is heard singing [Music 38b], before she and the rest of The Sprites (except The Haystack Woman of course) stream into the room.

They surround the bed and, as they work on Daddy, the two children, directed by Henry, flit about putting Star-dust on his papers and other things. As each of the other sprites does his bit and departs, The Laugher sings again [Music 38c] then re-calls The Sweep who collects up Daddy's discarded 'soot blacks' that have fallen on the ground. He is followed by The Gardener who sweeps up Daddy's unwanted 'dead leaves' before they both slip out once more. The Lamplighter returns next, touching Daddy with his flaming pole [Music 39], and then The Dustman. As long Sprite-calls are heard again, from within and without, the two of them depart [Music 40], off with the rest to deal with Grannie and The Governesses.

Though they have failed with Daddy tonight, 'We'll all be "OUT" tomorrow' says Jane Anne. But now the scene is becoming brighter: 'The Interfering Sun! Look out!' Jinny starts to bump into the furniture, then disappears suddenly. Henry and the children follow. A voice without is heard singing The Dawn Song [Music 41] and the curtain falls on Act Two.

Third Prelude

As the curtain waits to rise on Act Three, The Organ-Grinder enters and, for the third and last time, sings a prelude song as the troop of children dance about him [Music 42]. He tells now of his own immortal tunes, of the children that listen and dance to them, and of The Sprites that come to them in dreams.

Act Three: Scene 1

On stage, to the sound of cow-bells, we are back in The Den next morning [Music 43a]. The place looks quite tidy now, strangely 'un-wumbled', and there are bowls of The Gardener's 'yaller' flowers everywhere. Jane Anne is flitting happily about dusting (as ever) and singing The Gardener's song from the night before [Music 43b]. The Sprites are there too, hidden about the room. Mother enters, now contentedly wearing her clothes from The Magic Box. Like Jinny, she has been very busy from first light and, to her surprise, everything has come right for a change! Jinny, too, had found that the room had almost dusted itself. They both feel re-newed and Mother's faith in Daddy's work is alive again.

Jimbo and Monkey, who awoke with the sun also, enter with presents for Jane Anne. They now see their sister in a new light and want to share their secrets with her. The Organ-Grinder is heard in the distance[10] and soon Cousin Henry enters. He too has been up for hours, having a good think about his scheme, now focused, rather more clearly and closer to home, on 'un-wumbling' Bourcelles.

He tries to hide when they see Madame Jequier on her way, dressed in her finery from The Magic Box, but she is looking for him especially. Her life, she tells them, has changed overnight and she thanks Henry for paying her bills, a loan of course! He assures her that the money is a present for all her kindnesses. But she has sad news too: Miss Waghorn has died in her sleep [Music 44][11].

The Three Governesses call in next, beaming and bowing. Contentedly wearing the very things from The Magic Box which so dissatisfied them the day before, they too are transformed. As each one speaks, a sprite (first The Sweep, then The Lamplighter, and lastly The Dustman) pops his head out from a different hiding place, unseen by all except the children. After The Governesses and Madame have gone, Grannie arrives, wearing her shawl from the box and trying for a change and not without a little effort to be kind and amiable. Like the others her character is much improved and she shows a new generosity.

Not long after Grannie's departure, in comes Daddy at last. He too is starting to 'un-wumble' and looks as if he might burst, for he has found the pattern, the form, for his new book and the rest is coming if only he can find the way. The others encourage him, Mother with her new-found sympathy. As The Lamplighter stands unseen behind him, Daddy tells them raptly the beginning of his idea [Music 45]:

> The source of our life is hid with Beauty very, very far away . . .
> Our real continuous life is spiritual, away from self.
> The bodily life uses what it can bring over from this enormous,
> under-running sea of universal consciousness
> where we are all together – splendid – free – untamed;
> where thinking is creation,
> and where we see and know each other face to face.
> It will be bigger still, of course.

When Daddy finishes The Lamplighter disappears with a flourish of his pole. All the others are much affected by what they have heard and by the events of the previous night. Even Mother is starting to shed her worry. As the grown-ups talk eagerly about the children's future, and the practical help that Henry wants to give, Monkey and Jimbo discuss their own plans for helping Daddy get right 'OUT' the next night. With their own new-found respect for her, and the encouragement of The Sprites, they draw Jinny into their schemes for the first time and enrol her as Chief of The Star Society. The Sprites peep out again quickly as the curtain falls.

Interlude [Music 46]
and Entr'acte [Music 47a] leading to Scene 2

When the curtain rises again, following the waltz interlude and start of the entr'acte, we are back again in The Pine Forest at night just by The Star Cave, the entire golden interior of which, with the stone rolled away, is now visible in a blaze of starlight.

Most of The Sprites are there, loading up with Star-dust as The Dustman chants, and The Pleiades can be seen distantly through a luminous haze, dancing in the sky. After The Sprites have left to start their work, Monkey, Jimbo, Jane Anne and Cousin Henry enter through the trees [end of Music 47a]. They know that this is a special night and, as they wait expectantly, they look up to watch The Pleiades, Jinny's stars [start of Music 47b]. Madame Jequier is the first to join them and, as one by one The Sprites come and go again chanting, they all start collecting Star-dust, soon helped by The Governesses. Then The Laugher returns, singing [47c], and The Lamplighter chants again [start of 47d] before Mother enters, all soft-shiny like the rest. They tell her she is 'OUT' and that this is Daddy's cave. She has been looking for it all her life, she says, and now feels so happy and no longer apart from the rest of them as before.

They all wait expectantly for Daddy but the next to arrive is Mother's special sprite The Haystack Woman. She now gets 'IN' at last, with the help of The Little Winds, but again collapses in a heap. As the other sprites return and depart once more, to the further chanting of The Lamplighter [end of Music 47d], Henry and the rest go on with their collecting.

Then The Organ-Grinder enters and sings to tell us that 'They're all soft-shiny now' [Music 47e] before Grannie is seen approaching, ever so slowly [47f]. The children go and help her in [end of Music 47]. Only Daddy now to come! The spirit of Miss Waghorn passes, smiling and waving, and goes into The Star Cave, 'OUT for ever' [Music 48a].[12]

A faint radiance becomes visible in the eastern sky; Daddy is on his way [Music 48b]. He enters at last, even more brilliant than the rest [48c], and linking arms with Mother, steps forward to deliver his speech [end of Music 48].

> You all have led me to this perfect night,
> and, if I'm shining now – *you* brought me here.
> *You* swept the entrance divinely clear.
> *You* showed the way! You set me first alight!
> I only followed, half unawares;
> each helping hand, and this ineffable fire,
> I have but borrowed from a million prayers,
> to make this Pattern brave with *our* desire for Fairyland!

His inspiration is now complete. Mother realizes that his Fairyland is true; they will never drift apart again.

Jane Anne tells them to listen for the whole world is about to steal into their Fairyland [start of Music 49]. They all face the eastern horizon, where the light has been growing in intensity, and wait – for something wonderful is about to happen. The Sprites enter in Indian file, chanting, and Daddy leads everybody in a grand ensemble of verse, with A-Voice-from-The-Pleiades[13] taking the singing line, 'Oh, think beauty . . .'. Then The Pleiades themselves come down to earth and dance, throwing Star-dust about them [start of Music 50], and The Sprites, giving their Sprite-calls for the last time, stream out of The Star Cave and dance round The Pleiades.

A voice sings 'Dustman, Laugher . . .' [Music 50b], another 'Heart must be . . .' [Music 50c], and the two join.[14] As the duet ends, The Sprites and The Pleiades turn expectantly towards the east [start of 50d].

The Day-star rises; it lights up all the others and makes The Earth remember it's a star too. It is The Dawn, The Star-in-the-East, the source of Daddy's great light; it rose first when A Child was born, The Children's Star, Our Star, The Star of Sympathy, The Star of Love! They all face it reverently, the children with arms stretched out, The Pleiades in an attitude like that of Blake's angels . . . and the curtain falls.

Notes to Appendix 2

1. It should be remembered, however, that the role of The Organ-Grinder was combined with that of The Tramp during rehearsals leading to the elimination of the role of his original companion, The Gypsy, and the loss of their dialogue and stage 'business'.
2. The descriptions of the characters quoted are those originally devised by Violet Pearn (per Mrs Lavender M Jones). The realization at The Kingsway did not, of course, always correspond.
3. In the original version, The Gardener and The Tramp and The Gypsy call to collect their things – secreted in The Magic Box in advance because there is 'no luggage allowed' on The Starlight Express.
4. Originally, of course, The Tramp – accompanied by The Gypsy; and the two of them later appropriated The Magic Box in order to store Star-dust in it.
5. As E J Dent had predicted, the original line about 'Fraulein, Baby, and Mother' had been thus altered due to anti-German feelings.
6. The ensuing dialogue was probably cut, with the curtain falling as the curfew bell stops ringing.
7. Originally, of course, The Tramp and The Gypsy. (It must be said that it was really most inappropriate to bring on The Organ-Grinder at this point.)
8. As we have seen, this song was a later addition to the score.
9. Though not indicated, some music should be played here: No. 4 or (softly) No. 28 perhaps.
10. See note 9 above.
11. The death of Miss Waghorn in Act 2 was one of the cuts later in the run. This had further repercussions, both here and later in Act 3.
12. See note 11 above.
13. Sung by The Laugher at The Kingsway.
14. Sung by The Laugher and The Organ-Grinder at The Kingsway.

9 Shaw and Elgar

Ronald Taylor

On a Saturday in September 1930 George Bernard Shaw took the train to Crystal Palace, sat in the Main Hall of that great building (in a prominent seat it might be added), and listened to the same piece of music performed eight times in succession. At one point he was so carried away with delight that he insisted on congratulating conductor and players. Only a prior evening engagement and the need to catch a train to London prevented him from hearing four more performances of the same work. Shaw was not normally such a patient man, so what had brought him to this unlikely situation?

To find out we must go back to the beginning of the lives of Shaw and the composer Edward Elgar, Britain's premier living composer. They were almost exactly contemporaries: Shaw, born in Dublin in 1856, being ten months older than the Englishman. Shaw was born into a lower middle-class family but they had good connections in banking and law. Unfortunately, Shaw's parents were the poor relations and his father was all too often an unreliable alcoholic. His mother sought refuge from her rather unhappy life in music. She was a mezzo-soprano of considerable ability and the house had become something of a centre for musicians and singers. Mainly this was due to her friendship with a most unorthodox music teacher and local orchestra leader, George John Vandeleur Lee. GBS has described these early years in the long preface to his *London Music in 1888–89*:[1]

> Lee used our drawing-room for rehearsals ... My mother soon became not only prima donna and chorus leader but general musical factotum in the whirlpool of Lee's activity. Her grounding in Logier's *Thoroughbass*[2] enabled her to take boundless liberties with composers. When authentic band parts were missing she thought nothing of making up an orchestral accompaniment of her own from the pianoforte score. Lee, as far as I know, had never seen a full orchestral score in his life: he conducted from the first violin part or a vocal score ...

At a later stage Lee and the Shaw family moved to a jointly owned house. This was partly an economic arrangement, but there seems little doubt that Mrs Shaw was already planning to spread her wings and 'turn professional'.

GBS was 15 years of age when the break came. Lee moved to London, Mrs Shaw and her two daughters (both older than her son) joined him there, and the young boy was left with his father in Dublin. Mrs Shaw never returned to her husband or home. GBS's eldest sister had also shown vocal talent, a further inducement for the family to try their luck in London. As for poor George Bernard ... life with his father, usually in miserable lodgings, was a thankless one, though his father's addiction to alcohol seems to have diminished and he tried to do his best for his son. GBS finished his formal education and was employed in an estate office at a salary of 18 shillings a month.

Those familiar with Elgar's early years will already have noticed certain similarities, though with one very important difference. Elgar's village, and later cathedral town, background was in the security of a happy family, even if their social status was very modest. The fact that Elgar's father and uncle were both engaged in the music business and were both amateur musicians meant that, like Shaw, Edward was always conscious of music and singing. Although Elgar's parents could hardly be called intellectual, his mother had an abiding love for literature which influenced the mind of her second son. The fact that there was much music making in the family was not particularly remarkable in Victorian times, but Elgar showed a rare talent at an early age though his full development was many years ahead. Elgar too left school at 15 and entered an uncongenial period in a local solicitor's office. Two men, far apart, in the wrong jobs but both destined to influence their contemporaries and achieve international fame.

Their lives over the next few decades need hardly concern us here, but it should be said that after their early years the differences between them were greater than the similarities. Elgar was destined to become a musician whilst Shaw's interest was in the written and spoken word. Music to him was a pleasant aspect of life, not a career. Their progress too was to be different. Elgar's progress was slow, almost painfully so, but driven by a desire to compose. On the other hand Shaw showed early brilliance and conquered his own shyness (and a stammer) by sheer persistence. Both men were musically self-taught and most of their knowledge came from books. Elgar was a Catholic in a mainly Catholic family, but Shaw was already forming his own beliefs which owed little to any established religion and was motivated by an acute social concern. Whereas Elgar remained in the environment in which he was brought up, Shaw came to London following the death, from tuberculosis, of his younger sister. In his early 20s Shaw was a rising Socialist speaker and writer, giving great impetus to the newly formed Fabian Society. By the time he reached the age of 32 he was engaged as music critic on T P O'Connor's *The Star*, a radical London evening paper. Shaw could play the piano: self-taught, he used a piano score of Mozart's *Don Giovanni* as a primer! This and other works gave him enough knowledge to thoroughly understand music though without much technical skill. Like Elgar he read Mozart's *Succinct Thoroughbass*, but whereas it gave Elgar knowledge which he put to good use in composition, Shaw found it of little use.

The standard of musical criticism in 1888 was not high. Pedantry was the rule, and some critics seemed to scorn their chosen calling and often preferred to impress the reader with an excess of technical detail, omitting any sense of the musical occasion, or the qualities of the artists who were performing. When anything new appeared it was treated with great suspicion or patronising contempt. Shaw was to change much of this, and after him musical criticism was never quite the same again. A new breed of critic, literate, well-informed and enquiring, arose.

When Shaw accepted the task of writing a two-column weekly article for *The Star* (at two guineas a week) he sought a name which would not identify him as the Socialist agitator and Fabian. He chose the name Corno di Bassetto, for as he remarked 'nobody in England would know what it meant!' He was an instant success, his sharp observation and intolerance of bad performances being balanced by his obvious knowledge and love of many kinds of music. He particularly disliked the poor libretti of oratorios which many music festivals felt obliged to put on at this period. Part of a review from 1 November 1889 will suffice:

> Take it away, Messrs Novello, take it away. Burn the whole edition lest any choral society should waste its time on rhyme-jingling that never once rises to the level of blasphemy, and on music-mongering that is enough to make every intelligent student in England forswear counterpoint ... How their essential triviality must jar on all sincere Christians.

Shaw then joined Edmund Yates' *The World* at five guineas per week, and by this time he was writing with even more wit, knowledge and style. This is not the place to recall Shaw's many brilliant essays, but they may be read in the book mentioned above as well as in the collected *Music in London*.[3] In later years Elgar told Shaw that he had read the early reviews in *The Star*, though a radical evening paper seemed unlikely reading for the conservative man from Worcester. However, Shaw's articles coincided exactly with Elgar's first, and unsuccessful, attempt at making a name in the capital, and he may well have read them then even if only at a reading library.

There is no evidence that Shaw heard any of Elgar's music in the 1890s. Elgar was struggling to make his name, and such fame as he had was largely confined to the provinces though this was to change dramatically. The first evidence of Shaw's interest in early Elgar can be gathered from an article he wrote in 1920:[4]

> For my part, I expected nothing from any English composer; and when the excitement about *Gerontius* began, I said wearily 'Another Wardour Street

festival oratorio!' But when I heard the Variations (which had not attracted me to the concert) I sat up and said 'Whew!' I knew we had got it at last.

Shaw progressed to novelist and successful playwright. Equally, suddenly Elgar's music was everywhere. The two were bound to converge at some point, and Elgar's new enthusiasm for the theatre brought about his first contact with Shavian ideas. A letter to Troyte Griffith from Elgar after the latter had read the play *Man and Superman* in 1904, is the first that we know of Elgar's attitude to GBS:[5]

> Bernard Shaw is hopelessly wrong, as all these fellows are on fundamental things: – amongst others they punch Xrianity & try to make it fit their civilization instead of making their civilization fit it. He is an amusing liar, but not much more & it is a somewhat curious pt. that in the Don Juan scene he makes his characters 'live in the remembrance' (in figure, age, etc) just, or not just but very like Newman in Gerontius. Extremes meet sometimes.

Not perhaps the most promising beginning for a friendship and when, six years later, Griffith was involved with a Barker and Vedrenne production of *The Devil's Disciple*, Elgar was still not impressed:

> A poor play, with moments of power: *badly* acted all round – if they had frankly gone in for melodrama it wd. have been fine ... the thing lacks conviction: Shaw is very amateurish in many ways.

Both men grew in fame and stature, but they do not seem to have met socially until they were introduced by Lala Vandevelde in 1918. There are various accounts of this first meeting, though the most vivid was contributed by Shaw in the book *Flyleaves*:[6]

> It was a select little luncheon party, the only guests being Elgar, myself, and Roger Fry, then at the height of his reputation as Aesthetic Pontiff. He was a handsome man with a beautiful speaking voice, in which he was accustomed to lay down the law very impressively on questions of fine art. But, when it turned out that Elgar's favourite reading in his youth had been my articles in The Star ..., we two plunged into a conversation into which Roger could not get in a word; in fact we forgot all about him. At last Madam V., seeing that we were not only ignoring her distinguished guest, but forgetting also to eat anything, interposed and made it possible for Roger to pontificate. He began with the words 'There is only one art'. He got no farther: a formidable growl from Elgar stopped him. We all turned to him; and there he was, teeth bared and all his hackles bristling, glaring at Fry. 'Music' he thundered 'is written on the sky – and you compare it to a DAMNED imitation!!!! ...

The gentle Fry let the insult go and all passed off peacefully. From this point on the men met and corresponded. Shaw met the ailing Lady Elgar and visited Severn House several times.

In January 1920 a new publication called *Music and Letters* appeared. That first issue contained a frontispiece portrait of Elgar by William Rothenstein, and a quite remarkable assessment of Elgar by Shaw as its leading article. A typically Shavian frontal charge, humorous, but strikingly accurate:

> A young man from the West Country without a musical degree, proceeding calmly and sweetly on the unconscious assumption that he was by nature and destiny one of the great composers when as a matter of fact he had never heard of the supertonic, shocked and irritated the [London] clique very painfully ... To this day you may meet and talk to him for a week without suspecting that he is anything more than a typical English country gentleman who does not know a fugue from a fandango.

Shaw had attended one of the first private performances of the *Piano Quintet*, and wrote a long letter to Elgar which consisted mainly of critical praise. It was, in fact, just the kind of mixture which Elgar found most acceptable. He distrusted adulation but liked appreciation. Michael Kennedy has written that he believes this letter was the turning point in the relationship, turning acquaintance into friendship. Elgar's view may be judged in a letter which he wrote to Sidney Colvin in 1921:[7]

> I don't think we should have *liked* Aristophanes personally, or Voltaire (perhaps) but I cannot do without their works. GBS's politics are to me appalling but he is the kindest-hearted, gentlest man I have met outside the charmed circle which includes you.

The 1920s were years of increasing friendship and contact between the two men. Elgar's withdrawal to the Worcester countryside which he loved aided this friendship rather than made it more difficult. In the late 1920s the Malvern Festival was established, largely as a stage for the plays of GBS, and Elgar was a 'local' who could come and go with ease. The actors, actresses and producers who came to Malvern met the great man, and some, such as Cedric Hardwicke and Sir Barry Jackson, became fast friends of the composer. Shaw also helped to rekindle the flame of Elgar's inspiration, almost extinguished by the death of Lady Elgar in 1920. GBS was also a welcome guest in the recording studios (it was useful publicity for HMV to have such a distinguished visitor in the studio), and he was present on several occasions when Elgar made records. Just as Elgar attended at Malvern, so Shaw became a regular visitor at the annual Three Choirs Festivals. When Elgar was attacked in a German reference book, in an article by Edward J Dent, Shaw organized the defence: though in retrospect it would probably have been better to have ignored the insult which would have had little currency in this country otherwise. Shaw, however, was never one to dodge a fight.

When Elgar was asked to write the test piece for the 1930 National Brass Band Championships at Crystal Palace, he produced *The Severn Suite*, based largely on sketches made many years before. It is attractive music, and although not immediately taken into the bandsmen's repertoire, it is played more often today. Elgar made the dedication to George Bernard Shaw, much to that gentleman's delight. Elgar was unable to be present at the contest on the 27 September. The supposed attack of sciatica was, in fact, an early warning of the more serious disease which was to cause his death. Shaw went in his stead, hence his presence for many hours listening to 'his' music, played again and again. He wrote the next day:[8]

> It is a pity you did not hear them. They all worked like Trojans at the suite; and there was not a single slovenly or vulgar bar, not a note muffed or missed. All keen: no professional staleness.

Ironically, Shaw had to leave the hall before the eventual winners, Foden's Motor Works Band, had performed, though he certainly caught the flavour of the occasion.

Shaw's last piece of advocacy for the composer he had almost 'adopted' was to bully (it is not too strong a word) the BBC into commissioning another Symphony from Elgar. Alas, it was to prove too late . . . Shaw was increasingly convinced that orthodox medicine was not the answer to the body's ills, and Elgar's frequent attacks of sciatica were an ideal opportunity for him to suggest that a visit to an osteopath would be beneficial, or a course of homeopathic medicine. The knowledge, surely available to Shaw after Elgar's death, that there was a large, inoperable, cancer pressing on the sciatic nerve, would have made most men regret that they had persisted with such advice, but Shaw was unrepentant. In a note, published many years after Elgar's death, he stated:[9]

> When his spine began to go visibly wrong I tried to persuade him to have it handled by an osteopath; but nothing could induce him to consult an unregistered practitioner; and he died, I believe, before his time, a martyr to the scrupulous conventionality he felt committed to as King's Master of Music.

On Elgar's death, in February 1934, many tributes were paid by famous men and women in various countries. It is curious that Shaw said very little at this time. Perhaps the loss of a valued friend was too acute, or again he may have felt that comment was unnecessary. Certainly he admired Elgar greatly. In a copy of *Music in London* which I saw some years ago, Shaw wrote to Elgar: 'This title is wrong. There was no music until you came'.

Another view of this relationship is contained in some notes, as yet unpublished, which the critic H C Colles wrote on returning from the Memorial Service for Elgar, held in Worcester Cathedral in March 1934. Colles made notes of a conversation with W H Reed, as the two travelled back to London by train. Reed said:

> . . . after Lady Elgar's death he took up with a set of people who were not those of his old life at all and who made him think it was smart or up-to-date or something to be irreligious.

> Bernard Shaw, I suppose, said I.

Exactly; he was awfully flattered because instead of lampooning him Shaw gave out that he [Elgar] was the only great composer, the only man indeed who could do anything still in music ... It was not a real friendship. Elgar liked Shaw's brilliant talk. He took to asking me round because Shaw was going to be there and I used to go in afterwards whenever I could. I preferred that. I always knew that that sort of thing was not Elgar's real self ...

In view of these sentiments it is perhaps surprising that Reed paid tribute to Shaw for his encouragement and advice in the publication of *Elgar as I Knew Him* (Gollancz, 1936). In fact, in *Gollancz, the story of a publishing house* (1978), a letter of Shaw's is referred to, in which he claims to have 'gone through the MS and pruned it and rearranged it, taking care not to destroy its unprofessional naivete; so that it is now quite presentable'.

GBS survived Elgar by sixteen years, still holding that central stage which he had occupied for so long. He seldom talked or wrote of Elgar, stating in 1949, in response to a request from Basil Maine, that he had nothing more to say on the subject. He commented that 'the critics are getting tired of his music'.

But curiously, Elgar was to play a role in Shaw's last hours. When GBS lay dying he was visited by Lady Astor. According to her he asked that two pieces of music should be played at his funeral. They were *Libera Me* from Verdi's *Requiem* and Elgar's *We are the Masters*. Of course, there is no such piece as the latter and it was assumed that he had meant to say 'We are the Music Makers'. But a singer, Irene Jacob, suggested that Shaw had meant *We are the Ministers* from *The Apostles*, and Lady Astor agreed. However, it was *The Music Makers* which was played and whichever Shaw had intended to 'play him out' the music of Edward Elgar was heard in salute at the last.

Notes

1. Constable, London, 1937.
2. Logier, Johann Berhnard, 1777–1846.
3. *Music in London, 1890–94*, 3 vols. Constable, London, 1932.
4. *Music & Letters*, vol.1, no.1, January 1920.
5. *Letters of Edward Elgar*, edited by Percy M Young. Bles, London, 1956.
6. Shaw, Bernard, *Flyleaves*, edited by Dan H Laurence & Daniel J Leary. W. Thomas Taylor, Austin, Texas, 1977.
7. *Letters* ... See note 5.
8. *idem.*
9. *Flyleaves* ... See note 6.

10   Some Elgar interpreters

Michael Kennedy

There are many more interpreters of Elgar than some people think, and always were. Even if this article had been written twenty years ago, before the wider renewal of interest in his music had gained full momentum, readers might have been surprised by the number and variety of musicians who performed the works of a composer who many of his fellow-countrymen had come to believe had a narrow and limited appeal. Today the number of conductors alone who have explored his works constitutes a formidable array: not merely the third generation of British conductors: Del Mar, Groves, Handley, Davis, Gibson, Rattle, Loughran, Hickox, Mackerras, Thomson, Marriner, but their contemporaries from abroad. Thus, in the past decade, major Elgar works have been conducted (and in many cases recorded) by Solti, Barenboim, Haitink, Sinopoli, Bernstein, Dorati, Svetlanov, Kasprzyk, Rozhdestvensky, Jochum, Previn, Mehta, Ormandy, Stokowski and many others. There are outstanding omissions in this list which tell their own story, most notably Karajan and Giulini.

Yet the 'mystique' surrounding Elgar interpreters belongs to the first and second generations, those who pioneered and created in the early years of this century and those who tended the flame in years when performances and recordings were scarcer than they are now. This article will be principally concerned with them. Inevitably, discussion will largely devolve upon recordings. Even the interpretations of Sir Adrian Boult and Sir John Barbirolli can only mean anything to younger readers through their recordings. It is too early for an assessment of their present-day successors: the perspective is not yet in clear focus. It is, of course, only through recordings that we today can form any judgements about some of the legendary Elgarians. About some of the greatest we can rely only on written reports and hearsay. How tantalising it is that we have no idea of how Hans Richter phrased the First Symphony, or what his tempi were in the *Variations*. Notwithstanding his failure to come to grips with *The Dream of Gerontius* at the first performance in Birmingham in October 1900, it is clear that by the time he conducted it again in Manchester in March 1903, he had mastered it completely and was anxious to make reparation for his earlier shortcomings. Arthur Johnstone, critic of the *Manchester Guardian* and by far the most sympathetic and perceptive of the early writers on Elgar, wrote next morning that it was 'doubtless the most carefully prepared of the performances that have been given thus far in this country'. The Hallé Choir's contribution

> sounded spontaneous and unembarrassed, as though the singers were sure of the notes and could give nearly all their attention to phrasing, expression and dynamic adjustments. In the highest degree remarkable, too, was the orchestral performance. Passages of such peculiar difficulty as the rushing string figures that represent the strains of heavenly music overheard by the Soul and the Angel as they approach the judgment-seat came out with much greater distinction than we have ever heard before, and we had a similar impression at many other points in the performance, which was as delicate as it was precise in detail and broad in style.

Johnstone was writing with considerable authority and experience, for not only had he been at Birmingham, he had attended both the Düsseldorf performances conducted by Julius Buths. (Critics paid less attention to conductors' interpretations than we do today, so we are none the wiser about Buths as an Elgarian.) It is good to recall that Richter was so upset by the cool reception the Manchester audience gave to the *Introduction and Allegro for Strings* that he repeated it there and then, much to the listeners' chagrin, it would appear.

Nor is it Richter only whom we should like to have heard. Bruno Walter, Fritz Steinbach, Felix Weingartner, Franz Schalk and Artur Nikisch all conducted major Elgar works in the years up to 1914 (Walter after the war, too: the First Symphony at the Royal Philharmonic Society on 4 December 1924). What would one not give to have been in Carnegie Hall in 1910 and 1911 and to have heard Gustav Mahler conduct four of the *Sea Pictures* and the *Variations*? Alas, the New York critics of the day were unsympathetic both to Mahler as a conductor and Elgar as a composer, so no press comment on these occasions is of any significant value. If Mahler had lived, he would have conducted Charles Ives's Third Symphony in New York, and it is reasonable to suppose he might well have included Elgar's First Symphony in his programmes, although it would surely have been the Second (first performed in London six days after Mahler's death in Vienna) that would have appealed more strongly to him.

Some conductors active in the pre-1914 years have left us Elgar recordings, although of the four I have in mind only Sir Henry Wood would have claimed to be a thoroughgoing Elgarian. He recorded neither of the symphonies and we can judge him today by recordings of the *Variations* made in 1925 and 1936 and by the not very imaginative accompaniment to

Albert Sammons's performance of the Violin Concerto. Toscanini was one of the earliest interpreters of the *Introduction and Allegro for Strings*. When he visited London in the 1930s to conduct the BBC Symphony Orchestra he conducted, and retained sporadically in his repertoire, the *Variations* in a performance that led some of the critics of the day to describe it as 'un-English', which could be interpreted as 'This is an English masterpiece which Italians don't understand, so keep off our grass'; others waxed ecstatic over its 'absolute truth'. The recording made with the NBC Orchestra in the 1950s is outstanding for clarity and for faster tempi than those to which we are accustomed today (of which more anon). The violist Bernard Shore rated Toscanini's performance the best and recalled that he spent a long time on the theme itself, perfecting the phrasing and balancing the supporting harmonies. Pierre Monteux also recorded the *Variations*, late in his long career, when he was principal conductor of the London Symphony Orchestra. This is not the foreign conductor's statutory tribute to the host country, but a reading which has been deeply considered. I have often commented on the influence on Elgar of the French composers Bizet, Massenet and Saint-Saëns, so it is no surprise to find Monteux at home in this score and giving such winsome charm to 'Dorabella'.

The fourth of this pre-1914 quartet is a controversial figure in Elgarian studies, Sir Thomas Beecham. His savage cutting of the First Symphony and his likening it to 'the towers of St Pancras Station' are notorious. So is his ill-mannered ignoring of Elgar's suggestion that *Falstaff* might have been written for him. So far as I can discover he never conducted *The Dream of Gerontius* in Britain, but in June 1941 he conducted it in Montreal. A Beecham Demons' Chorus must have been worth hearing. But, generally speaking, big religious choral works were not his line of country, nor, for that matter, big late-romantic symphonies of the kind composed by Elgar, Bruckner and Mahler. It is fair to judge a conductor's preferences by the composers he most frequently included in his programmes, and Beecham did not often conduct Elgar. In any case he was at his best in smaller lighter works or in music where vignettes were part of the structure. So Elgar's *Variations* were always more likely to appeal to him than the symphonies, and his 1950s recording with the Royal Philharmonic Orchestra is one of the most fascinating there is. Like Toscanini, he lavished extraordinary care on the theme, which he takes slowly and expressively, broadening into a lyrically poetic 'C.A.E.' The 'Nimrod' is of profound solemnity (one would have expected him to de-mythologise it) and 'Dorabella' has a Gallic poise but is rather too slow. The drum-beats in the 'Romanza' for the six bars after cue 58 in the full score sound ominous, as if Beecham knew Elgar's secret and that *** stood only partly for Lady Mary Lygon. In this variation he lets us hear more clearly than most conductors the cello solo accompanying the solo clarinet's first two quotations of Mendelssohn. The impression of the performance as a whole is that Beecham excels everybody, including Elgar himself, in conveying that the music represents a personal portrait-gallery. Each variation is finely chiselled, there is a mellow and affectionate air to the proceedings as well as the characteristic Beecham elegance and charm. Such insights into the music must have sprung from wholehearted admiration.

As one would expect, Beecham's *Cockaigne* has a swaggering exhilaration that does not preclude a highly romantic approach to the quieter episodes. The coda is swept along at a great pace. His infallible touch with lighter works which are something less than masterpieces but are still first-rate music is shown in the *Serenade*, where the hesitantly delicate rhythms of the first movement are gracefully enunciated. But in the central *Larghetto*, Beecham again outguns his rivals in demonstrating that this movement is a microcosm of the bigger movements in the symphonies and concertos. It is played with an intensity that takes it into the realm of tragedy, its long-spanned melody passionately phrased, the climax underpinned by a throbbing bass. After this, the *finale* comes as a gentle epilogue. It is instructive to compare this performance with Elgar's, recorded in 1933 on his last visit to the HMV studios. The old man treats this favourite work of his youth with infinite tenderness and imparts a blithe spirit to its first and last movements.

There I have mentioned the outstanding interpreter of Elgar during his lifetime, the composer himself. He was the first composer to realise the potential of the gramophone both as a medium for study and as a means of preservation. So we have a large body of his work conducted on record by himself. It is interesting to observe the gaps in his recorded repertory. It is understandable, considering the limitations of 78 rpm recording, that there is nothing from *The Apostles* and *The Kingdom* (except the Prelude to the latter) and only extracts from *Gerontius* (although he was pressing for a complete recording from as early as 1917). But no *Introduction and Allegro* remains puzzling; no Triumphal March from *Caractacus*, nor the Woodland Interlude; no *Sospiri*; no *Grania and Diarmuid* funeral march; no *Imperial March*; no *Dream Children* and only a brief extract from *King Olaf*. But much else and, above all, the symphonies, concertos, concert-overtures, suites, marches and many of the lighter pieces.

It is perhaps superfluous to raise the hoary question of how good a conductor Elgar was, but obviously it has some bearing on discussion of his interpretations. One test of a good conductor is that he should be able to impress upon an orchestra exactly how he wants the music to sound and to 'go'. It does not really matter how he does it as long as he does it. There can be no questioning Elgar's ability in this respect. Sir John Barbirolli, who played in orchestras conducted by Elgar, said: 'He could make you feel exactly what he wanted if you were in sympathy with him'.

Sir Adrian Boult ascribed Elgar's production of tone quality that was 'highly personal' to the 'tension and lustre' added by his 'nervous, electric beat'. He maintained that most of the finest performances of Elgar's works he and others had heard were conducted by Elgar. But Sir Adrian was also emphatic that it was dangerous to accept Elgar's recorded performances as a yardstick. There was, he maintained, the constriction caused by the limit of four (later four-and-three-quarter) minutes for one side of a 78 rpm record. (This, as I will show later, may be disputed.) More important, Boult's experience was that Elgar's performances fluctuated both in tempi and dynamics. Boult would mark certain passages in his copies of the scores when he attended performances, 'Elgar 1928', for instance. But he gave it up because, as he told me, 'they were never the same'. It is dangerous, therefore, to speak of Elgar's recorded performances as 'definitive' in tempo, nuances, phrasing and dynamics. But they have much to teach us about the general atmosphere of the works, how they should 'go'.

Listening to Elgar's performances inevitably involves some understanding and acceptance of the performing practices of those days, particularly the string players' portamento or sliding, the absence or sparing use of vibrato and the tendency to hurry short notes. The use of portamento especially when it was 'heavy' (that is to say the slide was slow and was as loud as the two notes it connected) gives an old-fashioned sound to modern ears, but was obviously acceptable to Elgar, as can be heard in the playing of the theme in his 1926 recording of the *Variations*, when there are 18 slides in 17 bars! In the solo viola passages in this recording there is no vibrato on short notes and very little on others. This style also affected wind-playing, as can be heard in the long recitative-like oboe solo which weaves its way above the rest of the orchestra in the *Larghetto* of the Second Symphony. The change in orchestral styles of playing came in the early 1930s with the formation of Boult's BBC Symphony Orchestra and Beecham's London Philharmonic. It was not that portamento disappeared altogether, but it became subtler and less audible. Boult, recording the *Variations* in 1936, has 15 slides in the theme but they are scarcely noticeable. Soloists changed too: Menuhin's portamento in his famous 1932 recording of the Violin Concerto with Elgar is quick and light compared with Albert Sammons's recording of a few years earlier. When Elgar re-recorded *Cockaigne* in 1933 with the BBC Symphony Orchestra, the semiquavers were less hurried and were given their full value compared with the over-dotted dotted rhythms in the same passages in his 1926 recording. His *Froissart* with the LPO, recorded in 1933, has Leon Goossens as principal oboist playing with vibrato and much more expressive phrasing. Elgar thought his playing 'divine'.

Even more fundamental is the matter of tempi. Elgar (and other conductors) took his music a good deal faster than any modern conductors.

But, ignoring or extending indications in the score as the case might be, he greatly varied the tempo within individual movements, accelerating and decelerating in a manner that bore out his expressed wish that his music should be played 'mystically and elastically', not squarely. He had an entirely individual mastery of tempo rubato to which orchestras were clearly responsive (another indication of his technical effectiveness as a conductor) and a cavalier attitude to his metronome markings (some of which are mathematically suspect, such as 'W.N.' in the *Variations*). In his *Variations* recording, No 2 is taken at $\quad$ = 80, whereas the score gives 72 (though it was 84 in one of the sketches for the work). This variation provides a good example of the modern tendency to go slower. Recording it in 1936, Boult's speed was 86, in 1961 it was 68; Barbirolli in 1947 was 84, in 1963 the scores prescribed 72. 'Nimrod' was a source of particular trouble to Elgar. Originally the metronome mark was $\quad$ = 66, which Elgar altered to 52 after conducting the *Variations*. (He also altered the tempo direction from *moderato* to *adagio*.) In his recording he veers from 40 to 56. Similarly, in the First Symphony his variations of speed are much more extreme than in any modern recordings. Incidentally, although he speeded up the tempo in some of his pre-1925 acoustic recordings to fit the music on a side, it is doubtful if he did so for electric recording since there was often room left at the end of a side.

Elgar's volatility makes his performances of his own works more dramatic and exciting than almost anyone else's. In the works he recorded, with few exceptions (when he was obviously in one of his uninterested moods), the music glows and surges with an ardour that the limitations of recording techniques cannot prevent being transmitted to the listener. The intensity of his phrasing and the subtlety of his rubato in the theme of the *Variations* in 1926 are a revelation which has been approached in modern recordings only by Barbirolli and, perhaps more unexpectedly, by Menuhin. Here, too, is surely the right fluttering speed for 'Dorabella'. Elgar is remarkable in conveying some nameless menace in the 'Romanza'. Where Beecham does it with the timpani, Elgar emphasises the crescendo on horns and trumpets. He also attaches special importance to the rhythmic figure for trumpets which occurs twice in 'E.D.U.' between cues 73 and 74.

Of the symphonies, the finer recorded performance is that of No 1 in 1930. Something of the excitement of the 1908 premiere conducted by Richter can still be sensed from Elgar's exhilarating account. His pacing of the motto march-theme is a model for all in its dignity which eschews all lugubriousness. The *scherzo* flashes along, yet with wistful poetry in the 'down-by-the-river' trio and punctilious attention paid to the melodic counterpoints in cellos and violas which are obscured in most other recordings. His most marked changes of speed are in the *finale*, where he ignores the $\quad$ = 84 at the allegro in favour of 76. The Second Symphony was recorded in 1927, the year of his seventieth birthday, and is a less mercurial performance than that on his acoustic recording made in 1924. For example, the glorious coda of the *finale* seems almost perfunctory in the second recording compared with the superb swell and fade of the earlier version. Even so, there is much here to intrigue the modern ear, such as the prominence given to counter-melodies. Very personal to Elgar, too, is his treatment of the passage beginning at cue 33 in the first movement. This is the episode he described to Alice Stuart-Wortley as 'most extraordinary ... a sort of malign influence wandering thro' the summer night in the garden' and to Ernest Newman as like 'a love scene in a garden at night when the ghost of some memories comes *through* it – it makes me shiver'. In many a performance one is at a loss to discover anything 'malign' here, so insistent are conductors on letting us relish the luscious beauty of the string section. But Elgar makes us shiver, too, as some ghostly spectre lays an icy finger on the music. How does he do it? By making the texture transparent so that the listeners hear not only the high strings but the sepulchral harps, muted horns, the ascending semiquavers in the divided violas and of course the cellos' yearning melodic line above the rapid pizzicato rhythm of the basses and the side-drum's stealthy beat.

The tragedy of our not having a complete *Gerontius* from Elgar is underlined by the quality of the fragments we do possess. These have the additional value of having been made, as daring technical experiments, at public performances, one in the Royal Albert Hall with a bronchial February audience in 1927, the other later the same year in Hereford Cathedral during the Three Choirs Festival. Only Margaret Balfour's Angel is common to both performances among the soloists. With none of the constraints of the recording-studio, these precious glimpses of Elgar's interpretation of his greatest choral work reveal how he combined an almost operatic dramatic approach with a devotional spirituality that never carries the remotest suggestion of sanctimoniousness. Indeed, the performance of the Prelude is a marvellous advertisement for muscular Christianity, with its gathering impetus from a slow start, its theatrical pauses and the processional fervour of the 'Go forth' theme at its first appearance.

Elgar was fond of the word 'alive' in relation to his own music, and that is what we feel here, that it is constantly re-created, re-lived. The surges of tone on the repeated 'Amen' cadences as the choir chants its litany about Noah, David and Job, the blazing tone of the choral 'Go forth' and the continually varying pace of the 'Praise to the holiest' chorus are all outstanding examples of the elasticity and flexibility Elgar wanted. The critic in 1926 who wrote of his cutting his way through his own music 'in a fashion both nervous and decisive' put his finger on Elgar's secret as a self-interpreter. This decisiveness is most apparent in both recorded accounts of the Angel of the Agony's solo 'Jesu, by that shuddering dread', where the brass and drums are given licence vividly to illustrate the shuddering dread and the intensity of the strings brings Gethsemane into our sitting-room. The Three Choirs 'Kyrie' is beautifully sung. Elgar encourages a non-legato enunciation of each note of 'eleison' at six bars after cue 29 and he allows an effective if strictly unauthorised *rit.* at 'Prepare to meet thy God'. Although the marking in the score is triple piano, he also gives prominence (in both recordings) to the drum-roll which accompanies the choir's 'Lord, Thou hast been our refuge' and one does not always hear so clearly the horns' counterpoint to the orchestral statement of the 'Softly and gently' theme (cues 126–7). The *forte* on the second syllable of the last 'Amen' is heavily stressed, with the orchestra's final chord vibrating into silence. Clearly, a *Gerontius* performance conducted by the composer was concerned with essentials but the details fell into place naturally. In the Prelude to *The Kingdom*, which is all we have of it under Elgar's baton, the overwhelming impression is again of nervous energy and urgency and of the arched phrasing of the 'New Faith' theme. Extracts from *The Music Makers* leave no doubt as to the music's personal significance and importance: it is manifest in the shaping of every quoted phrase that 'in this I have really *shewn* myself'.

The other three major works which Elgar conducted for the gramophone are the concertos and *Falstaff*. The cellist Beatrice Harrison's portamenti are rivalled in emotional un-reticence by Elgar's orchestral rubato, especially in the second movement at cues 27 and 28. Elgar's first-movement *moderato* is faster than that of most other conductors and he and the soloist keep the *adagio* as a secret reverie rather than as the soulful burst of emotion to which we are more accustomed nowadays. As for the *finale*, vibrant is again the only word for Elgar's fluctuations of tempo and mood. In her autobiography, Beatrice Harrison reveals little of her attitude to interpreting this exquisite concerto (although we learn that she always wore blue knickers when playing it!) but quotes a remark made to her by the composer before a public performance: 'Give it 'em, Beatrice, give it 'em. Don't mind about the notes or anything. Give 'em the spirit'. They both do that on the records and the result is revelatory.

As for the Violin Concerto, the 1932 recording with the boy Menuhin is rightly one of the most famous events in gramophone history. Elgar had had his 75th birthday six weeks earlier and was evidently in good humour. No subsequent recorded performance of the orchestral part (and not many that one hears in the concert-hall) seems so absolutely right in choice of tempi and has so much fire, energy and brilliance. In the opening tutti, Elgar's interpretation has a spring in its step, a sense of barely contained excitement at all that is to come. Later in the first movement (from cue 25), there is a passage where the second subject (the 'Windflower' theme) enters quietly on the cellos and modulates into remote and wonderful regions of tonality while the solo violin performs ecstatic acrobatics. Elgar finds the exact nuances of phrasing for the orchestra. And so on, throughout the work, with Elgar and the 'wonderful boy' matching each other in penetrating to the heart of this generous music. Menuhin's later recording with Boult may have moments of more mature insights but there is an artistic joy in his youthful playing which is still moving to hear after the passage of over half a century.

The enjoyment Elgar felt while recording the concerto may also be savoured while listening to his *Falstaff* from 1931. Here was a work which, since its first performance in 1913, had had relatively few performances and had probably never been played to a full hall. It is a tribute to Fred Gaisberg's perspicacity that he over-rode any commercial considerations in order to commit Elgar's interpretation to disc. The result was worth the risk, a relaxed, genial performance, full of rhythmic zest and with the two Interludes (which Elgar had recorded separately with rather less inspiration some years earlier) played with infinite tenderness. The violin solo in the first is played by W H Reed, whose tone may sound thin today but who knew the expressive value of every note. The unforgettable co-operation between the two friends in this music is somehow symbolic of the art of Elgar's interpretation as it was in the golden age of his lifetime.

It is also a reminder that we are bereft of performances by many of Elgar's first interpreters. Richter has already been mentioned. But not a note exists of Kreisler in the Violin Concerto nor of Felix Salmond in the Cello Concerto. We have nothing of the original soloists in *The Dream of Gerontius* and no Elgar sung by Gervase Elwes, one of the famous exponents of Gerontius. Another notable Gerontius, whom Elgar preferred to Elwes because he sounded more worldly and less of a saint, was John Coates. His 1915 recording of *In the Dawn* tells us how suitable he must have been in the larger role. No one has yet discovered a recording by Muriel Foster, the leading exponent of the Angel from 1902 until her retirement. Both Elgar's daughter and Sir Adrian Boult described her to me as coming near to the timbre of Janet Baker.

But we do have a short example of the first *Caractacus*, Andrew Black, in the 'Sword Song', none too accurate, perhaps, but disarmingly vital and virile. We have Clara Butt in *Land of Hope and Glory*, far better than caricature may have led many to suppose, though Edna Thornton, who sang in the first London *Coronation Ode*, runs her close. Butt's 'Where corals lie' from *Sea Pictures* has a lightness that also distinguishes her brief *Gerontius* extract recorded in 1916, no big booming Dame Clara here.

I will return to some singers of Elgar later, but some conductors claim attention now. Sir Hamilton Harty's Elgar performances were much admired but we can judge them from only two recordings. His *Variations* with the 1932 Hallé has more portamento in the statement of the theme than Elgar's

1926 recording. He also takes the fast variations faster, and it says much for the Hallé woodwind in No 2 that they articulate the notes as well as they do. One of the refreshing aspects of this performance is that this is the last time on record that 'Nimrod' has no overtones of the Cenotaph or a memorial service. Harty's other recording is of the Cello Concerto, with W H Squire as soloist, made in 1930. This performance is less wayward than the Elgar/Harrison and the portamento is subtler. There is a deeply affecting performance of the *adagio*. Squire was a splendid cellist, yet his name is almost forgotten.

Of the second-generation Elgar conductors, Adrian Boult is more closely associated with his music than anyone else. Yet he was not an instinctive Elgarian. His youthful diaries disclose that he responded coolly to most of Elgar's works when he first heard them. Strauss, Wagner and Berlioz attracted him more and, among English composers, Parry and Vaughan Williams. Yet he saw the light at some time during the First World War and included *In the South* and the Second Symphony in the famous 1918 concerts with the London Symphony Orchestra, when he courageously introduced himself to London audiences by conducting four programmes of new or neglected works. The performance of the symphony removed the shadow that had hung over it since it was first played in 1911 and won Boult Elgar's gratitude. It remained a Boult speciality for the rest of his life and he recorded it five times. Oddly, he did not conduct the First Symphony until 1936 although he rehearsed it for Elgar. He did not record any Elgar (apart from the orchestration of Chopin's Funeral March) until the *Variations* in 1936, a period piece in respect of the portamento in the theme (although lightly applied) and the fast tempi. His finest Elgar recording is almost certainly that of the Second Symphony made in 1944. It has a blazing excitement and rhythmic drive combined with a rich layer of emotional fervour faithfully captured by the engineers. Although his tempi differed little in later year (a bit slower), his interpretation as recorded acquired an extra dimension of architectural splendour and dignity but, it may be thought, at some cost in imaginative flair. In the concert-hall, however, even when he was nearing ninety the blood could flow hot and strong. He was not always at his best as an accompanist in the concertos. True, he was wonderfully sensitive to a soloist's reading but there was a certain heaviness or staidness that sometimes prevented the music taking flight. Boult, one felt, was always slightly disconcerted by Elgar's uninhibitedly grandiose manner (it was not surprising that in the 1970s he refused to conduct *Caractacus* unless the text of the final imperialistic chorus was modified). He was more effective in the coda of the Second Symphony than of the First, and he rarely brought to the 'E.D.U.' *finale* of the *Variations* the swagger that Barbirolli and Sargent achieved effortlessly. Again, it is not surprising that some of his noblest performances of the *Variations* were those he conducted for the Royal Ballet where the original, less effusive, ending was used. In the delicious fancies of the *Wand of Youth* he was incomparable.

But no one did more to establish Elgar among the classic composers. Boult did this in the twenty and more years after the composer's death when Elgar's reputation underwent a decline and recording companies were not over-anxious to risk investment in him. In the eight years immediately after the war in Europe ended, Boult recorded only the Cello Concerto (with Casals), the First Symphony and *Falstaff*, major works it is true, but today one could expect more than one recording of each within one year. It was in this climate that Boult's dignified and superbly moulded Elgar held audiences' respect, and interpretations were perhaps purposely under-stated in order that the then less acceptable face of Elgar might not divert attention from the more elevated aspects.

In his old age he made the first complete recording of *The Music Makers*, with Janet Baker an incandescent soloist, and he revealed the beauty of the two oratorios, *The Apostles* and *The Kingdom*, so effectively in his recordings that performances of these works are today by no means uncommon, whereas in 1968, when *The Kingdom* was recorded, they were hard to find. Boult agreed with his and Elgar's friend Frank Schuster's opinion that *The Kingdom* was a greater work than *Gerontius*. Even if this is regarded as an eccentric judgement, he laid his conviction on the line in his recording and committed a deeply moving performance to disc, following it up some years later with a no less magnificent *The Apostles*. Then in 1976 he finally recorded *Gerontius*, not without personal qualms that it would be found 'boring' after Barbirolli's. Not boring, merely different and clearly the result of deep and critical study of the score. He would have liked, as Sargent had done in his first recording, to have two separate basses, feeling (as he told me) that the arias were written for such different types of singer that only in this way could their true greatness be revealed. Barbirolli's *Gerontius* was a visionary and personal religious document, Sargent's a spiritual journey, Britten's a relishing of the score's novelty and daring. Boult's was distinguished by its tremendous grandeur and lofty aims. We did not expect from him the nervous tension of Elgar's own conducting, but the music is susceptible of many interpretations and Boult's was born of an unshakeable musical integrity.

Barbirolli hero-worshipped Elgar from his youth, played in orchestras under him (including the ill-fated first performance of the Cello Concerto in 1919), was an early soloist in the Cello Concerto and began his Elgar-conducting career in public in 1927 with the Second Symphony and in the recording-studio with the first recording of the *Introduction and Allegro*, which he re-recorded two years later (and four times more after that). Elgar said of this recording that he had not hitherto realised it was 'such a big piece', a remark that has been interpreted as an implied criticism, although since he said the same thing about Casals' interpretation of the Cello Concerto it seems unlikely to have been intended adversely. Barbirolli's mixture of an English-Italian-French temperament was ideal for Elgar but his interpretations did not command universal approval. Just as Toscanini, Casals and Monteux were regarded as 'un-English', so it was felt that Barbirolli (who had made his name as an opera conductor) was too dramatic, too over-heated for this music. This attitude began as early as that 1927 performance of the symphony. Schuster wrote afterwards to Elgar that

> Barbirolli gave a remarkably good account of your No 2, playing it as it was written and, what's more, as it is felt. No point-making and no exaggeration but very cohesive and round and rich. But it appears that in spite of a most enthusiastic reception the highbrows don't agree with me.

And they never did. But Barbirolli's red-blooded approach to Elgar converted many thousands of listeners to the music. One had to be irreversibly out of sympathy with it not to be led into its most secret recesses by the power and proselytising zeal of Barbirolli's conducting.

Like several great conductors he was never fully himself in the recording-studio. Splendid as his Elgar recordings are (and none finer than those of the string music, the *Variations* and the Cello Concerto, with both Navarra and du Pré), they lack some of the remembered magnetism of the 'live' events. The nearest on record to what one heard in the hall are the 1954 Second Symphony with the Hallé and 1963 First Symphony with the Philharmonia. Here one feels the ebb and flow and hears the kaleidoscopic shadings of tone that were his distinguishing marks; and here there is the nervous energy with which he intuitively came nearer to Elgar himself than was the case with Boult. Barbirolli was frequently criticised for slow tempi, notably in his 1964 recording of the Second Symphony, where some feel that he jeopardised the work's main structure for the sake of a diversion along an emotional by-pass. Those in sympathy with him have no such qualms and are swept along on the floodtide of this impassioned performance, which is certainly 'elastic', and reached its most overwhelming moment at the climax of the *Larghetto*, when Elgar's request for vibrato and glissandi is met by conductor and players with the artistry that comes from deep understanding of the music. Barbirolli's slow tempi in any case are no longer remarkable when one compares him with Haitink and Bryden Thomson in this work. His recording of *Falstaff* is the next best to Elgar's in its zest, characterisation and structural unity.

In Barbirolli's *Gerontius* recording, the blend of dramatic and devotional is well caught, but a recording of a 'live' performance would have been even more memorable and truer to this conductor's genius. He never conducted the oratorios nor *The Music Makers* and, by a strange quirk, he overlooked *In the South* until the last months of his life when, if immodesty will be excused after this lapse of time, I persuaded him that this music of Italy might have been written specially for him, and was rewarded with a performance of a sumptuousness such as I have never experienced from anyone else, including Silvestri. He did not have Boult's Elgarian range, but on those works he loved he lavished an artistry that was born from the conviction that Elgar was one of the great composers of the world. Whenever he went abroad he took some Elgar with him and it is not his fault if the inhabitants of New York, Houston, Berlin and Prague, to name only a few, remain ignorant of Elgar's achievement. It is through him that Barenboim and Mehta came to Elgar's music. Of all the 'non-traditional' conductors of Elgar, Barenboim is perhaps the most musical, providing illuminating new insights into the symphonies.

Of Malcolm Sargent's Elgar performances I have mixed memories: of an *Apostles* that put all other interpretations in the shade; of interpretations of the symphonies that went no more than skin-deep, probably because of skimped rehearsal; and of how the brilliance of him and Heifetz in the Violin Concerto resulted in that heartless recording. Of the man's moving belief in Elgar's greatness there could be no doubt. He left a classic memorial to that belief in his *Gerontius* recording of 1944. This brings me conveniently to the role of Gerontius, which must have its place in any discussion of Elgar's interpreters.

It is a role which requires the tenor to be both a Verdian and a Handelian, and for many years it has had a succession of singers who have 'made it their own'. Coates has already been mentioned. Elwes, to judge from his other recordings, and Steuart Wilson, judged from a fragment recorded with Elgar, were episcopal in approach and tone as was Peter Pears. I was told by Boult that Elwes' voice was not big enough for Queen's Hall. From what one can hear of him as recorded at Hereford in 1927 Tudor Davies must have been near to ideal, dramatic, intense and with an appropriate baritonal quality. A tendency to Celtic lachrymoseness is detectable. Sargent's recording has Heddle Nash, not a big voice in the concert-hall, but as recorded here his interpretation has remained a touchstone by which a whole generation has judged other singers of the part.

Richard Lewis, the Gerontius on Sargent's second recording and on Barbirolli's, was the finest in my own experience, the complete Gerontius, from the agonies of dying to the anxious questionings of the Angel and the final ecstasy. The Australian Ronald Dowd most nearly rivalled him. I recall two marvellous performances by Parry Jones, not a great singer, but when he was inspired, as he was on these occasions, capable of greatness. Boult's daring choice of the Swedish Nicolai Gedda was justified by many interpretative insights, scrupulous observation of Elgar's markings and a clear distinction in vocal timbres between the Gerontius of Part I and the Soul of Part II. No tenor today is identified with the part. For the first time in its history it lacks a natural interpreter. The opposite applies to the role of the Angel, where any number of mezzo-sopranos have shown themselves equipped to succeed Janet Baker, whose performance is not only vocally supreme but manages to suggest a celestial being, sometimes stern and remote as well as sympathetic. (The present revival of the popularity of both *The Music Makers* and *Sea Pictures* may also be ascribed to this plethora of mezzos.) Too many singers of the Angel sound domestic and motherly dragging the music close to sentimentality. Of the generation that included Astra Desmond, Kirkby Lunn and Muriel Brunskill, we have records only of Margaret Balfour with Elgar conducting. A fragment, with piano accompaniment, is all that is recorded of Kathleen Ferrier. Her majestic performance contained a lightning-flash that will never be forgotten by those who heard it, her singing of 'It shall pierce thee, too'. The word 'pierce' was a rapier-thrust at our hearts. In the bass/baritone arias Elgar hoped for a Wotan voice and with Horace Stevens he found it. The 1927 Hereford account of the Angel of the Agony's aria should be studied by all who aspire to sing it, just as Dennis Noble's 'Proficiscere' on Sargent's first recording has a clarion quality all too often missing.

Before leaving the subject of *Gerontius*, I must make special mention of the recording conducted by Benjamin Britten, the only recording of an Elgar work conducted by a composer of comparable stature (unless it is really true that Strauss recorded the *Variations*). Whatever music Britten conducted, he approached from a composer's point of view and in some curious way he managed to give the impression that he had composed it himself. Detail in the orchestral score is highlighted with sometimes startling effect, and sometimes by composer's licence as when, during the Prelude (cue 9 in the score), he prolongs the drum-roll over the barline with exciting but inauthentic effect. Britten's interpretation conveys the sheer physical exhilaration of the music, his own relish of its daring and imagination and his obvious love of the melodies. When recording it, say those who took part, he was far fussier than over his own works. That he referred to Part I as 'Act I' is in itself significant. This is an opera-composer's interpretation and he brings out to the full the operatic element that is a very real part of Elgar's creation. Britten also recorded the *Introduction and Allegro* with a verve and brilliance that give the impression of a newly-cleaned old master. He was to have conducted *For the Fallen* at Aldeburgh but it had to be cancelled after the Maltings fire, so no one ever heard the composer of *War Requiem* in music with which he must have been in particular sympathy.

Menuhin's interpretation of the Violin Concerto has already been discussed. With the advantage of Elgar's conducting, he went to the heart of the score, as he did with Boult years later. Albert Sammons, with uninspired orchestral support, had a more difficult task in 1930 to leave an adequate record of his glorious interpretation, which I was fortunate enough to hear with Barbirolli conducting. The glow in his playing, the controlled emotional power, intimate and withdrawn yet brilliantly accurate in florid passages, is apparent even in the old records. Yet Sammons' insight into Elgar's music is apparent even more penetratingly in the still unequalled performance of the Sonata, recorded with William Murdoch in 1935. The playing in the slow movement ('Romance') has a tender, whimsical, breath-catching quality that no other violinist has yet approached. It was as if Sammons had written the music himself, he is so intimately bound up with every nuance. One is tempted to say that musicianship like this (and one can experience something similar in the Stratton Quartet's playing of the String Quartet) has vanished from the earth, for it had a spiritual innocence that it would be hard to emulate today. But there are moments in his playing of the concerto when Pinchas Zukerman suggests he might achieve something near to Sammons' quality. The concerto, eagerly welcomed by the world's virtuosi in 1910, has now attracted them again, from Perlman to Kremer, from Kyung-Wha Chung to Ida Haendel. In Britain Nigel Kennedy has arisen to claim the right to be compared with Sammons; his recording will surely not be his last, for his interpretation of the work is still developing, a sure sign that the music has him in thrall.

The Cello Concerto, too, is no longer the preserve of the few. Britain's clutch of young cellists, Robert Cohen, Colin Carr, Steven Isserlis, Julian Lloyd Webber and Alexander Baillie among them, is rivalled by a whole generation of European and American soloists. It will be time enough several years hence to analyse their performances as one did those of Casals, Fournier and Tortelier. To hear Tortelier and Boult in this concerto in York Minster or Worcester Cathedral was to enter a realm of Elgarian interpretation that has rightly become the stuff of legend. It was sad, then, that their recording failed to perpetuate the magic. (Tortelier's 1989 re-recording with Groves is near to ideal.) Boult's interpretation is more faithfully preserved in his 1946 recording with Casals. Yes, there is some Elgarian secret that eluded Casals, mainly a matter of his rather curious phrasing of the opening melody, but there is such authority and such magisterial command of every resource that only the kind of chauvinist who wrote musical criticism in London in the 1930s could fail to be won over by it.

We may count ourselves blessed, too, that we have two recordings by Jacqueline du Pré. She felt each note as a living organism. Part of the success of her interpretation lay in its breadth of conception quite apart from the brilliance of her playing. With Barbirolli at his most sensitive and accommodating as an accompanist, their performance together ranks among the supreme achievements in Elgar's name. Her performance recorded 'live' in Philadelphia, with her husband Daniel Barenboim conducting, is more indulgent in the matter of tempi and the playing has some tiny flaws. But the sheer outpouring of emotion in the *adagio* and the *finale* would melt a heart of stone. Such unstinted musical emotion is precious at any time and poignantly so in this case. Du Pré's playing epitomises Elgar's remark about his music: 'If you cut that, it would bleed'. In those seven words he betrayed the secret of interpreting his works because his music was his life's blood.

References

Moore, J Northrop (1974). *Elgar on Record*. OUP: London.
Philip, Robert (1984). 'The recordings of Edward Elgar (1857–1934), authenticity and performance practice.' *Early Music* 12 (4): 481–9.

Appendix   A select Elgar discography

John Knowles

This select discography gives details of the recordings referred to in Micheal Kennedy's chapter 'Some Elgar interpreters'. It has been prepared expressly for the purpose of illustrating the chapter and should not be regarded as a list of recommended recordings, nor as the suggested basis of a representative Elgar record collection.

Readers are directed to my complete Elgar discography (*Elgar's Interpreters on Record*) for a listing of all Elgar recordings issued up to the end of 1984.

	Key
78 rpm records	DB 1939
LPs	ASD 655
Tapes (reel & cassette)	*TC-ASD 2764*
CDs	**CDC 747329-2**

BARBIROLLI, Sir John (1899–1970)

(The) Dream of Gerontius op. 38

Dame Janet Baker, Richard Lewis, Kim Borg, Ambrosian Singers, Hallé & Sheffield Choirs, Hallé Orchestra, Sir John Barbirolli
HMV ALP 2101/2 ASD 648/9 SLS 770 *EX 763185–4* **CMS 763185–2**
(recorded Free Trade Hall, Manchester December 1964)

Falstaff – Symphonic Study op.68

237

Hallé Orchestra, Sir John Barbirolli
> HMV (*TA-*)ALP 2062 ASD 611 ASD 2762 SLS 5030 (*TC-*)SXLP 30279
> **CDM 769185-2**
> (recorded Kingsway Hall, London June 1964)

Introduction & Allegro for string quartet & string orchestra op. 47

International String Quartet, National Gramophonic Society Orchestra.
> Sir John Barbirolli
> Nat.Gram.Soc. NGS 94/5
> (recorded London October 1927)

Allegri Quartet, Sinfonia of London, Sir John Barbirolli
> HMV (*TA-*)ALP 1970 (*TC-*)ASD 521 ASD 2762 SLS 5030 (*TC-*)SXLP
> 30279 STAMP 1 (*TC-*) ESD 7169 **CDC 747537–2**
> (recorded Temple Church, London May 1962)

Symphony no. 1 in A flat op.55

Philharmonia Orchestra, Sir John Barbirolli
> HMV ALP 1989 ASD 540 ASD 2748 SLS 5030 (*TC-*)SXLP 30268 EMX
> 412084–1 (–*4*)
> (recorded Kingsway Hall, London August 1962)

Symphony no. 2 in E flat op.63

Hallé Orchestra, Sir John Barbirolli
> HMV ALP 1242 Barbirolli Society SJB 101
> (recorded Abbey Road studios June 1954)

Hallé Orchestra, Sir John Barbirolli
> HMV (*TA-*)ALP 2061/2 ASD 610/1 ASD 2759 SLS 5030 (*TC-*)SXLP
> 3028 7 EMX 412093–1(-*4*)
> (recorded Kingsway Hall, London April 1964)

Variations on an original theme (Enigma) op.36

Hallé Orchestra, Sir John Barbirolli
> HMV C 3692/5 C 7702/5
> (recorded October 1947)

Philharmonia Orchestra, Sir John Barbirolli
> HMV ALP 1998 ASD 548 SLS 5030 (*TC-*) ESD 7169 **CDM 769185–2**
> (recorded Kingsway Hall, London August 1962)

see also – DU PRÉ, Jacqueline
 NAVARRA, André

BARENBOIM, Daniel (b.1942)

Symphony no. 1 in A flat op.55

London Philharmonic Orchestra, Daniel Barenboim
 CBS 76247 78289 (*40–*)61880
 (recorded Abbey Road studios November 1973)

Symphony no. 2 in E flat op.63

London Philharmonic Orchestra, Daniel Barenboim
 CBS 73094 MQ 31997 78289 (*40–*)61988
 (recorded Abbey Road studios September 1972)

see also – DU PRÉ, Jacqueline
 ZUKERMAN, Pinchas

BEECHAM, Sir Thomas (1879–1961)

Cockaigne – Concert Overture op.40

Royal Philharmonic Orchestra, Sir Thomas Beecham
 Philips ABL 3053 SBR 6225 ABE 10041 GBL 5646 CBS (40–) 30055
 61660 61878
 (recorded Walthamstow Town Hall November 1954 – *parts with organ* location unknown December 1954)

Serenade for String Orchestra op.20

Royal Philharmonic Orchestra, Sir Thomas Beecham
 Philips ABL 3053 SBR 6225 ABE 10188 GBL 5646 CBS 61660 61878
 (recorded Walthamstow Town Hall November 1954)

Variations on an original theme (Enigma) op.36

Royal Philharmonic Orchestra, Sir Thomas Beecham
 Philips ABL 3053 SBR 6224 GBL 5645 CBS 61660 61878
 (recorded Walthamstow Town Hall November 1954 – *parts with organ* location unknown December 1954)

BLACK, Andrew (1859–1920)

Caractacus op.35 – Sword Song

Andrew Black with orchestra
 G & T 3–2324 Elgar Society ELG 001
 (recorded London 1906)

BOULT, Sir Adrian (1889–1983)

(The) Apostles – Oratorio op.49

Sheila Armstrong, Helen Watts, Robert Tear, Benjamin Luxon, Clifford
 Grant, John Carol Case, Downe House School Choir, London Philharmonic Choir & Orchestra, Sir Adrian Boult
 HMV (*TC-*)SLS 976 EX 749742–1 (*–4*) **CDS 749742–2**
 (recorded Kingsway Hall London October/November/December
 1973/July 1974)

(The) Dream of Gerontius op.38

Helen Watts, Nicolai Gedda, Robert Lloyd, London Philharmonic Chorus,
 New Philharmonia Orchestra, Sir Adrian Boult
 HMV (*TC-*)SLS 987 **CDS 747208–8**
 (recorded Kingsway Hall, London May/July 1975)

Falstaff – Symphonic Study op.68

London Philharmonic Orchestra, Sir Adrian Boult
 HMV DB 9603/6 (*TC-*)RLS 7716
 (recorded Abbey Road studios July 1950)

Funeral March (Chopin) (1933)

BBC Symphony Orchestra, Sir Adrian Boult
 HMV DB 1722 ED 290355–1 (*–4*) **CDH 763134–2**
 (recorded Abbey Road studios May 1932)

(The) Kingdom – Oratorio op.51

Margaret Price, Yvonne Minton, Alexander Young, John Shirley-Quirk,
 London Philharmonic Choir & Orchestra, Sir Adrian Boult
 HMV SAN 244/5 SLS 939 EX 749381–1(*–4*) **CDS 749381–2**
 (recorded Kingsway Hall, London December 1968/February 1969)

(The) Music Makers – Ode op.69

Dame Janet Baker, London Philharmonic Choir & Orchestra, Sir Adrian Boult
  HMV ALP 2311 (*TC-*)ASD 2311 *TCC-POR 54291* **CDS 747208–8**
  (recorded Abbey Road studios December 1966)

Symphony no. 1 in A flat op.55

London Philharmonic Orchestra, Sir Adrian Boult
  HMV DB 21024/9 DB 9456/61 ALP 1052 (*TC-*)RLS 7716
  (recorded Abbey Road studios September 1949)

Symphony no.2 in E flat op.63

BBC Symphony Orchestra, Sir Adrian Boult
  HMV DB 6190/5 DB 8967/72 ED 290355-1 (*–4*) **CDH** 763134–2
  (recorded Bedford Grammar School August/October 1944)

London Philharmonic Orchestra, Sir Adrian Boult
  HMV (*TC-*)ASD 3266 EX 290617–3 (*–5*) **CDC 747205–2 CMS 763099–2**
  (recorded Abbey Road studios November 1975/January 1976)

Variations on an original theme (Enigma) op.36

BBC Symphony Orchestra, Sir Adrian Boult
  HMV DB 2800/2 DB 8068/70
  (recorded Abbey Road studios January 1936)

London Philharmonic Orchestra, Sir Adrian Boult
  World Record Club T 158 ST 158 *TT 158* Classics for Pleasure (*TC-*)CFP 40022
  (recorded Abbey Road Studios August 1961)

London Symphony Orchestra, Sir Adrian Boult
  HMV (*TC-*)ASD 2750 EX 290617–3 (*–5*) **CDC 747206–2 CMS 763099–2**
  (recorded Kingsway Hall, London August 1970)

Wand of Youth Suites op.1a/b

London Philharmonic Orchestra, Sir Adrian Boult
  HMV (*TC-*)ASD 2356 *TCC-POR 54291* ED 291129–1(*-4*) **CDM 769207–2**
  (recorded Abbey Road studios April 1967)

see also – CASALS, Pablo
           MENUHIN, Sir Yehudi
           TORTELIER, Paul

BRITTEN, Benjamin (1913–1976)

(The) Dream of Gerontius op.38

Yvonne Minton, Peter Pears, John Shirley-Quirk, Choir of Kings College
  Cambridge, London Symphony Chorus & Orchestra, Benjamin Britten
  Decca SET 525/6 421 381 –2, –4
  (recorded The Maltings, Snape July 1971)

Introduction & Allegro for string quartet & string orchestra op.47

English Chamber Orchestra, Benjamin Britten
  Decca *(KSXC)*SXL 6405 411 639–1, –4, *KMC2 9003 414 049–4*
  425 160 –2, –4
  (recorded The Maltings, Snape December 1968)

BUTT, Dame Clara (1872–1936)

Dream of Gerontius op.38 – excerpts

Dame Clara Butt, Maurice D'Oisly, Chorus, New Queens Hall Orchestra,
  Sir Henry Wood
  Columbia 7128/31 7308/9 75005/8 HLM 7025
  (recorded London 1916)

Land of Hope & Glory (1902)

Dame Clara Butt
  HMV 03153
  (recorded London 1909)

Dame Clara Butt, Orchestra, Sir Dan Godfrey
  HMV 03510 HLM 7025
  (recorded London 1915)

Dame Clara Butt, Chorus, Orchestra
  Columbia 7156
  (recorded Hyde Park, London Empire Day 1917)

Sea Pictures op.37 – 'Where Corals lie'

Dame Clara Butt, Orchestra
  HMV 03299 HLM 7025 Olympus ORL 222
  (recorded 1912)

Dame Clara Butt, Orchestra, Sir Hamilton Harty
  Columbia 7246 7320
  (recorded c.1916)

CASALS, Pablo (1876–1973)

Concerto for 'Cello & Orchestra in E min. op.85

Pablo Casals, BBC Symphony Orchestra, Sir Adrian Boult
  HMV DB 6338/41 DB 9043/6 HLM 7110 World Record Club (*TH*)SH 121
  (recorded Abbey Road studios October 1945)

COATES, John (1865–1941)

In the Dawn op.41 no.2

John Coates
  HMV 02584 Elgar Society ELG 001
  (recorded Hayes 1915)

DU PRÉ, Jacqueline (1945–1987)

Concerto for 'Cello & Orchestra in E min. op. 85

Jacqueline du Pré, London Symphony Orchestra, Sir John Barbirolli
  HMV ALP 2106 (*TC-*)ASD 655 (*TC-*) ASD 2764 SLS 895 SLS 5068
  (*TC-*)SLS 154696–3 (*-5*) **CDC 747329–2 CMS 769707–2** EX 769707–1
  (*–4*)
  (recorded Kingsway Hall, London August 1965)

Jacqueline du Pré, Philadelphia Orchestra, Daniel Barenboim
  CBS (*40–*)76529 **MK 76529**
  (recorded Philadelphia [public performance] November 1970)

ELGAR, Sir Edward (1857–1934)

Cockaigne (In London Town) – Concert Overture op.40

Royal Albert Hall Orchestra, Sir Edward Elgar
   HMV D 1110/1 RLS 713
   (recorded Queen's Hall April 1926)

BBC Symphony Orchestra, Sir Edward Elgar
   HMV DB 1935/6 ALP 1464 RLS 708 World Record Club SH 139 BBC
   Records (*ZC–*) BBC 4001
   (recorded Abbey Road studios April 1933)

(The) Dream of Gerontius op.38 – excerpts

Margaret Balfour, Steuart Wilson, Herbert Heyner, Royal Choral Society,
   Royal Albert Hall Orchestra, Sir Edward Elgar
   HMV D 1242/3 RLS 713 Pearl OPAL 810
   (recorded Royal Albert Hall [public performance], February 1927)   .

Margaret Balfour, Tudor Davies, Horace Stevens, Three Choirs Festival
   Chorus,
   London Symphony Orchestra, Sir Edward Elgar
   HMV D1348 D1350 RLS 708 World Record Club SH 175
   (recorded Hereford Cathedral [public performance], September 1927)

Falstaff – Symphonic Study op.68

London Symphony Orchestra, Sir Edward Elgar
   HMV D 1621/4 D 7112/5 D 7493/6 BLP 1090 RLS 708 World Record Club
   SH 162
   (recorded Abbey Road studios, November 1931/February 1932)

Froissart – Concert Overture op.19

London Philharmonic Orchestra, Sir Edward Elgar
HMV DB 1938/9 RLS 713
(recorded Abbey Road studios April 1933)

(The) Kingdom – Oratorio op.51 – Prelude

BBC Symphony Orchestra, Sir Edward Elgar
   HMV DB 1934 RLS 708 World Record Club SH 139
   (recorded Abbey Road studios April 1933)

(The) Music Makers – Ode op.69 – excerpts

Three Choirs Festival Chorus, London Symphony Orchestra, Sir Edward
   Elgar
   HMV D 1347 D 1349 RLS 708 World Record Club SH 175
   (recorded Hereford Cathedral [public performance], September 1927)

Serenade for String Orchestra op.20

London Philharmonic Orchestra, Sir Edward Elgar
   HMV DB 2132/3 ALP 1464 RLS 713
   (recorded Kingsway Hall, London, August 1933)

Symphony no. 1 in A flat op.55

London Symphony Orchestra, Sir Edward Elgar
   HMV D 1944/9 D 7311/6 D 7620/5 RLS 708 World Record Club SH 139
   (recorded Kingsway Hall, London, November 1930)

Symphony no. 2 in E flat op.63

Royal Albert Hall Orchestra, Sir Edward Elgar
   HMV D 1012/7 Pearl GEM 116 EWE 1
   (recorded Hayes, February 1924/April 1925)

London Symphony Orchestra, Sir Edward Elgar
   HMV D 1230/5 D 7239/44 D 7558/63 RLS 708 World Record Club SH 163
   (recorded Queen's Hall, London, April/July 1927)

Variations on an original theme (Enigma) op.36

Royal Albert Hall Orchestra, Sir Edward Elgar
   HMV D 1154/7 D 7564/7 ALP 1464 RLS 708 World Record Club SH 162
   (recorded Queen's Hall, London, April 1926)

see also – HARRISON, Beatrice
            MENUHIN, Sir Yehudi

HARRISON, Beatrice (1892–1965)

Concerto for 'Cello & Orchestra in E min. op.85

Beatrice Harrison, New Symphony Orchestra, Sir Edward Elgar
   HMV D 1507/9 D 7455/7 RLS 708 **CDH 769786–2** World Record Club SH
   175 Claremont **GSE 78–50–31**

(recorded Kingsway Hall, London March/June 1928)

HARTY, Sir Hamilton (1879–1941)

Variations on an original theme (Enigma) op.36

Hallé Orchestra, Sir Hamilton Harty
   Columbia DX 322/5 Past Masters PM2 Cambridge Records (*ZC-*)IMP1
   (recorded Central Hall, Westminster March 1932)

see also – BUTT, Dame Clara
            SQUIRE, William Henry

HEIFETZ, Jascha (1901–1987)

Concerto for Violin & Orchestra in B min. op.61

Jascha Heifetz, London Symphony Orchestra, Sir Malcolm Sargent
   HMV DB 21056/60 DB 9533/7 ALP 1014 RCA LSB 4022 *GK 87966* **GD 87966**
   (recorded London June 1949)

KENNEDY, Nigel (b.1956)

Concerto for Violin & Orchestra in B min. op.61

Nigel Kennedy, London Philharmonic Orchestra, Vernon Handley
   EMI EMX 412058–1 (*–4*) **CDC 747210–2**
   (recorded Watford Town Hall March 1984)

MENUHIN, Sir Yehudi (b.1916)

Concerto for Violin & Orchestra in B min. op.61

Sir Yehudi Menuhin, London Symphony Orchestra, Sir Edward Elgar
   HMV DB 1751/6 DB 7175/80 (*TA-*)ALP 1456 RLS 708 HLM 7107 **CDH 769786–2** Claremont **GSE 78–50–31**
   (recorded Abbey Road studios, London July 1932)

Sir Yehudi Menuhin, New Philharmonia Orchestra, Sir Adrian Boult

HMV ALP 2259 (*TC-*)ASD 2259 (*TC-*)SXLP 290000–1 (*–4*) EX
290617–3(*·5*)
(recorded Kingsway Hall, London December 1965)

Variations on an original theme (Enigma) op.36

Royal Philharmonic Orchestra, Sir Yehudi Menuhin
    Philips 416 351–1, *–2*, *–4*
    (recorded London July 1985)

MONTEUX, Pierre (1875–1964)

Variations on an original theme (Enigma) op.36

London Symphony Orchestra, Pierre Monteux
    RCA RB 16237 SB 2108 VIC 1107 VICS 1107 Decca SPA/*KCSP*
    DPA 537/8 SPA/*KCSP* 536 *414 049–4* **417 878–2**
    (recorded London 1960)

NAVARRA, André (1911–1988)

Concerto for 'Cello & Orchestra in E min. op.85

André Navarra, Hallé Orchestra, Sir John Barbirolli
    Pye CCL 30103 GGC 4057 GSGC 14057 GSGC 15005 (*ZCGC*)GSGC
    2017 **PVCD 08384** Nixa *NIXMC 6006* **NIXCD 6006**
    (recorded Manchester May 1957)

SAMMONS, Albert (1886–1957)

Concerto for Violin & Orchestra in B min.op.61

Albert Sammons, New Queens Hall Orchestra, Sir Henry Wood
    Columbia L 2346/51 HMV HLM 7011 World Record Club (*TC-*)SH 288
    Novello *NVLC* 901 **NVLCD 901**
    (recorded London March/April 1929)

Sonata for violin & piano in E min. op.82

Albert Sammons, William Murdoch
    Columbia LX 379/81 LX 8163/5 Cambridge Records (*Z*)DIMP 1

(recorded February 1935)

SARGENT, Sir Malcolm (1895–1967)

(The) Dream of Gerontius op.38

Gladys Ripley, Heddle Nash, Dennis Noble, Norman Walker,
    Huddersfield Choral Society, Liverpool Philharmonic Orchestra, Sir
    Malcolm Sargent
    HMV C 3435/46 C 7611/22 RLS 709
    (recorded Huddersfield Town Hall April 1945)

see also – HEIFETZ, Jascha

SQUIRE, Willam Henry (1871–1963)

Concerto for 'Cello & Orchestra in E min. op.85

W.H. Squire, Hallé Orchestra, Sir Hamilton Harty
    Columbia DX 117/20 Cambridge Records (*ZC-*)IMP 1 Novello *NVLC 901
    NVLCD* **901**
    (recorded Free Trade Hall, Manchester November 1930)

STRATTON QUARTET
(Leader – George Stratton [1897–1954])

String Quartet in E min. op.82

Stratton String Quartet
    HMV DB 2139/41 Cambridge Records (*Z*)DIMP 1
    (recorded December 1933)

THORNTON, Edna (1875–1958)

Land of Hope & Glory (1902)

Edna Thornton with orchestra
    Odeon 66128 Elgar Society ELG 001
    (recorded London 1908)

TORTELIER, Paul (b.1914)

Concerto for 'Cello & Orchestra in E min. op.85

Paul Tortelier, London Philharmonic Orchestra, Sir Adrian Boult
   HMV *(TC-)*ASD 2906 *(TC-)*SLS 270001–3 *(–5)* EX 290617–3 *(–5)*
   CDM 769200-2
   (recorded Abbey Road studios October 1972)

TOSCANINI, Arturo (1867–1957)

Variations on an original theme (Enigma) op.36

BBC Symphony Orchestra, Arturo Toscanini
   HMV EH 291345–1 *(–4)* **CDH 769784–2**
   (recorded Queens Hall, London [public performance] June 1935)
   NBC Symphony Orchestra, Arturo Toscanini
   HMV ALP 1204 RCA VIC 1001
   (recorded Carnegie Hall, New York December 1951)

WOOD, Sir Henry (1869–1944)

Variations on an original theme (Enigma) op.36

New Queens Hall Orchestra, Sir Henry Wood
   Columbia L 1629/32
   (recorded 1925)

New Queens Hall Orchestra, Sir Henry Wood
   Decca K 837/40
   (recorded January 1936)

see also – SAMMONS, Albert

ZUKERMAN, Pinchas (b.1948)

Concerto for Violin & Orchestra in B min. op.61

Pinchas Zukerman, London Philharmonic Orchestra, Daniel Barenboim
   CBS *(40-)*76528
   (recorded Abbey Road studios April 1976)

Envoy

Jerrold Northrop Moore

It has been a moving experience to read this collection of able, informed studies by a group of scholars and lovers of Elgar's music. The scholarship and love often go together nowadays. It was not always so. Thirty and more years ago, when Elgar's music first drew me, friends wondered at such eccentricity: and the critics (mostly of the Anthony Blunt generation) backed them up. The ranks of those who carried Elgar's banner then were thin and mostly elderly. There was a feeling that enthusiasm for Elgar survived basically in those who had shared his world in his time.

The albums of photographs at the Elgar Birthplace drew my imagination into that world and time, and I dreamt of assembling a life of Elgar in pictures. When I asked the help of Mrs Elgar Blake she was characteristically generous. She took the occasion to deposit at the Birthplace further albums of private photographs until then hardly seen outside the family; and she invited me to draw on them without reservation. Once when we lunched together that first summer at an hotel I started to pay the bill. 'Certainly not,' she said with decision: 'it is the least I can do when you are doing so much for my father.' (At that stage I had done nothing at all.) At my request, she put me in touch with a long list of her father's surviving friends or their descendants, supplying most of the addresses from memory: twenty-five years after her father's death, she had kept in touch with them all.

And so it was that I was enabled to talk with Lady Bantock, Sir Barry Jackson, Agnes Nicholls, Beatrice and Margaret Harrison, 'Dorabella' (Mrs Powell), May and Madeline Grafton, Sir Percy and Lady Hull, Philip and Nella Leicester, Wulstan Atkins, Astra Desmond, Rutland Boughton, Herbert Howells and a good many more. There were few refusals. Ernest Newman's wife wrote to say that her husband was too old and ill (he died a few weeks later). Lady Bantock strongly recommended that I contact Havergal Brian; he replied that he had nothing to offer. The only outright refusal came from Elgar's secretary Mary Clifford though May and Madge Grafton pleaded my case. Miss Clifford sent pleasant, helpful answers to specific questions. But she was too crippled with arthritis, she said, to be seen.

She had been a beautiful woman and probably thought that I had seen her photographs. I hadn't then, but when I did I understood, though disappointment remained.

For the rest, they were kindness itself. They unhesitatingly invited me – a stranger and a foreigner, two if not three generations after them – into their homes. They gave me generous hospitality. They shared their relics and treasures (not always at the first visit). And they invited me back and back. Thus I became a sort of honorary nephew to May and Madge (though they had three real and wonderful nephews of their own and a niece too). Gradually I gained the confidence of Dorabella, who at last honoured me deeply by talking to me as an old and intimate friend.

At the Philip Leicesters' house in Worcester, The Homestead, where they had lived since 1926 (and thus became Elgar's neighbours when he moved to Marl Bank in 1929) I met the closest friendship of all. The Leicesters, like all of Sir Hubert's family, were devout Catholics: I was not. Philip was a man of seeming rigidity, and he was known to have seen off more than one Elgar enquirer with scant ceremony. But he and Nella took me instantly in, made me repeatedly welcome, and devised that I should return the following year (as it would be Worcester's Three Choirs Festival) to share their house party with May and Madge. A few months after that wonderful Festival Philip died; but Nella remained, and there followed a friendship of twenty years. She gave me the freedom of The Homestead whenever I liked to come to Worcester and Broadheath for research – as often as I wished, for as long as I could stay. Nella opened generously to me the wealth of her shrewd observations of the Elgar household – not only at Marl Bank but in earlier glimpses she had enjoyed, going back to Lady Elgar's time.

Nowhere and never in my life had I met such understanding and real friendship. When we drew close enough for me to ask the really hard questions, they answered with honesty, skill and also with (as I now see) affectionate regard for my tender years.

Why did all this happen? I often asked myself why, and sometimes I asked them. The answer was always the answer that Carice had given: you are doing this for the most wonderful being we ever knew. I think now they also saw in my youthful enthusiasm the future they wanted for the music of the man they had loved. And so I came to feel that it was Elgar himself, all those years after his death, who really opened those friendships for me. Nothing in my life up to now has meant more to me than they do still.

*   *   *

Another insight into the good will that Elgar engenders came after I had taken the suggestion implied in those Elgarian friendships and had come to make my home in this country. A friend of my own age in London, with the keenest musical ears, had and has tastes which extend to Elgar and much besides. He would come with me occasionally to an Elgar Society meeting when the London Branch was new in the early 1970s: and he never failed to remark what a friendly and happy group we all were in each others' company. Well, why ever not? I asked. I shall never forget his answer. He said he heard friendliness and good feeling in the textures of Elgar's music.

Then he took me to a Society he knew. They had an able and entertaining talk by a distinguished conductor. But after it that hapless man was taken rancorously to task by a committee member for sins of omission against what some of them had apparently received as holy writ and dogma. It was then that my eyes really opened to how lucky I had been to be attracted to Elgar and his music – and how lucky we all are. I came away from that meeting feeling my friend had been right: there is something of special kindliness in Elgar's music. No one has ever benefited more from the kindliness than I, but it took that contrast to bring it home to me.

*   *   *

Kindliness and good feeling are not so common in the world that even we can take them for granted. May I therefore bring this book to a close with a plea? It is to be keenly aware of our collective good fortune in the sympathy we ought always to feel for each other's endeavours. I think we still do fairly well at it. But just now and again, as the Society has grown, as the Birthplace Trustees have bought and built, a less than happy atmosphere has emerged. Once or twice recently the *Journal* has carried a letter written in a less than welcoming spirit about a younger colleague's work. My hope is for us all to remember constantly the generous spirit of the man who devoted his life to creating the music which has brought us together. Never lose the sound of that generosity. Take example from these memories of my Elgarian friends, if you will. Take it certainly from the wreath of chapters in this book. And treasure the fellowship that Elgar's music has brought to every one of us.

Index

Acland, Sir Henry W.   102
Acland, Sir Thomas D.   102
Acworth, Harry A.   49, 61–2, 64, 70
Alexander, Sir George   122
Anderson, Robert   vii, author of 118–
33
Aristotle   70
Armes, Philip   16, 32
Arnold, Ella (wife of RPA)   91–2
Arnold, Matthew   91–2
Arnold, Richard P.   89, 91–2
Arts Council of Great Britain   47
Ashwell, Lena (later Lady Simson)   142,
157, 159–62, 164, 172, 175, 176–8,
180–1, 183
Athenaeum, The   83
Atkins, Sir Ivor   50, 170

Bach, J. S.   19, 32, 38, 44, 52;
Phoebus and Pan   53
Bain, Robert N.   68, 69
Baker, Dame Janet   231, 234
Baker, Letitia J. D. (later Townshend)
97
Baker, Mary F. (later Penny)   98
Baker, Rev. Vincent   99
Baker, William Meath   96–9
Baldwyn, Edgar   42
Balfe, Michael   3
Balfour, Margaret   227, 234
Bannister, Canon A. T.   100
Bantock, Sir Granville: *Omar
Khayyám*   56
Barbirolli, Sir John   114, 221, 226,
231–3, 233, 237–9
Barenboim, Daniel   221, 233, 236, 239
Barnett, John F.   16
Barrie, Sir James   113
'Battle of Maldon, The'   66
Baughan, C. A.   83
Bayreuth 1,   10
Beauchamp, Earl   93–4
Beecham, Sir Thomas   165, 223–4, 239
Beethoven, Ludwig von:
Egmont 7; *Pastoral Symphony* 40;
Piano Sonata in C. min. 7; score in
Elgar's library 32; Works listed (in
Appendix 2)   19–20
Bellasis, Rev. Henry   92
Bellini, Vincenzo   3; *Norma*   13, 20
Bennett, Arnold   109
Bennett, Jim   39
Bennett, Joseph   61: *Analytical Notes
on King Olaf*   67, 68

Elgar, Sir Edward (Music index)